"No Place of My Own"

"No Place of My Own":

The 1920s California Diaries of May Ripley Diddy Maylone

Edited by Christine Laennec
with an Introduction, Family History and
Notes

ISBN: 978-0-9565313-0-8

The cover photograph shows May's 1926-1927 diary ("Compositions") below her 1925-1926 diary ("MRD"). Resting on top is a photograph from ca. 1923 showing Ethan Austin Papineau as a baby, being held on Olive Perryman Ripley's lap. Behind Olive are standing May Ripley Diddy Maylone and her daughter Amy Emma Diddy Papineau.

This book is dedicated to May, Amy, Ruth and Isabel:
all strong and loving women

Table of Contents

Acknowledgements

I am very grateful to my mother, Ruth Ann Papineau Williams of Portland, Oregon, for her help in reading May's diaries and understanding May's life, and for reading through my transcriptions. Mama and I have had some fun times staying up late to see what happens next! Arlene Wright of Sacramento, California has been an enormous help to me in my research into May's family background, and preparation of the transcriptions. My uncle Ethan Austin Papineau has helped me with his interest and encouragement. Thanks also to Gary F. Kurutz, California State Library, for his encouragement with this project. I owe a debt of gratitude to my Californian cousins Millie Hizer Cuellar, Eleanor E. Hizer Manning and Doreen Rothlisberger, who provided me with photographs, information, advice and encouragement in this project. It is a shame that neither Millie nor Eleanor lived long enough to see May's diaries published. For years Doreen has been the organizer and host of Hizer family reunions. In addition to her splendid hospitality, Doreen also gave me and my family an unforgettable backroads tour of El Dorado County, California, which brought the Fairplay sections of May's diaries very much to life.

I am also very grateful to Dan Mitchel of Sacramento, California, a fellow Ripley descendant whom I found via Ancestry.com, for long-distance correspondence, photographs, generous help and interest. Although we 'met' over the internet 6,000 miles apart, we discovered that his aunt had been in touch with my grandmother! I would also like to thank the Henry County Genealogical Society, Kewanee, Illinois, for allowing me to reproduce a section of the 1875 Cambridge township map. My thanks also go to the generous and helpful staff of the J.J. Jake Jackson Memorial Museum in Weaverville, California who leapt into action one summer morning when I strolled in, and gave me photocopies of everything they had on the Diddy family.

Here in Scotland I have been helped by my colleague Dr. Mary Pryor, whose editing prowess is second to none, and whose interest in May's life has spurred me on. My son Calum has helped by continuing to grow into a fine young man. My greatest thanks go to my husband Michael Syrotinski and my daughter Isabel, who have unfailingly supported me over the more than three years that it has taken me to complete this project. I hope that Isabel will be proud to have documentary evidence that she comes from a long line of interesting men and women!

I have been amazed at what I have been able to unearth about my own family history with the help of the internet. I have been as scrupulous as possible, and apologize in advance for any errors or misinterpretations.

Christine Laennec
April 2010
Aberdeen, Scotland

List of Illustrations

Introduction

I never knew my Great-Granny May, but growing up with my Granny's and my mother's stories about her, I had the sense that she was a strong and clever woman who had struggled with adversity to find a better life for herself and her three children. I was told that May was resourceful – a hard worker who ran a teamster stop near the Afterthought Mine at Ingot in Northern California. She was said to have been an excellent cook. I knew that she appreciated fine things and that she was a talented needlewoman. I also was aware that she valued education, as did my Granny, Amy. Amy told me that May was a gifted midwife who was familiar with Indian herbal remedies, and I wondered how many Indians May knew or directly learned from. I also knew that May kept goats. Amy told me that she and her two brothers had three patriotic goats: one red, one white and one blue. She showed me a black-and-white photograph of them with the goats out in the farmyard. My curiosity was never completely satisfied as to exactly how blue and red the goats were!

Although my life has taken me far from Oregon, where I grew up, I have been entrusted with several precious heirlooms from May, including her diaries. There are three of them, covering the winter periods between 1925 and 1928. They paint a vivid picture of a hard and uncertain life, lived in several locations in Northern California in the 1920s. When she wrote her diaires she was in her forties, a grandmother, and married to her second husband, George Washington Maylone. The diaries follow May and George as they go from one venture to the next.

Amongst other things, May's diaries provide an eloquent insight into the history of ordinary women at this time. It is clear that she had to be subservient to her husband. When her daughter Amy gets George to take them on a car ride to the opening of a new bridge, May comments "I never ask to go any where or do any thing, it is easier to go where he says we will go and do what he says we will do." (4 Dec. 1927) The truth of this observation is borne out by her record of life married to George. May often remarks on the changing roles of men and women. For example, in January 1925, she wrote that building fires was strictly a man's task: "my 'fire-maker' is on the job every morning he is well" (13 Jan. 1925) But less than two years later she remarked: "Never had to build fires befor in my life till the last few years. Always swore I'd never build fires for any man to lay and sleep while I did it, but I am getting to be quite a liar" (26 Oct. 1926).

The sheer amount of physical labor her life entailed will lead anyone who reads her diaries to agree with her lament that: "as a woman I did the work of two women and one man most of the time." (5 Nov. 1927) My mother, Ruth, believes that these three diaries are the only ones that May ever kept. My mother has also wondered whether the reason all the diaries were written during the winter months is because May did not have the time and the energy to write during the spring and summer. If this is the case, it is hard to imagine how May could possibly have worked even harder than she did when she found the time to write.

Her diaries also show us a woman who never gave up trying to find beauty in life. I have inherited one of the beautiful miniature quilts that May made for my mother's dolls. As a child, my mother's stories about her beloved Granny May made a deep impression on me. Although May died when my mother was only three, my mother adored her and still remembers her vividly. Ruth's descriptions of May made her seem quasi-magical. May would confect toys out of scraps, teach my mother simple needlework, make gardening interesting, and play games: anything one did with May became fun. Reading May's diaries has confirmed my mother's descriptions of her. She certainly was creative and loving, and she doted on small children. When she was writing her diaries, Ruth had not yet been born, but her older brother, Ethan Jr., was the apple of May's eye. Her diaries show that May was skilled in making do with little, and that she believed in making the best of things. Her love of nature and animals comes through very strongly. (I can now better appreciate the skill involved in raising goats.)

As a child I also knew that May was a bit of a renegade. I was told how, in about 1918, she had divorced her first husband and moved herself and her three children from the small settlement at Ingot to the state capital of Sacramento, leaving her life and many cherished possessions behind. Years later, Amy still remembered the trauma of the move. She had been fifteen at the time. She explained to me how unusual and difficult it was in those days for a woman to take such a drastic step. May's diaries bring out quite clearly how a divorced woman was made to pay a penalty for her social crime: "I met Mrs. Chandler, I have a fellow feeling for her, as she is enduring what I had to go thru for two years – the sneers and slurs of folks in glass houses. I lived thru it and found happiness, I hope she does." (Jan. 13, 1925)

No doubt May decided to marry George Washington Maylone in part because being married again would remove this stigma, and give her a chance of greater security. However, she had misgivings at the time. On their fifth anniversary, she remembered walking up the steps of the Yolo County Courthouse to marry George. On her way up the stairs, she had wondered if she was doing the right thing. Her inner struggle is expressed as a conversation between May (her first name) and Martha (her middle name):[1]

My husband did not think of Our Anaversary so I did not mention it.

I remember five years ago I walked up the long flight of step[s] at the Woodland Yolo Co. Court House and each step I said – Martha says to May – Bein a fool again, didn't have slavery enough with your first Master, bein' a fool again, and May said to Martha, "Oh leave me be you sour old maid".

With each step I said Will I be sorry? Will I be glad? (2 Dec. 1927)

Clearly the part of her personality that resisted being a "sour old maid" won out.

Although she was a rebel in leaving her first husband, in other ways she was conventional: loyal perhaps to a fault, always holding out hope for a somewhat romanticized vision of life. The poems she wrote during her first marriage may seem very sentimental to us now, but I have included them after the diaries because they express her longing for love and happiness. She had ambitions for her writing as well. My uncle Ethan ("Junior" in her diaries) remembers that May published some of her poetry in the *Sacramento Bee*.[2] I have not been able to track down any published poems (and she may not have published under her own name), but I was somewhat startled to find a rejection slip from an editor tucked in amongst the poems in her diary. Having received a few rejection slips as a writer myself, I felt a great closeness to my great-grandmother in that moment.

Although (unlike her poems) her diaries are often written somewhat hastily, in my opinion they show her love of language, and a skill in describing both her surroundings and the people who were part of her life. Her writing is lively, vivid and humorous. She clearly was alive to the poetic possibilities of language, but wrote from the heart in an unpretentious style. I realize I am not the most objective of editors in this case, but I consider her to have been a talented writer.

Another treasured heirloom in my possession is May's trunk, which is now in my bedroom in Aberdeen, Scotland. It was given to me when I was a teenager, in the 1970s. When I received the trunk, it was already a hundred years old. Its bashed corners are a testimony to the many travels it has been on – probably the easiest of its journeys was being air-freighted from the West Coast of the US over to Scotland. The inside of the trunk's arched and heavy lid is decorated by an illustration of a fashionable lady from the 1870s.

I was told by my grandmother Amy that the trunk had come to Oregon across the Great Plains in a covered wagon. For a while I wondered if this could be true, given that the trunk was made about 20 years after the great rush West in the 1850s. Because Amy had once described May's father to me as a "railroad man," I imagined that they had moved west by train. However, I was recently given the obituary of one of May's aunts, which describes May's grandparents and family moving their possessions in a covered wagon from Illinois to Nebraska in the fall of 1887.[3] I realized then that May's trunk probably had indeed made its way to Oregon in a covered wagon, albeit in the 1880s and 90s.

This wasn't the first time in my research that family oral history – however unlikely it seemed – was ultimately confirmed. I am very fortunate to have notes from conversations about our family history that I had in my teenage years with my granny Amy. The process of researching May's family background has in many ways been like a kind of conversation with both Amy and May. Often, after going on what I'd thought would be a wild goose chase, sparked off by things scribbled on various scraps of paper, or by May's diaries themselves, I have found myself saying out loud: "You were right! I'm sorry I doubted you."

There have also been some uncanny coincidences in the course of my research. For example, in 2008, my sister and my own family travelled to places May had lived in California. Avoiding the heat of Redding, we stayed two nights in Weaverville, in the Trinity mountains – without knowing at the time that it was where May married John Diddy in 1899, or that his family had connections to the place as well. Travelling south, we just happened to stop for a break from the heat in Woodland, where we turned the corner and saw the impressive steps of Yolo County Courthouse, which May described climbing on her way to marry George Maylone. It was one of those spooky moments that felt absolutely right.

Now that I am about the same age as May was when she began the first of the three diaries, reading them I am constantly struck by how positive she is, how alive she is to nature, and how deep her desire is for self-expression. Having come to know her through working on her diaries, now when I think of May, the word "spirited" is what characterizes her most for me: she was not just independent and lively, but she was alive to the spiritual dimension of life, a free thinker who was constantly searching for meaning beyond what meets the eye.

A Note Regarding My Transcription:

I have tried to strike a good balance between, on the one hand, remaining faithful to May's somewhat idiosyncratic spelling, and on the other, rendering her diary entries and poems in a way that makes them easy to read. I've introduced sentence and paragraph breaks, as May's rather breathless writing doesn't always indicate these. I have corrected slips of the pen and put in apostrophes where I felt these helped to make May's meaning clear. Otherwise I have left her writing to speak for itself.

Part One:

May's Family History

May had a great deal of pride in her family background, and this gave her a sense of worth when facing adversity. In 1926 a woman in Knight's Landing repeatedly refused to acknowledge May on the street. This woman was a supervisor's daughter-in-law. May fumed in her diary: "I can match relation with her any day. I was a supervisor's daughter and among my short-tail relation[s] I can number Bank Presidents, Railroad Presidents, [a] College President, Soldiers, cops, secret service men and better yet I'm Geo. Washington's wife." (15 Dec. 1926) Although May, in her annoyance, was allowing herself to exaggerate a bit, my research has found quite a few "short-tail relations" that verify her claims.

The "bank president" may well have been Robert Goodin, married to May's father's cousin Harriet Perryman. In the 1880 census Robert Goodin had risen to a high position in a bank in St. Louis, where his sons were eventually also employed.[1] As we shall see, there were numerous Civil War soldiers in May's family tree, and her brother Ray Asbury Ripley was a policeman. The Railroad President and College President continue to elude me – and surely the identity of the secret service men will never be found! However, I have learned that there is a family story amongst the Ripleys that a scholarship was established by a Ripley in either Pennsylvania or Ohio.[2] Although I haven't been able to confirm the existence of this scholarship, I am rather inclined to think there may be a grain of truth in May's mention of a College President.

When as a teenager I asked Amy about our family, she told me that May was originally from John Day, Oregon, and that her father was a Kansas railroad man who came west to Oregon with his brother, after a few years mining in French Gulch, California. She said that May's mother Olive was from the South, and had been taken to safety during the Civil War – she remembered family tales of how as a young child, Olive had hidden in the skirts of her black Mammy to escape from raiding soldiers. Thanks to the wonders of the internet, I've been able to trace quite a bit of May's ancestry. Most of it does corroborate family oral history, although there are some points which remain veiled in the mists of time.

Family Tree of May Martha Ripley Diddy MacLane   CmL

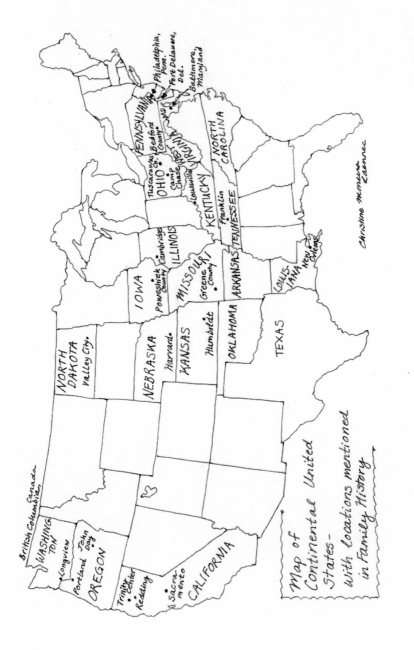

Map of
Continental United
States –
with locations mentioned
in Family History

Christine Moreau Laenac

1.

May's Maternal Line

The Perrymans and the Mulanaxes in Missouri
(1778 to 1860)

To begin with, May's maternal line is one of multiplicities: of spelling, names and births. The Perrymans are sometimes the Perimans or the Perrimans; the Mulanaxes are also Mullinaxes, Mullenaxes and several variations thereof; and both family trees contain many marriages resulting in numerous children, often given the same names as their cousins. This has made research interesting to say the least, but I have managed to trace May's maternal line. May's mother was Olive Almeda Ann Perryman. She was born four months after the outbreak of the Civil War in August 1861, in Cave Spring, Greene County, Missouri.[3]

Olive's parents were William Alexander Perryman and Mahaly (or Mahala) Jessyphy (or Josephine) Mulanax. William Alexander and Jessyphy, to use the names that Amy knew them by, were married on the 21st of October 1860 in Cass Township, Greene County, Missouri.[4] Three months later, William Alexander's sister was to marry Jessyphy's brother[5], so the Perrymans and Mulanaxes were doubly linked.

Jessyphy Mulanax was born in Missouri in 1842, the second of ten children.[6] Her parents had come to Missouri only a few years earlier. Her father, Joseph Mulanax, was born in Pendleton County, West Virginia in 1795, which is as far back as I have been able to trace this branch of the family.[7] As mentioned, the Mulanaxes were prolific. For example, Joseph Riley Mulanax (Jessyphy's brother) and his wife Mary Louise Perryman (William Alexander's sister) - who married three months after William Alexander and Jessyphy did - eventually had 13 children. Another brother, Alfred Constantine Mulanax, had ten children. Many of these families left Missouri to make a living farming further west, in Arkansas, Oklahoma and Texas. Some Mulanaxes (for example Mary Louise Perryman Mulanax) even ended up in California.[8]

Olive's father's side of the family, the Perrymans, had arrived in Missouri over a decade before the Mulanaxes, and were amongst the founding families of Greene County. Jacob Perryman, Alexander Perryman's grandfather, was born in 1778 in Rockingham County, North Carolina. He and his wife, Margaret "Peggy" Knight, had ten children as they moved west via Tennessee. They arrived in Greene County, Missouri sometime in the 1830s.[9] One of their eldest sons, Absalom Perryman, remained in Tennessee. But at least two of his brothers came to Greene County and settled there: Benjamin F. Perryman and Thomas Knight Perryman, William Alexander's father.

R. I. Holcombe's 1883 History of Greene County tells us that "Cass township was first organized by the county court, May 1, 1846.... At the head of the petition asking for the creation of the township was the name of Jacob Perryman."[10] Holcombe writes that Cave Spring – still a small settlement to the west of Springfield, Missouri – took its name from "a large spring flowing out of a sort of cave on Asher creek near by". The families who arrived in Cave Spring in the 1830s had to live without many amenities. The first store in Cave Spring was established in 1845, but there was not to be a post office or high school there until 1868. Mt. Zion Presbyterian church was established in 1839, although it met in parishioners' homes until a church building was built in 1845. Holcombe tells us that it was "one of the very oldest Presbyterian churches in Missouri," and the first west of St. Louis.[11]

William Alexander's cousin, John G. Perryman (eldest son of Benjamin F. Perryman) also made his way into the history books. Holcombe gives him his very own entry for his role as founding father of the community of Ash Grove in Greene County. After telling us of John G. Perryman's two marriages and 13 children, Holcombe concludes: "Mr. Perryman owns one of the best farms in his section, well stocked, in a high state of cultivation, and the best orchard in the township. He and his wife are members of the Missionary Baptist church at Ash Grove. He is regarded as one of Greene's most substantial citizens, and is a gentleman of integrity."[12]

Slavery and the Civil War (1850s – 1860s)

R.I. Holcombe was writing his history less than twenty years after the Civil War ended, for readers whose families would have fought on both sides. What he does not mention about John G. Perryman is that a year before the outbreak of the Civil War in 1861 he was a slave owner. The 1860 US Federal Census Slave Schedule tells us that he owned a 45-yr-old female slave, a 16-yr-old female slave and a 3-yr-old male slave.[13] In the 1850 Slave Schedule, Sarah Wood Perryman, John G. Perryman's mother and William Alexander's aunt, was listed as owning eight slaves, from ages one to 35.[14] Writing of events in Greene County in the 1850s, Holcombe discusses slavery in a section subtitled "The 'Peculiar Institution'". "Shocking" rather than "Peculiar" might be the word that leaps to the mind of a contemporary reader:

> Slaves were worth a good price in Greene county
> this year [1857]. About the first of January there
> was an auction sale of this species of property in

Springfield. One "likely" negro man, 35 years of age, brought $1,000. Two women were put upon the block and sold fairly; one, 26 years of age, brought $830; the other, aged 30, brought $715. March 30, a negro woman, 40 years old, with a child of two years, sold for $900; another, about 30, with a two-year-old child, brought $860.

Occasionally slaves escaped from their masters about these days, and struck out toward the north star, or for the abolitionists in Kansas, or for the Indians in the western part of the Indian Territory. One or two were said to have been spirited away by interested parties and taken to California.[15]

Interestingly, when the Civil War began, John G. Perryman fought for the Union, alongside many other men in the Perryman family, as well as Olive's uncles Joseph Riley and Alfred Constantine Mulanax.[16] It may strike us as strange that a man who owned three slaves in 1860 should fight for the Union a year later. However, Holcombe's description of those Greene County men who supported abolition fits John G. Perryman to a tee: "[T]he majority were originally from Kentucky and Tennessee, and, reared amidst slavery, they had grown to dislike it, and to be opposed to its further extension."[17]

Neither William Alexander Perryman, nor his father Thomas Knight Perryman, nor Jessyphy's father Joseph Mulanax, are listed as slave owners in the 1850 or 1860 Slave Schedules. However, the family story I was told of the "black Mammy" hiding the young Olive under her long skirts suggests that Olive's family did have at least one African-American – slave or freed, we will never know – working for them. If the story is true, there must have been enough of a tie of loyalty for the servant or slave to protect a young white child in danger.

In his History, R.I. Holcombe makes the case that slaves were generally well-treated in Greene County, Missouri:

> While many of the people of the county were
> slaveholders, the majority of the class was
> merciful toward this species of their chattels and
> treated them with much consideration. A hard and
> cruel master was almost unknown. There was a
> stringent law against mistreating slaves, and in this
> county it was enforced. In January of this year
> (1860), the grand jury of Greene county indicted
> C. S. Bodenhamer for "cruelty to a slave," and he
> was duly arrested and held upon the charge.[18]

The reader is left wondering whether Holcombe intends to be
ironic when referring to African-American slaves as "species of
their [masters'] chattels". We are fortunate to have the testimony
of a man who himself escaped slavery in Missouri in the 1840s:
"Though slavery is thought, by some, to be mild in Missouri,
when compared with the cotton, sugar and rice-growing states,
yet no part of our slaveholding country is more noted for the
barbarity of its inhabitants than St. Louis."[19]

    As the very fact of the publication of William W. Brown's
story in 1847 shows, debates about the abolition of slavery had
been taking place for decades before the Civil War. In the late
1850s, some of the "debates" could be very violent indeed. As a
border state between the Confederate South slave states and the
newly-opened western free states, Missouri was plagued by
bands of vigilantes for several years before Civil War actually
broke out in April 1861. Jayhawkers and Bushwhackers had been
doling out their own version of justice on the local population
since 1856.[20] The History Net website gives this definition of a
Jayhawker: "A Jayhawker was one of a band of anti-slavery, pro-
Union guerrillas coursing about Kansas and Missouri, impelled
by substantially more malice than charity. Jayhawkers were
undisciplined, unprincipled, occasionally murderous, and always
thieving. Indeed, Jayhawking became a widely used synonym for
stealing."[21]

William Alexander and Jessyphy began their married life only months before the war began. In the words of History Net, "The Civil War came early to Missouri and Kansas, stayed late, and was characterized at all times by unremitting and unparalleled brutality. More than anywhere else, it was truly a civil war."[22] William Alexander and Jessyphy were living in one of the most dangerous parts of the bitterly divided country: in the southwest corner of Missouri, Greene County lies less than 50 miles from the borders of Kansas, Arkansas and Oklahoma Territory – all areas where in 1861 slavery was not allowed by law.

Two weeks after William Alexander and Jessyphy's marriage, Abraham Lincoln was elected President. According to Holcombe, "Great was the astonishment of everybody when it was learned that in Greene county 42 votes had been given to 'Abe' Lincoln". He recounts how Lincoln's supporters had met in secret before the election, and gives a partial list of these men:

> Among the Republicans of Greene county in 1860 were ... John Reynolds (murdered afterwards for his politics), Joseph Goodwin, Alexander Goodwin, George Cooper (killed by guerillas), Joseph Cooper, Wesley Matherly, Alexander Hammontree, John Hammontree, Joe Mullinax, J. R. Mullinax.[23]

The last two on his list are Jessyphy's father and brother. As the fates of those killed for their beliefs amply demonstrate, it was a dangerous time to support the abolition of slavery.

When war was declared on April 15th 1861,[24] Jessyphy was four months pregnant with Olive. It must have been a terrible time to be expecting a baby. Describing events of August 1861, which presumably he had witnessed himself, Holcombe writes:

> And now the people of Greene county had come to realize what civil war meant... What a change

in a few brief months! The peaceful citizens of one year ago were now soldiers, with arms in their hands seeking to blow out one another's brains or cut one another's throats. Peaceful fields were converted into military camps; dwelling houses were made hospitals; peaceful plow horses were harnessed to cannon carriages, the rumble of whose wheels, mingled with those of the "army wagons," was to be heard at all hours in lieu of the cheerful rattle of the farmer's wagon a year ago; bands of illy-disciplined soldiers of both armies were ravaging the country, killing stock, plundering gardens and smoke-houses, "pressing" this, that, or the other article of property, terrifying the inhabitants out of their wits—while a great battle, sure to be fierce and bloody, was imminent and to be fought on Greene county soil, accustomed aforetime only to the pleasures and delights of a time of peace.[25]

Sadly, history tells us that Holcombe's prose does not seem to be painting a wildly exaggerated picture. According to the Missouri Civil War Museum, "27,000 total Missouri citizens (Confederate and Union loyalties) are estimated to have been killed in the Civil War."[26]

On August 9th 1861, just a few weeks before the birth of William Alexander and Jessyphy's baby, the bloody Battle of Wilson Creek raged around Springfield, just a few miles east of Cave Spring. But Olive arrived safely. Presumably the family continued to farm as best they could as the war raged around them. However, the next year William Alexander enlisted with the U.S. Army. He joined Company M of the 8th Cavalry Regiment Missouri, which was formed in July 1862. The history of this regiment tells us that: "from the time of its muster ... until the following summer it was on duty in the locality where it was recruited, and was then attached to Gen. Davidson's cavalry division for the Little Rock [Arkansas] campaign."[27] William Alexander and Jessyphy's family life thus truly came to an end when their first, and as it turned out only, child was just a year old.

Divided Loyalties, Divided Families

Although William Alexander, two of his uncles and his brother-in-law all fought for the Union, not all the Perrymans were pro-abolition. The sons of Benjamin and Sarah Wood Perryman (the owner of eight slaves in 1850) fought on both sides of the war. As we have seen, their eldest son John G. Perryman, although a slave owner in 1860, chose to fight for the Union when Civil War broke out. However, his younger brothers Thomas Jefferson Perryman (1831- before 1870), Owen Franklin Perryman (1837- before 1870), James M. Perryman (1840 – at least 1910) and William Perryman (1842- before 1870) all fought for the Confederacy.[28] Three of the brothers (Thomas, Owen and William) spent time as prisoners of war in such vile prisons as Fort Delaware, where the soup was full of white worms, prison wardens threw rats to the starving prisoners, and diseases such as smallpox, measles and dysentery raged.[29]

The youngest of the four Perrymans who fought for the Confederacy, William, was just two years younger than his cousin William Alexander Perryman (Olive's father). In 1860, the census indicates that the widowed Sarah Perryman and her family lived very nearby Thomas Knight Perryman and his family, so the two cousins would have grown up together. One can only try to imagine the deep and lasting rifts caused within families when war was declared and differences of opinion were no longer a private matter. One hopes that the cousins who grew up together never actually had to face one another in battle.

William was captured in Franklin, Tennessee, on December 14th 1864, and was forwarded to Louisville, Kentucky on February 24th, 1865.[30] On March 3rd, 1865 he was transferred to

Camp Chase, near Columbus, Ohio.[31] Conditions at Camp Chase were said to be "harsh" and as in other camps, disease was rife.[32] On May 2nd, 1865 he was taken to New Orleans to be exchanged.[33] He was one of thousands of Confederate prisoners exchanged towards the end of the war:

> At about this time [February 1865] negotiations resumed to arrange an exchange of prisoners. Several thousand sick prisoners had been exchanged the previous fall and public pressure was mounting to free the rest. ... With the collapse and surrender of the Confederacy [in April 1865], the remaining prisoners of both sides were released over the next several months.

When the war was finally over, it was determined that more than 56,000 men had died as prisoners of war.[34]

There is no more trace of William Perryman after the record stating that he was transferred to New Orleans. Perhaps he died there; perhaps he made it back home for a while. It is significant that neither Owen nor Thomas, also Confederate prisoners of war, seem to have survived beyond 1870.

William Alexander does not seem to have survived the Civil War either. I have not been able to find any record of his participation in the Civil War beyond his enlistment. His experience, like his cousins', must also have been horrendous. We know, for example, that his regiment lost 26 enlisted men in battle, but that an incredible 352 enlisted men in the regiment died from "disease or accident".[35] After the campaigns in Missouri and Arkansas, William Alexander's regiment was mustered out at the end of the war, in July 1865.[36] Sometime before 1869 Jessyphy filed for a widow's pension.[37]

Even after the war officially ended, life in Greene County continued to be dangerous. Holcombe tells us that in August 1865, the august citizen John G. Perryman, along with Jessyphy's father Joseph Mulanax, were arrested by a band of men called "The Regulators" who took the law into their own hands:

> Other work of the "Regulators" was the assisting of Deputy Sheriff Isaac Jones in the arrest of some parties near Walnut Grove, who were charged with stealing. Seven of those arrested were confined in jail. The names of all arrested were Joseph Mullinax … John Perryman…. These men were arrested about the 6th of June. Some of them were afterwards bailed out …[38]

Unlike some of the other victims of the rough-and-ready justice meted out by "the Regulators," Jessyphy's father and William Alexander's uncle survived this particular ordeal.

What Little We Know of May's Mother's Childhood (1861 – 1876)

The war had devastated Missouri, and particularly the borderlands where Greene County was located. Holcombe gives us this description of the months immediately following the war. A Mrs. Phelps had been given $20,000 by the Federal government to set up a Soldiers' Orphans Home "wherein the orphans of Federal soldiers who had died in the civil war could be cared for until they reached an age when they could care for themselves." Holcombe waxes poetic in describing the retreat of the Federal army in September 1865: "The ex-Confederate soldier, at work in his field, striving to repair his wasted farm and mend his broken fortunes, heard the bugle call, saw the little cavalcade in blue, knew what it all meant, and, resting upon his implement, mused a long time."[39] Perhaps by September 1865, Jessyphy and Olive had long ago fled to safety.

On January 13, 1874, a subsequent entry was made on William A. Perryman's Civil War pension form. It lists Albert M. Sewell, William Alexander's brother-in-law, as guardian of a minor (and this minor can only be Olive).[40] Albert was married to William Alexander's sister Martha Adeline Perryman, and himself fought for the Union.[41] Albert and Martha went on to have a large family, and after Martha's death, Albert remarried and eventually moved to Texas. What Albert and Martha Sewell's involvement with Jessyphy and young Olive was at the time of the Civil War and its aftermath, is hard to say.

I have not been able to find either Jessyphy or Olive in the 1870 census. They are not living with the Sewells. Where had they gone? Who were they living with? Had Jessyphy perhaps remarried? And does the pension form entry in January 1874 signify that Jessyphy died in this month, leaving Albert as sole guardian of twelve-year-old Olive?

The next thing we know for certain is that Olive married Jehu Beal Ripley on September 14th, 1876.[42] I haven't been able to find out where their marriage took place. Olive had turned 15 just two weeks earlier.

2.

May's Paternal Line

Jehu Beal Ripley, May's father, was born on a farm in Cambridge, Henry County, Illinois, on January 19th, 1855.[43] Two more of the odd coincidences that have come up in the course of my research are that my own daughter's birthday is the 19th of January; and also that during the four years that I lived and taught in central Illinois, I enjoyed visiting the village of Bishop Hill, which is less than ten miles from Cambridge. One of the few keepsakes I have from our Illinois years is a pen-pot made in Bishop Hill with "Henry Co. Illinois" written on it. When I discovered – years after having left – that I had often, without knowing it, been very close to where my ancestors were born and bred, I did feel a little shiver!

Jehu's father was Asbury Ripley, and his mother was Elizabeth Eleanor Owings. Both Asbury and Elizabeth were born in Ohio, and they were married there in 1848.[44]

The Owings Family (1300s to 1806): from Wales to Maryland, with a Dash of Scotland and Barbados

Let us begin with Elizabeth Owings, May's paternal grandmother, for hers is a very proud and interesting lineage. Elizabeth was born in 1828, in Harrison County, Ohio, the daughter of Beal McKenzie Owings (born in Baltimore in 1804) and Maranda Young.[45] Elizabeth was one of eight children, of whom it seems that only four lived past childhood.[46] Sadly, her parents also died young. Beal McKenzie Owings died at 35, and Maranda Young Owings at 38. Elizabeth was about 16 when she was orphaned, but did not marry until she was 20. It would seem that (unlike, perhaps, Olive Perryman) she did not have to marry in order to survive. Presumably her relatives took care of her.

Elizabeth Owing's mother, Maranda Young, was born in 1806, the daughter of Mary McKenzie from Wales or Scotland, and Denton Young, from Maryland.[47] Mary McKenzie and Denton Young were married in Maryland in 1798, and had moved to Ohio by 1820.[48] Family trees indicate that Denton Young's father William was born in Maryland in 1740; further back than that I haven't been able to trace.[49] One of Denton Young's great-grandchildren, Denton True 'Cy' Young (1867-1955) was a famous major-league baseball pitcher.[50] His sister Ella married James E. Ripley, a descendant of May's great-great-grandfather, so the Youngs and Ripleys were connected by more than one marriage.[51]

I have found out much more about the family of Beal McKenzie Owings' father.[52] The Owings family, who fortunately for myself have done a great deal of genealogical research, can trace the family tree back to Richard Owings, who was born in Llanllugan, Montgomeryshire, Wales, and came to the colonial outpost of Baltimore, Maryland in 1716, along with some of his brothers and sisters. In fact, this Owings family apparently goes as far back as the 14th century, to families living in Caernarvonshire, Marionethshire and Monmouthshire in Wales.[53]

Having arrived in the English outpost of Maryland, Richard Owings married Rachel Beale.[54] Rachel was born in Maryland in 1662, and it seems she was the daughter of a Scotsman, Ninian Beall.[55] Ninian Beall is a fascinating character. He was born in 1625 in the fishing village of Largo, in Fife.[56] He fought in the Scottish army against the forces of Oliver Cromwell, who invaded Scotland in 1650. However, his was the losing side, and along with many others he was "barbadosed" – sent to Barbados as an indentured slave.[57] Passenger and Immigration Lists, 1500s – 1900s on Ancestry.com have records of Ninian Beall arriving in Barbados in 1650 and later that same year arriving in Maryland.

Ironically, the former slave went on to become a prosperous slave owner in the New World. Ninian fought in the Indian Wars and became Colonel Ninian Beall of the Maryland Militia in 1694. Remaining true to the majority faith of Scotland, he donated land for a Presbyterian church to be built in Upper Marlboro, Maryland. He also built a rather grand house named after his home farm back in Scotland. This house is now Dumbarton Oaks Research Library and Collection, located in Washington D.C. but part of Harvard University. In recognition of his military services, Beall was granted hundreds of acres of land. The area of Georgetown, now part of Washington, D.C., was named after his son George Beall. Thus May's father's middle name (Jehu Beal Ripley) came originally from a Scottish founding father of Maryland. The family clearly had a long memory as to their origins.

The Owings family was prosperous and successful in colonial Maryland. There are documents currently on open access on the internet that give us a picture of their lives in the early years of the newly-formed United States. Richard Owings' grandson Stephen Hart Owings (1715-1801) lived in Baltimore all his life. He married Sarah Gott in 1742, was a constable of the "Soldiers Delight Hundred" – an area of land – in November 1739, owned 60 acres of Bachelor's Hall in 1750, and was churchwarden of St. Thomas' Parish in 1744 and 1756.[58] There is still a waymarker for the Garrison Forest Church, (St. Thomas Parish) located in Owings Mills, Baltimore, Maryland.[59] Owings Mills is now a suburb of Baltimore boasting the large Owings Mills shopping mall, but it takes its name from the Owings family mills, which had been established in the 1700s.[60]

The 1806 will of Stephen Hart Owings' son Richard Gott Owings – May's great-great-great-grandfather – makes for interesting reading:

> In the name of God, Amen, I Richard Owings of Baltimore County State of Maryland, being weak in body but of sound mind and understanding calling to mind the uncertainty of this life and certainty of death do make and constitute this my last will and testament in manner and form following to wit. I commend my soul to God who gave it my body to the earth to be buried in a christian like manner at the discretion of my Executors hereafter named my desire is that all my just debts together with any funeral expenses shall be fully paid and satisfied.
>
> Item. I give unto my loving wife Ruthey Owings my negroe man James to do with him at her own election and my negroe woman Mariah to belong to my wife while she remains a widow and at marriage or death which shall first happen the said Mariah to be sold and the money arising from such sale to be equally divided between my two sons Samuel and Esaah. I also give unto my loving wife a feather bed and furniture of her own choice of all my beds likewise my riding mare...[61]

Again we see that slaves were truly "chattels" on a list alongside featherbeds and furniture. In another section of his will, Richard deeds his blacksmith shop to his eldest son Beal Owings. Clearly

May's ancestor Richard Gott Owings was well-off. However, a browse through some of the other Owings' wills from the same period in Baltimore demonstrates that he was a comparatively poor member of the Owings family. Another Richard Owings (not a close relative of May's ancestor) bequeathed hundreds of acres of land along with his mills to his nine children in 1818.[62]

The blacksmith Richard Gott Owings had seven sons and one daughter. His son Nicholas Owings (1772-1851) married Sophia Dorsey, who was a descendant of Edward Darcy of Hornsbye Castle in Yorkshire, England. The Dorseys had come to Maryland in 1619, even earlier than the Owings.[63] A hundred and fifty years later, Nicholas Owings did not have a castle and did not even inherit the blacksmith shop. He and Sophia headed for Tuscarawas County, Ohio, where in 1804 Beal McKenzie Owings, May's maternal grandfather, was born.[64] Ohio had only become a state the year before, and its constitution prohibited slavery, so presumably Nicholas Owings was happy to leave slavery behind in Maryland.[65] Thus, although May's paternal grandmother, Elizabeth Owings, was an orphan by the age of 16, she had a long and proud family lineage and she was provided for until she married Asbury Ripley at the age of 20.

Ruppels and Ripleys (1656 – 1840s) : from Germany to Pennsylvania and Ohio

Let us look now at May's father's family history. The earliest Ripley that I have been able to trace – thanks to Dan Mitchel's genealogical research – is in fact not a Ripley but a Ruppel. According to family trees on Ancestry.com, in 1656, in Gedern, Germany, Anna Elisabetha Lang married Engelhard Ruppel. Their son Johann Joachim Ruppel lived in Gedern all his life (1670 – 1739). He was married to Catharina Oberheim, and one of their children was Johannes Ruppel, born in 1704.[66] Johannes Ruppel married Anna Maria Best, and they had a son, Ludwig

David Ruppel. Sadly, Anna Maria died the same year that Ludwig David was born, in 1735. She may well have died in childbirth. The next year, Johannes sailed for America.[67]

Why did he leave his family and young motherless son behind in Germany? Many of his Protestant compatriots from what was called Palatinate Germany (the lands belonging to the Count Palatine of the Holy Roman Empire) had emigrated to Pennsylvania in 1709 after the Palatinate had suffered religious persecution, invasions from the French, and finally an exceedingly harsh winter that killed off orchards and vineyards. As one historian explains:

> The scene was set for a mass migration. At the invitation of Queen Anne in the spring of 1709, 7,000 harassed Palatines sailed down the Rhine to Rotterdam. From there, about 3000 were dispatched to America, either directly or via England, under the auspices of William Penn [the Quaker founding father of Pennsylvania]. The remaining 4000 were sent via England to Ireland to strengthen the Protestant interest.[68]

Nearly thirty years after the mass emigration of 1709, Johannes' 13-year-old son Ludwig David followed his father to America. Ludwig David's voyage is documented, and parallels the same pattern of the earlier migration. On Sept. 15, 1748, he sailed on the ship "Two Brothers," captained by Thomas Arnott. Following the same route as the emigrants of 1709, the ship sailed to the New World from Rotterdam via Portsmouth, England. Upon arrival in Pennsylvania, young Ludwig David took an Oath of Allegiance to his new country.[69]

I would like to think that Ludwig David joined his father. Ludwig appears on a Pennsylvania Census in 1748, the year of his arrival, and is listed as residing in Philadelphia.[70] He must later have travelled to Somerset County, hundreds of miles to the west, as both he and his father apparently died there.[71] At some point Ludwig David changed his last name from "Ruppel(l)"(or "Ruepfel") to the more American "Ripley". He was married (to whom is not clear – perhaps to Unity, and/or to Sybil?), and had five sons: Jacob, Valentine, Henry, Lewis and John Ripley. The youngest of these was May's paternal great-great-grandfather.

John Ripley married Elizabeth Sheets Casebeer in Pennsylvania in 1785, when he was 21 and she was 16.[72] Elizabeth, who was born in Bedford County, Pennsylvania, was a second-generation American. Her mother, Catherine Dibert, was probably from French stock. The German side of her family had also Americanized their name, from "Kasebier" (Elizabeth's grandfather was Gottfried Kasebier) to "Casebeer" (her father, John Casebeer, was born in Bedford County, Pennsylvania in 1745).[73] Elizabeth's father John was a blacksmith. He is mentioned in the 1884 History of Bedford, Somerset and Fulton Counties, Pennsylvania: "In the spring of 1771 the county of Bedford was organized ... and the residents and lot-owners of Bedford... were as follows: Anthony, Adams, Carling & Casebeer, blacksmiths..."[74] John Casebeer left Pennsylvania for Tuscarawas County, Ohio – not far from the western border of Pennsylvania – sometime after 1800 and before his death in 1813.[75] He probably accompanied or followed his daughter Elizabeth and his son-in-law John Ripley there.

Elizabeth and John went to Ohio between 1808, (when their twelfth child, Andrew Stephen Ripley, was born in Pennsylvania) and 1812, when their eldest daughter Catherine was married in Tuscarawas County.[76] In the early 19th century, Ohio was a popular destination. Soon after America had declared its independence from Britain in 1776, white Europeans began to settle in Ohio. It was granted statehood in 1803.[77] Tuscarawas County, where John and Unity settled in the township of New Philadelphia, was formed in 1808.[78] Early settlers in New Philadelphia, when shown around their new township by its founder John Knisely, had a surprise in store:

> Reaching the forks of the trail, the present juncture
> of Beaver Avenue and East High Avenue, [John
> Knisely] said: "You are now in the town, this is
> the Lower Market Square, and this (pointing
> Westward) is High Street!" Looking around, the
> newcomers could see no town, nothing but bushes
> and trees. The houses were yet to be built. From
> this square, they followed Mr. Knisely west on
> High Street, where the enthusiastic proprietor
> pointed out the Courthouse Square, where he
> stated the Court House and Public Buildings
> would be erected. This square was like the former,
> with the exception that some bushes were cut and
> some corner stakes driven.[79]

John and Elizabeth must have worked very hard to establish
themselves. They had 15 children, of whom twelve were still
living in 1846 when he drafted his will.

My grandmother Amy left me a copy of this will, which
indicates that he and Elizabeth had prospered:

> I, John Ripley .... give, devise and bequeath to my
> beloved wife Elizabeth Ripley, the plantation on
> which we now reside, containing about eighty
> acres be the same more or less, for the rest of her
> natural life. And all money or interest in my
> possession at my death and all the livestock,
> horses, cattle, sheep, hogs etc. by me owned or
> kept thereon ... [80]

Special mention is made in the will of the fact that he had already
given his two of his sons, John and Jacob Ripley, land worth
$150 each. John Ripley, his eldest son, was May's great-
grandfather.

This John Ripley, born in Pennsylvania in 1795 but as we
have seen already farming in Ohio in 1846, married Unity

McBride in 1821.[81] Unity had been born in Delaware in 1795. All I have found out about her parents are that they were both born in Ireland.[82] John and Unity settled and farmed in Guernsey County, Ohio, which adjoins Tuscarawas County. They had four sons: Ezekiel Cooper, Asbury, Isaiah and George Washington. Their second son, Asbury, born in 1827, was May's grandfather.

May could count at least two Civil War soldiers on her father's side (along with the many on her mother's side). Her uncles Ezekiel Cooper Ripley and Isaiah Ripley both fought for the Union and in fact joined the same regiment on the same day. Ezekiel died of disease while fighting in Kentucky in 1862.[83] His younger brother Isaiah was luckier, and was mustered out in 1863.[84] Isaiah and George Washington Ripley stayed in Ohio the rest of their lives, as did their parents. John died in 1872 at the age of 77 (not quite reaching his father's 90 years of age), and Unity died in 1888 at the age of 93.[85]

Ripleys in Illinois, Nebraska and Beyond (1848-1960s): May's Father's Family

Unlike his brothers, Asbury Ripley didn't stay in Ohio to farm. As mentioned earlier, he had married Elizabeth Eleanor Owings (the descendent of the prosperous Maryland Owings family and also of Ninian Beall) in Ohio in 1848.[86] Asbury and Eleanor had ten children between 1849 and 1867, of whom seven reached adulthood.[87] Their third child, May's father Jehu Beal Ripley, was born in 1855 in Henry County, Illinois. Sometime between 1851 and 1855,[88] the family had moved west to farm near Cambridge township in Henry County. This area of Illinois has gently rolling and very fertile farmland. I used to enjoy my visits to Henry County because there were roads that curved and went off at angles – unlike the endless grid of the cornfields further to the south.

The 1870 census shows that Asbury Ripley was a successful farmer with real estate valued at $6,000, and a personal estate valued at $2,500. He was able to employ a farm laborer.[89] However successful they may have been, their years in Illinois were marked by loss. In common with other parents of the time, they had already lost two children in infancy. In 1871, their son Denton died at the age of 14. The family stayed in Illinois until at least 1880: their land, less than a mile to the north of the town of Cambridge, appears on the 1875 township map, labeled "A. Ripley".[90]

The Ripleys did not settle in Illinois, however. A number of the family went to Nebraska. Asbury and Eleanor moved to Harvard, Nebraska along with three of their children (aged between 20 and 28) in a covered wagon in 1887.[91] Their eldest, Margaret Unity Ripley Spencer, was in Harvard, Nebraska by 1900. Another daughter, Edith Ella Ripley Curry, was there in 1890.[92] Sadly, Edith died in 1898 at the age of 37, leaving three young children and her husband behind. Asbury and Eleanor spent the rest of their days in Nebraska, cared for by Fannie May, the youngest Ripley (known as "Aunt Fan").[93]

What of the Ripleys who didn't settle in Nebraska? Sarah Maranda Ripley, Jehu's sister, married John Critchlow in Trinity County, California in 1877. She spent the rest of her days in California, living to the ripe old age of 92 and no doubt witnessing some amazing changes since her arrival 66 years earlier. Jehu's brother John Henry Ripley, who followed his parents to Nebraska when he was 28, married Ann Armfield the next year. They had 13 children, all the while leading a restless existence that led them to the gold mines of French Gulch in Trinity County, California, then to Eastern Oregon, and finally to British Columbia in Canada. John Henry seems often to have followed (or preceded) his older brother Jehu Beal. They mined together at French Gulch, and the two families lived nearby in Eastern Oregon for at least nine years.[94]

Although the various Ripleys settled in far-flung places (Nebraska, Oregon, California, British Columbia), connections were maintained, and there was a great sense of family pride. My Granny, Amy, felt a loyal attachment to the Ripleys: she always told us that her full name was Amy Emma Ripley Diddy Papineau -- something we would recite to amaze our schoolfriends. It now strikes me as unusual for a girl at the start of the 20th century to claim her mother's maiden name as part of her own.

May had some complimentary things to say about Ripley good looks. She wrote:

> I went to the Victor where we found Austin my youngest born (who has decided to add a year to my age by claiming twentyone years instead of twenty) is growing handsomer every day. He is the best looking Ripley since Aunt Fannie's time, for he is all Ripley. (5 Jan. 1925)

Indeed, my great-uncle Austin remained dapper until the end of his days. It should be said that May's praise for the Ripleys was not completely unqualified. Reflecting on problems which afflict families, she refers to her Uncle John's gambling habit: "he was a cancer on the happiness of one generation of Ripleys" (27 Nov. 1927). The inference here is that he was the exception to the Ripley rule.

My grandmother Amy kept in touch with at least two branches of the Ripley family besides her own immediate Ripley relatives. I have inherited correspondence between Amy and her Canadian cousins (John Henry's children), and on at least one occasion my grandparents travelled a thousand miles north from Redding, California to a Ripley family reunion in British Columbia.

The other Ripley link that Amy kept alive eluded me for nearly a year of my research. I remembered being taken by my grandparents, at the age of about four, to visit an elderly lady named Elizabeth Hendricks in Longview, Washington. I recalled a kind, grey-haired lady who lived in a high-rise, and then after our visit being taken to a place like a carnival, being lifted up onto a brightly colored merry-go-round horse, and held there safely. My Granny always kept Elizabeth Hendricks in high regard, and I knew that Elizabeth had some connection to May and the Ripleys. After many hours of searching and combing, I found that Elizabeth Hendricks had begun life in 1890 in Harvard, Nebraska as Mary Elizabeth Curry, whose mother Edith Ella Ripley Curry, Jehu's sister, had died when Elizabeth was only eight.

Elizabeth Curry went on to marry Bernard Clifford Hendricks, a Chemistry professor at the University of Nebraska. They retired to Longview to be with family, and Bernard was tragically killed in a car accident there in March of 1965.[95] Granny and Grampa must have taken me to visit Elizabeth that first summer of her widowhood, the summer I was four, to express their condolences and see how she was. Indeed there may have been more than one visit to Elizabeth, as she outlived both my grandparents.

I believe there was a sympathy between my Granny and Elizabeth that went beyond the family connection. They kept in touch over the years (my Granny's papers record her correspondence with Elizabeth) and I believe they had a bond of friendship. I also suspect my Granny enjoyed knowing a Ripley cousin who had married a college professor, because like May, Granny very much valued education.[96] Not only was Elizabeth's husband an academic, but in 1964 her son-in-law had become the President of the Women's Medical College of Pennsylvania.[97] Although I never located the "College President" ancestor May referred to in 1927, years later there was at least one in the extended Ripley family tree!

And now finally, patient reader, all the strands of family history have come together and we have arrived at May's own parents. In 1876, Jehu Beal Ripley (age 21) married the barely-15-year-old Olive Perryman (Civil War escapee and quite possibly an orphan by then).[98] As mentioned, I don't know where they wed, but the 1880 Census finds them in Humboldt, Allen

County, Kansas. Jehu "works on [the] farm," Olive "keeps house" and they have an eight-month-old daughter, May, born in Kansas.[99]

Part Two:

May's Life Before her Diaries

1.

Growing-up Years: from Kansas to Oregon (1879 – 1899)

As a child I was told that May's family had come west to Oregon, bringing her trunk in a covered wagon. What I hadn't understood was that this journey had taken the family nearly twenty years. When I first read May's 1920s diaries, I was very struck by the instability of her life: she and her second husband were constantly on the move. But when I looked into her history I realized that in fact she (along with her very young mother) had been moving all her life, like so many women who had no choice but to follow the head of the household to "pastures greener".

In telling me about Jehu, my grandmother said that he was a "Kansas railroad man".[1] I haven't been able to find any evidence that specifically states that Jehu worked for the railroad, but that in itself doesn't mean he didn't. Despite my best efforts, I still have no clear picture of the path that took Jehu from his family farm in Illinois (where he appears at the age of 5 in the 1860 census)[2] to his wedding to Olive in 1876 – and indeed I still have many unanswered questions about the years when he moved his growing family further and further west.

In the 1870 census, when Jehu was 15 years old, he is mysteriously absent from the enumeration of the members of his family's household in Henry County, Illinois. This could simply mean that the census taker – or whomever was answering the questions – made a mistake. Or it could mean that Jehu had left home. Curiously, his younger brothers Denton, age 13, and John, age 11, were listed as having the occupation of "Farm Laborer," whereas Margaret, age 20, and Sarah, age 19, were both "At school".[3] If the Ripley boys were allowed, or made, to leave school at an early age in order to work, it is possible that Jehu had left home at 15. However, I can't locate him anywhere else in the 1870 census, so it is also quite likely that he was still living at home and was simply missed out.

We know that Jehu married Olive in 1876, that May was born in 1879 in Kansas, and that in 1880 Jehu, Olive and baby May were living in the town of Humboldt, Kansas. According to my grandmother's recollections in "The Diddy Family of Flintlock Inn," May was born in Yates Center, Kansas.[4] Yates Center is less than twenty miles from Humboldt, and according to a 1912 history of Kansas, was "the railroad center of the county".[5] So it is quite possible that Jehu was working for the railroad when he met and married Olive. Certainly the 1870s was a boom-time for the railroad's expansion. Louis Reed's "Railroads in Kansas" states that: "The five year period ending in 1873 was one of feverish railroad building in the U.S..... Kansas was a perfect example of the railroad mania which seized the country."[6] In 1870 the Leavenworth, Lawrence & Galveston railroad was run through Humboldt – so Jehu and his family were living near at least one railroad in that town as well.[7] However, Jehu's occupation was listed as farming in the 1880 census.

Olive Almeda Perryman Ripley (age 18) with baby May on her lap, early 1880. I am very taken with Olive's splendid shawl!

Jehu and Olive did not stay in Kansas and it would seem that, if Jehu was employed to some extent by the railroad, he left that behind as well. By 1885, the family was living in Sheridan Township, Poweshiek County, Iowa. They now had two daughters: May (listed as Martha), 6 years old, and Nora, born there the year before. Jehu's occupation was again listed as "Farmer" and indeed all his neighbors were also farmers.[8] Iowa is well-known for its rolling, fertile farmland. By 1885 Sheridan Township was fairly well-established. It had a school (built in 1858), a Methodist church (built in 1877) and a post office (also built in 1877). However, the first general store was not to arrive until 1887.[9]

What was life on the farm in Iowa like for 6-year-old May? I presume she went to school. My Granny said that May had "read the Bible completely through by the time she was seven years of age."[10] It may well have been the case that the Bible was one of the only books the family owned. If May was a keen reader, she may have turned to it for its stories rather than out of any precocious religiousness. May also had to work hard helping her mother bring up the younger children. Jehu and Olive's third child, Margaret, was born in Iowa in 1886. Fifty years later May recalled: "As a child I did the work of a grown person from the time I could stand on a box and bend over a washtub of dirty didys" (5 Nov. 1927). Olive's obituary states that "to [Olive and Jehu] were born nine children."[11] As my family only knows of seven children, it is possible there were two other babies who did not survive.

The Ripleys didn't stay long in Iowa. Three years later they had moved again, to Valley City in Barnes County, North Dakota, where Ray Asbury Ripley was born in 1889.[12] Once again Jehu was living in a railroad town: Valley City was founded in 1872 when the Northern Pacific Railway arrived.[13] (In fact, one of the tourist attractions of Valley City today is "Rosebud," the "1881 Northern Pacific Superintendent's railcar with original furnishings".[14]) However, Valley City also developed as a fertile agricultural center.[15] Whether Jehu farmed or worked on the railroad I don't know.

The Ripley family was in North Dakota at a critical moment in its history – particularly critical for its native people. After the Battle of the Little Big Horn in 1876, Native Americans had been steadily rounded up onto reservations by the Bureau of Indian Affairs. It was in 1889 that the Lakota signed away nine million acres of tribal land.[16] I wonder whether the Ripleys saw any of the Indians who participated in the Ghost Dance religion which swept across the tribes of the Plains in 1890? I wonder if they read or heard accounts of how the U.S. military put a stop to the ghost dancers at Wounded Knee in South Dakota? As mentioned, my grandmother told me that May was a gifted midwife who was familiar with Indian herbal remedies. I think it is far likelier that she came into direct, friendly, contact with Native Americans in Oregon and California than in her childhood moving across the Great Plains.

Within five years, Jehu and his family were on the move again. They ended up in Oregon, but via an interlude in Northern California – an interlude that I nearly missed. While researching May's family history, I found a note from a conversation I'd had with Amy that said: "[Jehu] came to French Gulch [California]. John his brother went to John Day [Oregon]. After 2 yrs Jehu took his family." I didn't remember anyone speaking of May's family being in California prior to May's life there with her first husband John Diddy – the story had always been that the Ripley family came west to Oregon. (I hadn't yet received my Granny's reminiscences published by Shasta County Historical Society.) For a while I began to wonder if she had not been mistaken. However, I eventually found a typescript of an 1894 voter registration record from Shasta County, California. And on it I read:

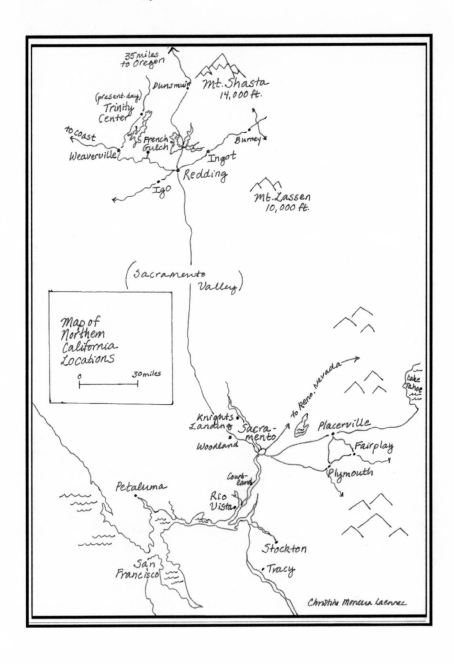

35 miles to Oregon

Dunsmuir

Mt. Shasta 14,000 ft.

(present-day) Trinity Center

to coast

French Gulch

Burney

Weaverville

Ingot

Redding

Igo

Mt. Lassen 10,000 ft.

(Sacramento Valley)

Map of Northern California Locations

0   30 miles

to Reno, Nevada

Lake Tahoe

Knights Landing

Sacramento

Placerville

Woodland

Fairplay

Plymouth

Court-land

Petaluma

Rio Vista

Stockton

San Francisco

Tracy

Christine Moneera Laennec

Ripley, Jeahu B. [age] 38 [born] IL [residence] French Gulch

[registration date] Mar 14 1894
[height] 5' 6 ¼" [eyes] Blue [hair] Brown

Ripley, John H. [age] 35 [born] IL [residence] French Gulch

[registration date] Mar 14 1894
[height] 5' 10 ½" [eyes] Blue [hair] Light[17]

I now had evidence that the two brothers were, just as Amy had told me, in French Gulch. (I apologized out loud then and there for doubting her.) My Granny's words as I noted them were: "After two years Jehu took his family [to John Day, Oregon]". The next thing I know for certain is that on March 23rd 1895, Olive and Jehu's fifth child, Leo Henry, was born in John Day, Oregon.[18]

I do not have absolute confirmation that Jehu brought his wife and family along with him to French Gulch, because women were not allowed to vote in the United States until 1920, so no women are listed on the register of voters. The fact that Olive was pregnant with Leo for the latter half of 1894 is a good indicator that she and the children did accompany Jehu to the mountains of Northern California. May was 13 years old, Nora ten, Margaret eight, and Ray five.

Jehu had moved his family many times before, but this was by far the longest of their moves: about 1,750 miles to travel between Valley City, North Dakota and Northern California. As well, it must have been quite a change of environment for all the family. In Kansas, Iowa and North Dakota they had lived in open farming country. But, as I know from visiting the area, French Gulch is in a mountainous, densely forested region, at the foot of the Siskyou – Trinity wilderness area. Winding roads along lakes and twisting rivers lead one quickly up from the town of Redding, at the head of the Sacramento valley, into the mountains. French Gulch, now at the end of a spur off the road between Redding and the coast, lies along Clear Creek. It got its name from the French Canadian prospectors who had found gold there in the 1848 gold rush.[19] Fifty years on the gold had run out, but as in so many other places in Shasta County, there was copper to be mined.[20]

Jehu and John Henry were not the first Ripleys to go to California. Their sister Sarah Maranda Ripley Critchlow had been married in Trinity Center, Trinity County (which adjoins Shasta County) in 1877, and as we shall see at least two of Jehu's Owings uncles were also in Trinity County prior to 1894. The distance between French Gulch and Trinity Center was not easily covered, being about 60 miles of very windy mountainous roads – or in those days paths and trails. So it is difficult to know how much contact Jehu and John Henry would have had with their sister and uncles.

What were Jehu and John Henry doing in French Gulch in 1894? The information that Amy gave to Elouise Shuffleton was that "Jehu ... had come to California to work in the Gladstone Mine".[21] A look at the 1900 census pages for French Gulch (frustratingly, the 1890 census is currently unavailable) shows 450 inhabitants living in the township, followed by a poignant list of 13 Indians who had received American citizenship. The great majority of the men are listed as having the occupation of "Miner (ores)". There are also a few farmers and ranchers listed, as well as two blacksmiths, two carpenters, three mail-carriers, several wood-choppers and teamsters, and more than a few saloon and hotel owners and employees. (Luke and Thomas McDonald, born in California of Scottish and Irish parents, both list their occupation as "Capitalist"!)[22] There was a schoolteacher in French Gulch in 1900: John J. Dailey, age 27, who was also the census-taker. If indeed May and her brothers and sisters were living in French Gulch in 1894, I wonder what kind of schooling they were able to have?

Once again the Ripleys moved on – to the John Day Valley in Oregon, a mere 500 miles to the north. And this time, after twenty years on the move, Jehu and Olive stayed. They lived in or near towns that were all in close proximity of one another in the area: Canyon City, Marysville, the town of John Day. The Ripleys came to Eastern Oregon a few years before yet another gold rush. Gold was found in Canyon City in 1898.[23] Martha Gay Masterson's impressions of arriving in Canyon City in 1874 make one wonder how the town could have supported a sudden boom:

> We were sadly disappointed. We had hoped to see an inviting place, but instead we saw a little mining camp built in a narrow canyon. There was only room for one street, the houses being built on either side of it. Freight wagons coming into the town had to drive the entire length of the street and out of town to find room to turn around. What a barren-looking place it was to us after living in the verdant Willamette Valley. .... We liked the place better [once we became] accustomed to the wild, weird aspect of the surrounding country.[24]

The discovery of gold affected the nearby settlements of John Day and Marysville as well. Here is an extract from the March 1898 diary of Effie Brandt of Canyon City:

> There is quite a bit of excitement in town about the mine on the mountain. It is owned by a German named Guger [sic]. They took out one piece worth $1,500 yesterday. A very rich mine, it makes me hungry for such good luck. Papa has a 1/2 interest in a mine in Marysville, which John is thinking of leasing and working for a while. If he does, I will be alone again this summer, but if only we could make money at it, it would be grand![25]

The town of John Day, as well as the John Day River, was named after an early explorer of Oregon.[26] In the second half of the 19th century, John Day was also home to one of the largest Chinese populations in Eastern Oregon. Many of the Chinese were miners.[27] As the mining dried up, the John Day valley became increasingly important as an agricultural area, and is now known as "cattle country".[28] It is an area of high desert, with famous fossil beds and amazing rock formations of many colors. Again, it would have been quite a change from the Ripleys' most recent home in the forested mountains of French Gulch.

May was 15 years old when her brother Leo Henry was born in John Day, Oregon in March 1895. As we know, the family had only recently arrived from Northern California. Her uncle John Henry Ripley and his family were in John Day as well.[29] Her youngest surviving sibling, Lela, was born three years later (March 1898) when May was 18 years old.[30] Presumably May was still helping out with washing diapers, and possibly she was still receiving some schooling.

The 1900 census shows the family living in Marysville, a few miles east of Canyon City and the town of John Day. Jehu's occupation is listed as "Road Supervisor" – so May was not exaggerating years later when she said that she was a supervisor's daughter. In 1901, Jehu and Olive had a son named Perryman (after Olive's father's family) but he did not live. His existence was unknown to my mother until 2007, when she visited the cemetery in Grant County, and found his grave.[31] The next year the family suffered more heartache when 16-year-old daughter Maggie died.[32]

However, May was no longer in Oregon when these sad events occurred. Her life changed forever when she married John Diddy in Trinity Center, California on November 14th, 1899. Her departure from the family home in Oregon continued to be of significance to her in later years, and there is a great sadness in her recollections. Of the three diaries that she kept, two are written during the fall months, and in both of these May remembers leaving Oregon. On October 30th, 1926 she reflected:

"Twenty-odd years ago my young friends gave me a farewell party. 'Surprise' – I being on the eve of flight from the home nest. Life has contained a great many surprises since then, some of them not as jolly as my farewell party from the John Day Valley." A year later, she wrote: "Tonight is Halloween, the anaversary of the night I left my father's care to intrust myself to the care of another man; a thing I regretted in less than a year and continued to regrett untill I grew old enough to understand it was only a kind of school where in I received needed training in order to make me a good mother; and a better wife to the one whose name I now bear." (31 Oct. 1927)

As far as I know, May only returned to Oregon on the rare occasion, perhaps only once in 1931. What were the events that led up to her first, unhappy marriage?

**The Jehu and Olive Ripley family, John Day, Oregon, ca. 1899
Standing, left to right: May (abt. 19), Ray (abt. 10), Nora (abt. 15)
Seated, left to right: Jehu Ripley (abt. 44), Leo (abt. 5), Lela (abt. 1
½), Olive Perryman Ripley (abt. 38). Maggie (abt. 13) is not in the
photograph, presumably because she was unwell.**

John Diddy (age 42) and May Ripley Diddy (just 21)
Redding, California, October 1900

2.

Married Life in California
(1899 – 1925)

Ripleys and Diddys

As we've seen, in March 1898, the same month that May's youngest sister Lela was born, Effie Brandt was excited about the prospects of her father's mine in the John Day Valley. May turned 19 in September of that year. This must have been a very turbulent period of her life. The story my grandmother told my mother is that May fell in love with a Catholic boy. Certainly the John Day area had been flooded by prospectors that year, so there would have been a sudden influx of available men from all parts of the world. My grandmother said that May's liaison with a Catholic so disgraced the Ripley family that May was married off to John Diddy, a man twenty years her senior.

Less than two months after her 20th birthday, May married 41-year-old John Diddy on November 14th , 1899 in Weaverville, Trinity County, California, about 60 miles northwest of French Gulch. We know from her diaries that she left John Day, Oregon on the 31st of October. The 500-mile journey would probably have taken the better part of two weeks in those days. Did she travel all that way unaccompanied? (It seems unlikely.) Had she ever met John Diddy before arriving in Weaverville to marry him? Had she known him when she was 13 and 14 years old, living in French Gulch? Clearly the marriage took place far from her family and friends.

In her diaries, May does not seem to judge or blame her parents for whatever role they played in this first marriage. Her inscription on the photograph that she sent home to Oregon a year later is as melancholy as the expressions on her and John Diddy's faces. I think her words express deep homesickness, and a desire to please or even placate her parents:

> To Mr and Mrs J. B. Ripley from their faraway children sent with loveing thoughts and fond wishes Mr and Mrs John Diddy, Oct 26 1900, Redding Cal.

> We may cross the tossing billows
> We may sail the wide blue sea
> But the old folks ne're forget us
> Where ever we may be

Certainly John Diddy was far from being like a child to Mr and Mrs Jehu Beal Ripley.

In later years, May identified with her own mother when she reflected on the paths their lives had taken and the limited choices that they had in life. She remarked: "I had to be forty years old to realize my mother is a wiser woman than I" (26 Oct. 1927) and "Poor Mama. I think in some life Mama and I must have failed to do our duty, but we have sure paid for our sins in the life we are now liveing." (4 Nov. 1927) Although she was increasingly unhappy in her second marriage, May's diaries reflect the reality of how economically dependent women were, and she was philosophical about the benefits of being (re-)married: "...what would life be if I had not married [again]. I'd [have] been just like Mama and Aunt Julia, at every one's beck and call, no home of my own and oh so unhappy." (29 Nov. – 2 Dec. 1927)

Who was this John Diddy, and what was his connection with Jehu and Olive Ripley? What I don't think my grandmother knew was something that I, peering at a computer screen in my kitchen in Scotland one winter evening, was amazed to discover. On the 1870s census form listing the relatively prosperous Asbury Ripley / Elizabeth Eleanor Owings family of Henry County, Illinois (real estate valued at $6000, personal estate valued at $2500, parents of 13-year-old Jehu Beal), were some neighbors only a few farms away: the William Diddy family, with 11-year-old son John. The 1875 Cambridge township map shows the two farms: A. Ripley to the north of the town, and W. Diddy to the west. William Diddy's son John grew up to be the man to whom Jehu and Olive Ripley married their eldest daughter thirty years later. John Diddy was a childhood friend (or at least associate) of Jehu Ripley. I don't think that my granny Amy was aware of this fact, partly because my mother was unaware of it and I was never told it by Amy, and partly because Amy described Jehu to me as a "Kansas railway man".[33] It makes me wonder whether May herself knew of the boyhood connection between her father and the man that her parents married her off to.

Here also I must admit to a streak of long-nurtured prejudice against John Diddy – the first husband that so hurt my granny Amy and great-granny May. May herself, perhaps understandably, did not speak well of the Diddy family. When she wrote of her youngest, Austin, that he was "the best looking Ripley since Aunt Fannie's time" she continued in scathing vein about the Diddys: "If he has any of his father's blood in him it is all on the inside, for I never saw a good looking person in the whole family." (5 Jan. 1925) Certainly Amy – who generally followed the rule of saying nothing at all if you didn't have anything nice to say – communicated to me that she didn't think much of her own father. We will never know what disappointments and frustrations John Diddy faced with his strong-willed and possibly very ambivalent young wife, or why he agreed to marry her.

Who were the Diddys? John's father, William Diddy, was a farmer, born in New York.[34] John's mother, Margaret Bull, was born in Ireland.[35] In Henry County, Illinois in 1870, their real estate was worth $800 and their personal estate valued at $400: a total worth which was 1/8 of that of their neighbors the Ripleys. John had three brothers – George, Charles and Thomas – and two sisters, Mary and Margaret. I would love to know more about the relationship between the Ripleys and the Diddys, because their paths intertwine at several points down the years. Both families came to Illinois from Ohio in the 1850s and 1860s.[36] John Diddy's sister Mary married John Mark Owings, Elizabeth Eleanor Owings' brother and thus Jehu Ripley's uncle. John Mark Owings was farming in Trinity Center, California at the time of the 1870 census. But he travelled back to Ohio at least once, because he married Mary Diddy there in 1874. In 1880 John and Mary Owings were living in Trinity Center, along with McKenzie Owings, another of Jehu Ripley's uncles.

William Diddy, John and Mary Diddy's father, also came to Trinity County, California. Sometime between 1880 and 1896 (thus when he was between the ages of 64 and 80) he and his wife Margaret travelled thousands of miles from Henry County, Illinois to Trinity Center.[37] My mother remembers that her parents used to take the family for picnics up in Weaverville. She was told that John Diddy's father had some connection to one of the shops there with the cast-iron staircase winding to the upper floor. I haven't been able to determine what this connection was, and clearly William Diddy was getting on in years by the time he arrived in California. Notes from a conversation I had with my grandmother Amy say that William Diddy was working at Scott's Ranch in Trinity Center, 40 miles north of Weaverville.[38]

Section of 1875 Cambridge Township Map, Henry County, Illinois.
Asbury Ripley's land is near the top left, and William Diddy's land
is near the bottom right.

Reproduced with kind permission from the Henry County
Genealogical Society,
Kewanee, Illinois. This is one of several 1875 Henry County
Township maps available on the Henry County Genealogical
Society website
(http://www.rootsweb.ancestry.com/~ilhcgs/)

It is possible that William Diddy went west before his wife did, because in 1895 she appears on the Iowa census as living in (or visiting) Belvidere, Monona County, Iowa – no doubt she was with her son George Diddy who settled there.[39] She did not live long after travelling to (or back to) California, for she died in Trinity Center in 1896. She and William were living with their daughter and son-in-law, Mary Diddy Owings and John Mark Owings, at the time. A typescript kindly supplied to me by the Trinity County Historical Society records her death: "DIDDY, MARGARET. Died at residence of John M. Owing in Trinity Valley July 9, 1896; beloved wife of Wm. M. Diddy, aged 75 yr 2 mo 7 dy. (TJ Sat. Aug 1, 1896)."[40]

How long had John Diddy himself been living in California? He had been there since at least 1880, when he was listed on the census as farming in Trinity Center. Interestingly, he is living in the same house as a Chambers Owings in 1880.[41] I can't find a connection between Chambers Owings and the Owings / Ripley family – but this isn't to say that there isn't one. In the same census, McKenzie Owings and John Mark Owings (Jehu Ripley's uncles) are listed as living next door to one another in Trinity Center, and were both listed as farming. John Mark Owings was sufficiently well-off to employ a farm laborer.[42]

Jehu's sister Sarah Maranda Ripley Critchlow and her family had left Trinity Center by 1880 and had moved to Redding. Sarah's husband John was working as a teamster, and they also employed a servant / nurse.[43] The 1885 Trinity County Directory lists the same families living in Trinity Center:

> Diddy, John [no occupation listed]
> Owings, Chambers - farmer
> Owings, John M. – farmer
> Owings, McKenzie - 200 acres[44]

Trinity Center in 1885 was an important town in Northern California. According to the Shasta Historical Society (whose website also lists 1885 township directories for other counties)

Trinity Center was "the second place of importance in the county, and the only point having telegraphic communication with the outside." Unlike today, it was located on the main route north to Oregon, and the stagecoaches of the California and Oregon Stage Line passed through it daily. In 1885, "the prevailing interest, as elsewhere in the county, [was] mining, although several good sections of farming land [were] found in the neighborhood, mostly all cultivated and realizing handsome returns to their owners from the good prices received for their product."[45]

I presume that John Diddy stayed in Trinity Center from before 1880 (when he was 22) until his marriage in Weaverville to May nearly twenty years later. Whether or not he met May in her teenage years (ca. 1894) when her family came to French Gulch, sixty miles away from Trinity Center, will probably never be known. Regardless, her parents had connections to him through various of their relations. As we have seen, the Ripleys and the Diddys had been connected in several ways since at least the 1860s.

May's feeling that she was married below her station in life is confirmed to some extent by the economic differences between the two families in 1870.[46] Also, it would seem that the male Diddys never met with huge success in life. In the 1900 census we find Charles Diddy, age 45 and single, as well as Thomas Diddy, 39 and single, in Monona County, Iowa, listed as working for their brother George Diddy on his farm.[47] George seems to have been successful in life at this point: he was married with two children and he had a boarder, as well as employing his brothers. However, in the same month (June 1900) the very same George Diddy (with exactly the same birth date, place and two parents born in New York) was in the Iowa Hospital for the Insane.[48] Five years later he was back in Monona County, but now living on his own.[49] Surely a very sad story lies behind these bald facts. John Diddy, as we've seen, was married to May and living in Trinity Center, California by 1900. In the next decade Charles followed John to California, and worked as a hired hand.[50] In

1920, 61-year-old Thomas Diddy was an "inmate" in Woodmere Old Folks Home in Portland, Oregon.[51]

It is sad to reflect that it was the pride (and religious prejudice) of the Owings and Ripleys that drove May into exile and a loveless marriage. But at the very same time, her family pride was also what gave her a sense of worth in years to come.

May's First Marriage: from Trinity Center to the Flintlock Inn near Ingot (1900 – 1918)

On the 6th day of June, 1900, the census taker in Trinity Center listed May M. Diddy, age 20, wife of John Diddy, age 42 and a farmer. They had been married for seven months and were living next door to John Mark Owings, age 71 (May's great-uncle) and Mary Diddy Owings, age 44 (John Diddy's sister) and their daughters.[52] What the census does not reveal is that May was expecting her first child. And what no-one that day could have known was that this first child, Lyle Beal Diddy (the last Beal of the Owings/Ripley line to my knowledge) was either to be still-born or to die shortly after birth a month later. No wonder May looks so very sad in the photograph taken in Redding in October of that same year.

The existence of Lyle Beal Diddy, who was born and who died July 10th, 1900, might never have been known to our family if it hadn't been for the 1950s feats of hydroelectric engineering that were to transform much of Northern California. In 1961, the original town of Trinity Center was flooded and relocated to higher ground when the Trinity Dam was built.[53] I remember my grandparents taking me to see it as a child. They pointed out to me the contours of the water's edge which had once been forested hillsides, and told me that far down below had been the graveyard of some of the family. The thought of ghostly trees and cemeteries under the water made me shudder. In the late 1950s, before the waters were let loose, my grandmother Amy had to go and identify the Diddy family graves before they could be moved. She was very surprised to find the grave of her older brother Lyle Beal, because May had never spoken about him. It is hard to imagine how painful those years must have been for May.

May and John didn't stay long in Trinity Center. By the end of 1900, they had moved to the small settlement of Ingot, east of Redding. Here they ran the roadhouse, or teamster's stop, called the Flintlock Inn.[54] The site of the roadhouse is now a forest fire station called Diddy Wells. The first years of the new century were marked by great sadness. John and May had another son, Everett Oliver Diddy, who was born and died on the same day on April 12, 1901.[55] The news from the Ripleys in John Day at this time would not have been any more cheerful, as May's youngest brother, Perryman, was born and died in 1901, and her 16-year-old sister Maggie died the next year.

May and John were not to remain childless, however: Leslie arrived in 1902, Amy in 1903, and Austin in 1905. Amy always told us that she'd been born "in Ingot, near the Afterthought Mine," which caught my imagination as a child: in my mind, it was the gold mine that was nearly undiscovered. Only recently was I able to see Ingot for myself. In 2008, it was still very much in the shadow of the closed copper (not gold) mine. Up the road a mile or two, the fire-fighters (very busy that summer) kindly let us walk around Diddy Wells fire station: it was difficult to know where the Flintlock Inn once was.

I grew up hearing about Amy's childhood in the teamster's stop. Here is Amy's memory of it in 1974:

> My mother named the place [the Flintlock Inn]. It was a stopping place for the teamsters that hauled ore from the Afterthought mine at Ingot to Bella Vista. The original house was like two houses with a covered porch in between. On one side was the living room, dining room, kitchen and one bedroom. On the other five bedrooms and a room we called The Fireplace as it had a fireplace in it,

> and was the teamsters' living room. There was a
> well near the house and the one where the fire
> guard station is [was] where we had our garden.[56]

I knew that Amy and her brothers had the red, white and blue
goats, and I remember seeing photographs of my grandmother
feeding the chickens in Ingot. I always pictured May running the
teamster stop more or less singlehandedly, but according to my
Granny's recollections as published in The Covered Wagon, John
Diddy "shod horses, repaired and made harnesses, built wagons
and sleds, and did other repairs as needed. He was also a fine
carpenter."[57] May was certainly kept busy. She did the cooking,
baking and washing for the paying guests, and made all the
family's clothes (John made their shoes). She looked after the
animals (goats, chickens and a milk cow) as well as growing
vegetables in the garden, gathering wild berries, making
preserves, smoking meat and making sausages.[58] My Granny also
told me that in addition to her other responsibilities, May worked
as a midwife during these years.

One of the stories that I heard from my Granny about the
roadhouse years was that May kept a myna bird whose tongue
had been cut so that it could talk. Apparently it could imitate
May's voice perfectly. It used to lift the old-fashioned phone
receiver off the hook and speak into it, fooling most people for an
initial minute. In her recollections of the Flintlock Inn, Amy said
that "May had a good voice and often sang or whistled as she
worked. The family didn't have a piano or any type of musical
instrument." Also, May "walked the three miles on the thick
dusty trail along Cow Creek to teach a Sunday school class at the
Ingot Elementary School."[59] The dusty trails occasionally turned
to knee-deep mud (the school once closed for two weeks as a
result), and during cattle drives they were no place for children:
"Another source of excitement was the cattle drives. One
neighbor after another would start the telephones ringing down
the canyon to get the children in because the cattle were coming.

The Diddy children would scamper to safety and peer out of the windows."[60]

As a girl I was given an accidental insight into another side of Amy's life at the teamster stop. When I was about 9 years old, I learned some bad words. In 1969 there were a lot of new words, like "groovy" and "cool" and "far out". And I thought that all the new words I had learned had been recently invented, including some of these bad ones. So one day, on a visit to my Granny and Grampa's house, I tried out one of these new (bad) words. My granny put her hairbrush down: "Christine! Where did you hear that word?!! I ought to wash your mouth out with soap right this minute." But I in my turn was completely astonished: "Granny! How do you know that word? I thought they didn't say those words when you were growing up." "Didn't say those words! Of course they said those words, and a lot more too. I heard plenty of words growing up at the teamster stop, and men saying, come here little girl and sit on my knee. But I never did, I knew better than that." Luckily for me I avoided the soap treatment on that occasion, but it gave me another picture of my white-gloved and church-going granny's Wild West upbringing.

The family did not often get to Redding, the nearest town:

> Visits to Redding were few and far between. ... Amy said the most remembered adventure was her father's bringing the children to Redding to see the circus. It was an experience that they talked about for many years.
>
> Amy had dental problems. When her teeth needed attention, her mother and she would come to town by horse and buggy for several days and stay at the Golden Eagle Hotel and eat at Oyster Grotto. Dr. Fred Eaton would do her dental work, which never proved as exciting as the circus.[61]

John and May Ripley Diddy, ca. 1904
with Leslie (born 1902) and Amy (born 1903)

I rather imagine that Amy's dental problems proved to have a bit of a silver lining for May, who was far more sociable (and twenty years younger) than her husband. The Covered Wagon article tells us that "May walked to Ingot to attend dances, card parties, and any other of the many activities that went on at the school, the hotel, or the 'hospital' ... John Diddy rarely went with her, for his interests were more in creating things in wood, metal, or leather with his hands."[62]

The Diddy family appears in Ingot on the 1910 census: John (age 52, farmer) and May Diddy (age 30), Leslie E[dward] Diddy, age 8, Amy E[mma] Diddy, age 6, and Austin I[van] Diddy, age 5.[63] And this brings me to another family story, which will no doubt forever remain unconfirmed: that Leslie was not May's child. Amy's reminiscences in private were not always as positive as they were for the Shasta Historical Society interviewer. She told my mother that her father John Diddy was a philanderer, and had got a woman in Redding pregnant. When the baby was born – so May had told her– May went to her house and demanded the baby, saying "that is my husband's child and I will raise him".

If this story is true and Leslie was not born to May, at his birth in January 1902 she was a woman who had already lost two babies and whose husband had been unfaithful.[64] I think it is very possible that this is what happened, although the census records all imply that May is Leslie's mother.[65] Also, my grandmother told my mother that Leslie was constantly teased by his contemporaries in Ingot about being illegitimate. According to Amy, his true origins were an open secret in such a small community.[66] Years later May, visiting what seems to have been the site of the roadhouse, wrote about the "hours of work, pain, misery, shame and grief" she had had there. She wrote that her hard work over the years there "should have saved me from insults that are the lot of an unloved wife." (4 Nov. 1927) When writing a teasing letter to her brother about her second husband George having an interest in the Copper Queen – a mine, not a woman – she commented wryly: "Leo [knows] that I'd never whimper if my husband was chasing a dozen yellow, black or red hussys." (22 Nov. 1927)

As my granny told the story, Leslie's birth mother handed him over without argument. What the feelings on all sides really were – not to mention the effect on Leslie – will probably never be known. May certainly loved him and brought him up as her own child. She wrote often in her diary of how he was in her thoughts while he was away in the military: "Dreamed last night that Leslie came home. I was so happy. I told the dream as soon as I woke to test the old saying 'tell a dream before breakfast and it will come true.'" (7 Feb. 1925). But whereas she mused in her diary about Austin's Ripley vs. Diddy characteristics, and recalls (10 Feb. 1925) the weather on the day that Austin was born, there were no such reflections about Leslie.

I remember my great-uncle Leslie. I was always a little frightened of him as a child, because he didn't have an easy way about him. As I grew older, I was very impressed with my grandparents' great love and tact towards him when he lost his closest friend and the man he had lived with for years, Lewis. In hindsight it is easy to think that there was always something different about Leslie. His legacy to me is his red and black Pendleton shirt, which I treasure.

May had a very busy life running the roadhouse and bringing up her three children. Her marriage to John Diddy was loveless and difficult. May's poems, written between 1908 and 1913 (which I have placed after the diaries), show a great longing for happiness in an unhappy situation. Many of them, though not all, are on the theme of an impossible and forbidden love. Because the poems are very conventional for their time, it is hard to know how much they are based on the reality of May's life. However, some of them are so specific (for example the poem "I watch you lad ride down the road," 1915) that one wonders whether May actually was in love with another man during these years. There are initials (E.M., M., JF) by many of the poems, but who these refer to remains a mystery to me.

**May in the garden at the Flintlock Inn,
near Ingot, Shasta County, California ca. 1914**

The roadhouse years came to an end in about 1918, when May left John Diddy and took the children with her to Sacramento to start a new life. Her father, Jehu Ripley, had died three years earlier, and I wonder if this made it more possible for her to leave John Diddy.[67] She must have left Ingot before November 1918, because in her diaries she recalled being in Sacramento (along with a neighbor from near Ingot) at the Armistice on November 11th, 1918: "I can hear yet the Old Western Pacific Shop whistle and its endless screaming, and not till the rest of Sacramento's countless whistles joined in did any of us dream what was wrong untill Addie Colby yelled at me 'Oh it's Peace, it's Peace'." (11 Nov. 1927).

May's Life Between 1918 and 1925: Divorce, Single Parenthood, and her Second Marriage

When my Granny talked to me about her parents' divorce, she always spoke of it as May's decision to free herself from a desperate situation. She told me that May suffered a great deal in the process, losing a lot of linens and china that she had put into storage, and being looked down upon as a bad woman – but that in the end it was worth getting away from John Diddy. The version that appears in The Covered Wagon, perhaps not surprisingly, speaks of their divorce in veiled terms:

> When the three Diddy children were old enough to go to high school, May took her children and moved to Sacramento. She could not bear to board them in Redding. John and she differed in their thoughts regarding the need for higher education. May and her three children, therefore, moved from Flintlock Inn to make a new life. She worked in the butter room of the Crystal Dairy in Sacramento

and as a mid-wife to support and educate her children.[68]

May herself recollected this time in her diaries. She talks about leaving everything she had worked so hard for: "I kicked it all from my path once... on any frantic way to freedom" (4 Nov. 1927). As we have seen, she also writes about the scorn and derision that she was treated with as a divorced woman.

May and her children appear in the 1920 census. May is listed as May R. Diddy, living in Sacramento on Y Street. On the census form (completed on January 5th, 1920) she is the head of the household, 40 years old, living in a rented house. She is listed as married, so the divorce must not have been finalized. With her are Leslie E. Diddy, age 17, not employed, Amy E. Diddy, age 16, working as a stenographer at a dry-good store, and Austin Diddy, 14, working as a delivery boy for a drug store. All three children are also listed as having attending school "anytime since Sept. 1, 1919". It would seem that Leslie, Amy and Austin went to high school and also held down jobs. It is difficult to read what is written as May's occupation and working place but it looks to me like occupation "weigher", working in "cannery".[69] Others listed on the same census page work in the cannery. She supplemented her cannery income with midwifery. In her 1927 diary, May refers to her work as a midwife in Sacramento: "I've manage[d] to live with less sleep on this fleet than I ever had to even when nursing, one at least had a few hours off then." (16 Jan. 1927).

What happened to John Diddy? In the 1920 census he is 62 years old and living in Anderson, near Redding. He is married to Marie A. Adams, and her son William K. Adams is listed as being John Diddy's son. (Presumably this was not actually the case?) His occupation is "Labor[er]" working on a "Farm," and his wife's occupation is "Manager" on a farm. He died in 1925. There is some mystery surrounding the exact circumstances of his death. My grandmother heard rumors that he was found shot in a creek because he had been horse-stealing. Perhaps this story is true, or perhaps it simply reflects what other people were prepared to believe about him.

We have now nearly caught up with the opening pages of the three diaries that May wrote. In July of 1921, Amy (just two weeks past her 18th birthday) married Ethan Alexander Papineau. He and Amy lived in Sacramento. Their son Ethan Austin Papineau, known as Ethan Junior or just Junior, was born on March 3, 1923.

In between these two events, on December 2, 1922 – little more than two years before the start of her first diary – May married her second husband, George Washington Maylone. He was 8 years younger than May, and a cousin of Ethan Papineau's. The Maylones and the Papineaus had had nearby homesteads in Fairplay, El Dorado County, California, although Ethan's parents had since moved to Amador County. George's mother, Mary Esther Papineau Maylone, was Ethan's father's sister. An account of George Washington Maylone written by one of his cousins says:

> He didn't want to go back to the mountains (after seeing Paree [in World War I]) so settled in Sacramento and went to work in the ice house... He was finally transferred to the delivery routes, and on one of his deliveries he became acquainted with a lovely lady, Mae [sic] who surprisingly had roots in the Fairplay area too.[70]

We know that George and May met on January 11, 1920, because she marks the anniversary in her diary. Also, in February 1925 she mentions fixing the drawer in the kitchen at Cedarville ranch (the Maylone home near Fairplay), which she says has been broken since she first came there "almost five years ago" which would again be early 1920. Clearly George made as big an impression on her as the broken drawer – only a more positive one, to begin with.

May (abt. 40), Leslie (abt. 17), Amy (abt. 15) and Austin (abt. 14) Sacramento, California ca. winter 1918/1919

When the diary opens in January 1925, May and George or "G.W." are living in a cabin near Fairplay. Amy, Ethan and Ethan Jr. (a year and a half old) are living in Sacramento. They often go to visit Ethan's mother Louise Papineau in Amador County, and sometimes drive further east to visit May in Fairplay – though not as often as she would like. Taking out an old ledger book that she had written poems in back in 1908, May marked the beginning of a new year by starting a diary.

**May Ripley Diddy Maylone and George Washington
Maylone ca. 1922**

Amy Emma Diddy (just 17) and Ethan Alexander Papineau (nearly 19) 26 June 1920
They married the following summer.

Part Three:

May's Diaries

1.

May's 1925 Diary:

Homesteading in El Dorado County

This diary begins on page 25 of a black ledger book, following 24 pages of poems that May wrote beginning in 1908. May had painted a wide band of gold on the black front cover, with the letters MRD [May Ripley Diddy] formed by leaving some of the black cover unpainted. Inside, May had written her name in ink, and later when she used the book for her diary, she added "Maylone" in pencil. (In this edition I've put the poems in Part Four, following all three diaries.)

In January of 1925, May (age 45) and George Washington Maylone (age 37) had been married for just over two years. It was a second marriage for each of them. They were living in a cabin that May calls "Woodchucks," somewhere near Fairplay in El Dorado County, California, where George's parents and some of his brothers and sisters lived. On New Year's Day, May and George went from "Woodchucks" to visit Cedarville, a large hand-hewn cedar house in Fairplay that belonged to the Maylones. May's daughter Amy, and her husband Ethan Papineau, lived in Sacramento with their first-born, Ethan Jr., ("Junior") who in January 1925 was a year and 9 months old.

Jan 1 1925
Woodchucks

Sunshine, warm. Drove up to Cedarville, Geo., C.P.C., Orin and I. Stayed at the ranch to cook dinner, G[eorge], C., O[rin] & F[erdinand] went hunting. At noon my latest sweetheart R.C. came up there to keep me company – he played with Elwin's toys. I sorted papers to take to Dad at the store, at 4 o'clock Geo & F[erdinand] returned to the house, C.P.C. & Orin going home. We four, Ferd., Ray, Geo. & I, ate New Years dinner together. Geo. & I drove to F[air]P[lay] and spent the evening with Dad, Mother, Daisy & Elwin. Talked "try ranch". I can't see it yet, but maybe come out O.K. later. Letter from Amy. Let my ferns die.

❖ C. P. C. – Charles P. Croft, listed in the 1920 census of Cosumnes Township, El Dorado County, as a "farmer" working on a "general farm".[1] In 1925 he was 51. Eleanor E. [Hizer] Manning, George's niece, noted on a typescript of May's diaries: "Saved my life – brought medicine after snake-bite".

❖ Orin – Charles Croft's son Orin, 12 years old.

❖ Ferdinand – Edgar Ferdinand Maylone, George's older brother. In January 1925, Ferdinand was 40. Ferdinand had married Elizabeth "Bessie" Hizer in 1906. The Hizers had a homestead in Fairplay nearby the Maylones and Papineaus. The wedding in 1906 was a double one: Frank Hizer married Gertrude Maylone (George and Ferdinand's younger sister) on the same day. But things didn't go well for Bessie and Ferdinand. Bessie was only 15 when she married, and by 1925 Ferdinand was on his own. Their two children, Elwin E. and Daisy Idell Maylone, lived with their grandparents (see below).

❖ R. C. – Ray Croft, Charles' youngest, 10 years old. Elwin's toys – Elwin was 12.

❖ Dad at the store – George's father, Edgar Maylone. Edgar and Mary Esther Papineau Maylone ran the general store in Fairplay.

❖ Dad, Mother, Daisy & Elwin – Five years earlier, in the 1920 census, Edgar's household consisted of: Edgar Maylone, 57, head; [Mary] Esther [Papineau] Maylone, 56, wife; Louis E. Maylone, 30, son; Earl A. Maylone, 26, son; Theodore R. Maylone, 18, son; Daisy I. Maylone, 9, granddaughter; Elwin E. Maylone, 7, grandson, and Joseph N. Papineau, 79, father-in-law.[2] Mary Esther and Edgar had eleven children between 1884 and 1907, of whom nine lived. Mary Esther Papineau Maylone was the paternal aunt of Ethan Papineau, May's son-in-law (and my Grampa).

❖ Daisy and Elwin: Daisy Idell Maylone and Elwin E. Maylone, children of Edgar Ferdinand Maylone and Elizabeth "Bessie" Hizer. In Jan. 1925, Daisy was 14 and Elwin was 12. In 1998, Daisy Maylone Miller's memories of growing up in Fairplay were featured in the *Mountain Democrat*. "[T]he town of Fair Play at the time wasn't much... 'It consisted of a store and a post office.' But Miller said the community was close knit. 'Whenever a family decided to butcher a large animal, neighbors would come by to help out...' Work wasn't the only reason Fairplay residents got together 'For about five years, my family hosted a weekly dance...'"[3]

❖ Talked "try ranch" – the ranch is Cedarville.

Jan. 2, Fri.

G.W. [and] F[erdinand] cut wood. I just fiddled around with my housework. Sunny and warm. G.W. got an awful cold. Plan to go to Sac[ramento], want to get some ferns for Mary. If we do go Amy needs her black satine pants dusted [adjusted?], my own fault; should tend to my own Christmas giveing. No doubt she had enough of her own to tend to.

- ❖ G.W. - George Washington Maylone
- ❖ Mary was a friend in Sacramento, whose husband was Robert.

Sat Jan 3

Sunshine still, can see low bank of fog down in the valley – just heard Miss Fox, the new teacher has arrived. "They say" she is O.K. I sure hope she not only can handle these hillbilly roughnecks, but I more sincerely hope she will teach some of these kids just a little of the common garden variety of good manners. Worked on Amy's belated Christmas gift, nearly done.

Sun. Jan 4

We are ready to start to Sac[ramento]. I have nearly broken my shins, got my arms all torn on rare thorns, fell in the water and am mud to my eyes, getting some ferns, roots & all for Mary. They are beauties tho. Mrs. C.P.C. gave me a beautiful bunch of cedar in bloom to take to Mary. All ready 11:25 a.m.

- ❖ Mrs. C.P.C. – Hattie E. Croft, Charles' wife.

Jan. 5

Just got back home to the Woodchucks – Towser, Topsey, Tommie & Blue, all here to welcome us home. We had sunshine yesterday untill we got to a few miles below Plymouth. Met the coldest nastyest fog and nearly froze all the way to Sac[ramento].

Found Amy, Ethan & Jr. out in back yard cleaning, also Albert Hansen there. My Jr. just rushed to me yelling, "Gaggie and Goggums," so I don't know if it was I or the dog Buddie he was the most delighted to see; he is perfectly darling now, how I hate to think of him as a smarty with his thumb to his dear little snubby nose in a few years more.

We had a good visit tho, after supper we Amy, Ethan, Jr., Geo & I went to the Victor where we found Austin my youngest born (who has decided to add a year to my age by claiming twentyone years instead of twenty) is growing handsomer every day. He is the best looking Ripley since Aunt Fannie's time, for he is all Ripley. If he has any of his father's blood in him it is all on the inside, for I never saw a good looking person in the whole family. He, Austin, is remodling the plumbing of the house. I fancy he thinks he is feathering his own future nest. No doubt will be asking me to sell some day. Maybe I will tho I think I want more for it than he will care to pay.

After we had seen the show, went down to Japtown and had Chow – <u>Minnie</u> as G.W. calls it. All at Ethan's expense. We were broke. I always feel ashamed to [blow?] the kids that way. They were awful nice to us: gave us a lovely wool & chally comfort, besides the lovely aluminum pitcher and carton of good things to eat they sent up Xmas. After breakfast this morning Amy and I visited around while G.W. finish[ed] pruning trees & grapes that he started on yesterday. Then he went down town to attend to some business. Amy, Jr. & I call'd on the Darts. Mrs. D. bobbed or rather trimmed my hair and marcelled it. We then called on Mrs. Prothero. I had already seen Mrs. Jordon. Toots gave me a lovely glass bon-bon dish & Buster a hand-made calendar, very cunning; by eleven G.W. was back, we drove to Mary & Robert's, had lunch. Mary & I waited until G.W. & R[obert] made a trip somewhere. About one o'clock we started for Oak Park, got our traps from Amy's (Jr. was asleep), bought some things at Aratas, and by two was on our way. Lo after 5 found us home. Tired and glad to get here.

❖ Towser, Topsey, Tommie & Blue – Topsey is a dog; the others may be goats.

- ❖ Plymouth – town in Amador County, on the way to Sacramento from Fairplay.
- ❖ Albert Hansen – unidentified
- ❖ Aunt Fannie – Fannie Mae Ripley, youngest child of Asbury Ripley and Elizabeth Eleanor Owings. She was born in 1867 in Illinois, and died in 1959 in Nebraska. Fannie was Jehu Ripley's sister and thus May's paternal aunt.
- ❖ "never saw a good-looking person in the whole family" – referring to her first husband's family, the Diddys.
- ❖ Austin remodeling the plumbing to feather his own future nest – May's youngest, Austin Diddy, was in fact a month from turning 20. He was living with his sister Amy and her family in Sacramento at this time. May's remark implies that Amy, Ethan, Ethan Jr. and Austin were living in May's house on 6th Avenue. This is further confirmed by the fact that the following year Amy and Ethan move from Sacramento to Redding just when May sells the property.
- ❖ hair marcelled – the "marcel wave" was an early kind of permanent curl.
- ❖ the Darts / Mrs. D[art?], Mrs. Prothero, Mrs. Jordon, Toots, Buster – these must all have been friends in Sacramento. May writes about Mr. & Mrs. Jordon on 14 Oct. 1927: "They were in their sixty and seventyth years, yet I saw them build a new home on an empty barren lot, and in less than five years it was a beauty." I have not been able to identify them.
- ❖ Oak Park – neighborhood in Sacramento, just south of the city center. 6th Avenue is in the Oak Park area.
- ❖ Aratas – a store in or near Sacramento (which doesn't open until 8 am, as we find out on Jan. 20th!).

Tues. Jan 6

Cloudy and cold. G.W. & F[erdinand] are splitting and cording wood. I forgot to say yesterday we found the sunshine right where we left it the day befor[e], right below Plymouth, was so glad to get out of that cold damp fog. I never realized there was so much nasty cold weather in the Sacramento Valley untill I came to the lovely mountains again. I'll sure never go back to the Valley to live, am trying awful hard to find "a spot that['s] known to us alone, up here in the whispering pine, A sweet little spot, that the rest have forgot, A nest that's just yours & mine." - - - - and maybe sooner or later I'll find it.

Have a nasty, blowey, sniffling cold and am cranky. Ray & O[rin] came down this evening – brought a letter from Ida and one from Amy that's a week or two old. Going to bed.

❖ Ida – I believe this is Ida May Baker Calkins, as we have a photograph (of May and her youngest, Austin) addressed by May to "Mrs. Ida M. Calkins" in about 1909 / 1910. Ida was born in 1871, married William A. Calkins in 1887, and lived in Buckeye, Shasta County, California at the time of the 1900, 1910 and 1920 censuses. Their son Ralph was born in Round Mountain (the district where Ingot is situated) in 1889. An online source (see note) states that William Calkins ran a store in Ingot, so presumably May met Ida there during the roadhouse years, and had stayed in touch. Ida also had a daughter Gladys, born in 1893.[4]

Wed. Jan 7

Sunshine, lots of frost last night, cold in my head worser. G.W. got breakfast. He don't like to cook or do house work, and of course don't like to see me sick, but the few times I have stayed abed and let him get breakfast give him a great thrill, he gets a kick out of letting folks know he is "cook," loves to run out with a dishrag and frying pan in his hand if any one is passing. A big overgrown loveable boy that one woman almost ruined; my youth wasted by a grouch and his by a shallow, unstable vamp. Queer world. Some reason for it tho I guess.

❖ "a big overgrown loveable boy that one woman almost ruined" ... "shallow, unstable vamp" – May's family records at the back of this diary (which are records of George's family rather than her own) state that George Washington Maylone married Therese Schenck on July 3, 1912. George's WWI draft registration in May 1917 listed him as living in Shingle Springs, [El Dorado County] California, working as a builder, with a wife and child under 12 years dependent on him.[5] The 1920 census shows Therese Maylone, age 30, divorced and working as a waitress in a hotel in Placerville, El Dorado County. The 1930 census of Placerville showed Charles F. Maylone, born about 1915, living with his mother Therese Veenewitz, his step-father Ellis A. Veenewitz, and his grandmother Hattie V. Schenck.[6] Nothing in May's diaries gives any indication that G.W. had a son, and I was surprised to discover his existence. In her recollections of George Maylone, his niece wrote: "Upon his return from the [First World] war, George made no attempt to see Theresa or Charles as he knew before he enlisted that their marriage was over."[7] However, she also noted on the typescript of May's diaries: "He visited with us & kept in touch".

❖ "my youth wasted by a grouch" – a reference to May's first husband, John Diddy, who was more than 20 years older than her, and seems to have been her parents' choice of husband, rather than her own. (See Part Two, "Married Life in California")

Wood cutting goes on right merryly, if this good weather holds a week or so we will do fine. Right here is as good a place as any to list my Christmas gifts, that I may remember them and where they came from.

From Mama – lunch cloth;	to Mama – slippers
R & M – Photo of E.R.	R & M – towel
L-F – book & Photo B.L.	L-F – towel
N & E – "	N & E -towel
Leo – nothing	Leo – keyholder
Betty L & Erma R – Photos	B.L. & E.R. – books
Amy, Ethan, Jr., Austin –	Amy – dresser c[loth?]
comfort,	Ethan – tie
pitcher,	Jr. – teddy & duck
Xmas box	Austin – card case
Mary & Robert – towel,	ferns
hand[kerchief], tie	
Toots – bon-bon dish	ferns
Buster – calendar	nothing
Ida – Arloma set	centerpiece
Mother – nothing	col[l]ar & towel
Dad – [duck? desk?]	box of eats
Ferd – hand[kerchief]	box of eats
Daisy & E –hand[kerchief]	handkys
Ray C. – hand[kerchief]	home-candy

Gave my husband pair of slippers. Will leave this page for gifts overlooked or yet to come.

- ❖ Mama – May's mother, Olive Almeda Perryman Ripley, who was 63. May's father Jehu had died in 1915. The 1917 draft registration document for Ray Ripley, May's brother and the eldest Ripley son, stated that his mother was solely dependent on him.[8] The 1920 census showed Olive, age 58, living in Portland with her daughter Leila Chauvin, age 21 and married.[9] Mr. Chauvin, however, was not listed as residing with them. In most other census forms, Leila's name is spelled Lela.
- ❖ R & M – May's brother Ray Ripley and his wife Maude, who married in 1919 and from at least 1920 lived in Portland, Oregon. Ray was a policeman, 35 years old in January 1925. He and Maude had a 4-year-old daughter, Erma Ray. The next year they would have a son, Guy. The 1930 census shows that Ray had become successful enough to own a house on S.E. 51st Street that was worth $5000.[10] I remember meeting my Great-Aunt Maude Ripley in Portland as a child. She was friendly and kind to me.
- ❖ photo of E.R. – this must be a photograph of Ray and Maude's daughter Erma Ray.
- ❖ L-F – I think this must be May's youngest sister Lela, as it comes in the list of May's siblings, and because the initials "B.L." fit those of Lela's daughter Betty Lee. In January 1925, Lela was 26 and Betty Lee about 4. (The 1930 census lists her as born in 1921.)
- ❖ N & E – May's sister Nora and her husband Edwin Hall. Their son Roy Edwin Hall was born in 1915 in Portland, Oregon, but Nora and her family appear to have lived mainly in or near John Day (they are there in the 1910,

1920 and 1930 censuses).[11] In January 1925, Nora was 40, and her son Roy was 10.

❖ Leo – May's brother who was almost 30. He had left John Day and in the 1920 census had been living in Lane County, Oregon, working as a laborer.[12]

❖ Betty L. & Erma R. – May's nieces, Betty Lee Chauvin (Lela's daughter), about 4 years old; and Erma Ray Ripley (Ray's daughter), about 4 years old.

❖ Toots and Buster must be friends in Sacramento. Toots may be a neighbor near May's house on 6th Avenue – when she was cleaning it out in 1926, she wrote that Toots gave her some breakfast and gave them both dinner (Oct 13).

❖ Ida – Ida May Baker Calkins, May's good friend from Ingot.

❖ Mother and Dad – George's parents Edgar and Mary Esther Papineau Maylone.

❖ Daisy & E – Daisy and Elwin Maylone, 14 and 12 years old, who lived with their grandparents Edgar and Mary Esther Maylone.

❖ Ray C. – Ray Croft, about 10 years old.

Thur. Jan. 8

Went to bed last night wishing I could go somewhere for a moonlight walk. The moon was lovely. Got up this morning and found a gray world – no sun, no blue sky. So cold the water froze in the pipes after G[eorge] & F[erdinand] went to work. Cleared off about eleven and the rest of the day was warm and sunny, with the bluest sky, and a thin gray-blue haze among the distant pines. I ask[ed] the woodchucks [i.e. George & Ferdinand] what it was – fog or smoke? I don't think they knew what it was. Such questions don't seem to ever bother <u>them</u>. They know it is "something" but as it don't bother them they worry not, any way it was beautiful. I walked over where they were cutting down and trimming trees, got a lot done since I've been laying off. I've a bum finger, don't know what ails it. The woodchucks say it is a "run-a-round" what ever <u>that</u> is.

G.W. and I went over and burned brush after supper. I tried my hand at making bread again, got in <u>too</u> much yeast and it's coarse & dark. Maybe I'll regain the lost knack of bread-making again. Got a letter of thanks from Mr. Baxter & his mother for the Christmas ferns I sent them. "Greens" he calls em. That['s] the Scotch for it I guess.

G.W. went up to C.P.C. after the letter and isn't back yet, been up there nearly two hours, said he would be only gone a moment. I am afraid that he will make me dislike C.P.C. for the latter is the first person I've ever realy had a reason to be jealous of. G.W. will leave me any time, any how, any place to go do most any thing, hunting, mineing, or just gabbing with C.P.C. Reckon I'd best be glad C.P.C. is not a she-male. Huh.

❖ "the lost knack of bread-making" – May baked bread daily at the roadhouse in Ingot, but when she and the children moved to Sacramento in about 1918 she must have begun buying bread. Her remark seems to imply that she didn't have to make her own bread in the first few years of her marriage to George either, which makes me think they had left Sacramento for El Dorado County not long before she started this diary. A few weeks later (Jan. 22nd) she comments that it's been six or seven years since she made bread, but before that she had done it for 20 years. Happily by the end of the month she has made a "realy lovely batch of bread" (Jan. 29th).

❖ Mr. Baxter and his mother – probably "Toots" and "Buster" on the Christmas list.

Fri. [Jan.] 9

We burned brush this morning till time for F[erdinand] to come. Mother phoned for the Chucks to kill a goat, wanted us to come over for supper, but G.W. says "No" he'd be to[o] dirty to eat supper over there. Huh. There is a new coon in town you know. The school teacher, she is making quite an impression on the male Maylones. My husband is never <u>too</u> dirty to eat dinner with his wife & mother, in fact I could not get him to clean up at [all] on Christmas day when we were to eat dinner with the old folks. Maybe I'd better watch this knifewielding schoolma'am who claims she can clean up on the biggest of em. Men are funny animals, aren't they?

Supper is waiting the return of the Woodchuck. He and the Other Chuck left at three o'clock to go up to Cedarville to kill a goat. It is a wonderfull moonlight night. I've done-did my chores & most of my team-mate['s], carried in my flowers, the wood, kindling & water, and turned the water out of the pipes, for it will sure freeze tonight.

Sat. [Jan.] 10

Hazy this morning, not so cold tho as last night. Had the funniest dream last night. Saw Geo. run out in the garden at home and knocked Jr.'s Teddy-bear over in the dirt. The Teddy got up and made the funniest face, ran his finger around inside his mouth and dug the dirt out. He looked just like a child that had taken a mouthfull of something sour: had a hurt, surprised, amazed & disgusted look, and looked right up at Geo. I was just yelling with laughter & woke up fairly whooping. Geo. was shaking me and wanting to know what in H--- was the matter. I laughed till I cried, and ever time I wakened I laughed all over again.

I wrote letters last night to Floy, Jessie, Emma Harrow, Tom Brock (for G.W.), a card to Amy, business letters to R-G, Mrs. J., M-C. How I hate to think of Gladys getting a divorce from Jim. Of course liveing in a glass house I can not say much. Jim may have changed in the last ten years, but I know he was good to her once and I know she dearly loved him, but I firmly believe had he kept her with him she'd love him just as dearly yet. Never never will I let my other half leave me. Nor will I [leave] him to go live in a more comfortable quarters. Where his work takes him there I will go. I am sorry for Gladys and sorry for Jim. They have been weaned away from each other. She may have found some one that finds more favor in her eyes. Otherwise as long as Jim is in one place and she another why should she want a divorce. Maybe there is a Reason in the case, one with a wad of money.

❖ Floy[d?], Jessie, Emma Harrow, Mrs. J., M-C - unidentified

❖ Wrote to Tom Brock (for G.W.) – I haven't identified Tom Brock. May writes a lot of correspondence for George, something she later points out in an acerbic draft of a letter to A.F. Johnston: "Thank You A.J. for your good opinion of my honesty, for you are well aware that G.W. Maylone is like A.F. Johnston, he leaves his writing as well as thinking to some one else. If G.W. Maylone and A.F. Johnston had not both married more Brains than they already had, they would as Will Rogers might say be in a Helluvafix." (back of 1927 diary)

❖ business letters to R-G – Robertson-Govan, agents who are involved in the sale of May's house in Sacramento.

❖ Gladys and Jim – could this be Ida Calkins' daughter Gladys?

Sun. [Jan.] 11

Was awful cloudy – very – last night, we burned brush untill dark. I never tire of watching those big bon-fires, sending millions of stars heavenward. They are a sight not to be forgotten, just as it is getting dusk, either against a blue velvet sky or the soft gray plush of the clouds, or later on a clear night it is black velvet. After we came in and had a lunch, then went to bed. Both were tired. Daisy called up for a chat; said she saw Don, also mentioned seeing little C.F.M. is able to go to school again.

This morning is sunny, but very hazy; is warm tho. Dad and <u>The</u> Woodchuck plan on going to Placerville tomorrow concerning the Ranch. I had planned to go to Mrs. C.'s and tie my comfort that Amy gave me, but Mother wants me to help her in the store. Guess I can tie the comfort next day. Lord I hope G.W. hurries. I must get my work done. I notice the man-handling teacher is no longer Miss F. to Elwin, she is Elizabeth. Sounds promising, like the girl who was named Mary, became May – then Mae, and at last was just plain Ma.

❖ Don and little C.F.M. – unidentified (I don't believe C.F.M. can be Charles F. Maylone).

❖ the Ranch – Cedarville. This is the conclusion of the "try ranch" talk of January 1st. May writes the next day that Cedarville is a "real log house" and George Maylone's boyhood home. It isn't clear how long it's been since Edgar and Mary Esther had been gone from Cedarville (presumably to move closer to the store in Fairplay, where George and May meet them the next day). Later in the month May takes "everything belonging to Mother" and puts it upstairs. On Feb. 3rd she writes: "G.W. got his Homestead Right back, so I guess we get our '40' O.K." A homestead was 40 acres. Eleanor Manning's recollections confirm that May and George spent some time in Cedarville: "[they] moved on the Maylone ranch for a time."[13]

Jan. 13 [in margin: Sunshine]

Well Mr. Book, I miss'd a day. We "riz" at 5 o'clock and wended our way to Fairplay, got there just as Mother had builded a fire. Dad was still in bed. Nothing doing in that line here, my "fire-maker" is on the job every morning he is well. When he is ailing I willing[ly] tumble out and make a fire, but as long as he is as well as I am – nothing doing.

Well we had breakfast and I met "<u>The</u> Fighting Elizabeth." For the first time in my life I liked at first sight someone I had heard praised to the skies. I had my mind made up to <u>not</u> like her, but she is a joy. I got the biggest kick out of her that I have had in ages. She is <u>Real</u>, there is not a bit of petty put on flapperism about her. I only hope she wears well. I'd hate to be disapointed in her, and oh how I hope she tames some of these bigheaded nuts going to school. I am glad she likes my Penrod, but then I don't see how she could help it.

The Woodchuck & Dad returned late in the afternoon. All's well. We will as far as I can see be the owners of Cedarville, I shall have to call it Woodchucks-at-Cedarville. I shall at last have a log-house – and better still my husband's boyhood home. My lovely hills, my pines and cedars, mine for the rest of my days.

I met Mrs. Chandler, I have a fellow feeling for her, as she is enduring what I had to go thru for two years – the sneers and slurs of folks in glass houses. I lived thru it and found happiness, I hope she does.

Today the Woodchucks have settled on just what basis we are to be one family; I don't know yet how it will end. I know I can hold up my end of the bargain, but men are not to be depended on. The Woodchuck leans against the collar all the time, is right up on the bit and rarin' to go, while the Other Woodchuck steps just the same gait at evening that he started out at night. That makes rather a jerky unsteady team. I suppose I'll have to be the harness that hold[s] them together, but I fancy it will be a strain sometimes. I will be glad tho to get in a real house again.

- ❖ I haven't been able to identify the marvelous Elizabeth Fox.
- ❖ Flapperism – young women in the 1920s were nicknamed "flappers". They shocked the older generation by cutting their long hair, smoking and wearing short skirts.
- ❖ Penrod must be a nickname for Elwin.
- ❖ A log house – Cedarville was a substantial cedar house. We are very fortunate to have Daisy Maylone's recollections of Cedarville:

"[My grandparents] lived in a hand-hewn log house, built by my great-grandfather Joseph N. Papineau on a 160-acre ranch." The local red clay was used to fill in the spaces between logs, then whitewashed, Miller said. "That house is still standing today, and people are living in it." Miller said that four generations of her family sometimes lived in the house. "My great-grandfather Joseph was there for a time, [Joseph Papineau died in 1921] and my uncles would often stay at the house during the winter, when the logging camps they worked at would be closed." The family fed itself from the gardens, orchards, and livestock it raised, Miller said. ... Miller and her brother Elwin were required to do a number of chores around the ranch, including shepherding the 300 goats the family raised for mohair to and from their ranges.[14]
Descendants of the Hizer, Papineau and Maylone families fought hard to save the house when the land was sold to a logging company, but very sadly they lost this battle and Cedarville was

destroyed in about 2006. Doreen Rothlisberger of Somerset, El Dorado County, a Maylone-Hizer descendant, showed me a corner of Cedarville that she had rescued. It is a great pity indeed that the house could not have been saved.

❖ Mrs. Chandler – unidentified. May is referring to the treatment that divorced women received in those days.
❖ "today the Woodchucks have settled..." – this is the agreement that George and Ferdinand make to go into ranching together at Cedarville.
❖ the Woodchuck – George W. Maylone
❖ the Other Woodchuck – Edgar Ferdinand Maylone

[in margin] Tues 14: hard rainstorm, some snow

Weds [Jan.] 15

Sunshine weather. Moved to Cedarville, first load. Thought at first we'd stay at the Cabin nights for the time we were moveing. But F[erdinand] wanted us to get our bed and stay so we went back after the second load and stayed here. G.W. is in his glory. Everything is allready Our Place, Our Cattle, Our goats, Our This-and-That. I only hope his New Broom never wears out.

~~Thurs~~ Fri [Jan] 16

Today is a beautiful day. I opened the whole house. Am not going to wear my "new broom" out at the first whack. So many folks in stepping in another's shoes, try to show off. I shall just do what I have to do every day and add a little extra work. I shall make what changes I do make so slowly the folks won't notice I am making any. That way I will not hurt any one's feelings or make any one say "My you'd orter see how May has just turned the place up side down".

I took everything belonging to Mother out of her room and put it upstairs. Also partly cleaned up F[erdinand]'s room. That for me was a big day's work, with getting three meals for two Woodchucks, three dog[s] and five cats.

Sun [Jan] 18, 10 o'clock A.M.

A cold, cloudy morning, sun trying to shine thro wintery-looking clouds. The Woodchucks & C.P.C. gone hunting. I've done the chores and writ[t]en to Amy. Found out the mail leaves this 11 A.M. so dictated a postal to Miss Fox over the phone to Amy so she won't worry – as it is a week tomorrow since I mailed a letter to her. I intend to write several letters today, if I can find any envelopes up here.

Mon [Jan] 19

The Woodchuck took a sudden notion to go to Sac[ramento]. A lovely morning. Drove to F[air]P[lay], got our order from the Gen. Man. there. Left the Cabin at nine o'clock A.M., sunshine all the way to Sac[ramento]. Found every one well. Amy washing, Jr. asleep. Austin in his pajamas – Ethan at work, is a bookkeeper now.

Saw Mrs. D and the girls. Dolo's baby is cute as can be but she's spoiling his looks with an old pacifier, sucks on it all the time. We saw the movie "America" at the Victor in the evening. Had a good visit, broke the news of our ranch venture to the kids. Don't think they think we have right good sense, but I know they hope we will do well for it means we won't want the 6th Ave. house any more.

❖ Ethan was working for Zellerbach Paper Company.

❖ 6th Avenue house – May's house in Sacramento, 3067 6th Avenue. May must have managed to buy property in the early 1920s while working there (in the 1920 census she is listed as living in rented property). I was told by Mildred Hizer Cuellar that George Maylone's family suspected that he married May for her money. This is reflected also in Eleanor Hizer Manning's recollections: "Mae [sic] owned a modest home in Sacramento, but George wanted to return to Fairplay and persuaded her to sell her home and back him in a mining venture. This was contrary to the wish of her family but George could be very persuasive."[15]

Tues. [Jan.] 20

Left Sac[ramento] about eight o'clock. I tried to tell my husband the stores did not open till eight, but he just fussed at me to hurry up as he wanted to get out of town by seven. I didn't have time to enjoy my breakfast. Then we had to fiddle away a whole hour standing around in the back of Aratas store. I didn't say any thing but I guess I looked my thoughts pretty plain, as Himself asked me if I wasn't feeling well. When he pulls a stunt like that, and is afraid of a scolding, he gets very anxious about my health and general comfort.

We had a flat tire at the big Prune Orchard, and when we got to the Jack place we ran out of gas and had to pull all the hills backwards; passed a Johnnie Gibson, who drawling said "G-o-i-n-g o-r c-o-m-i-n-g". When we got to the cabin we had a little gas there, so made it to PF[Fairplay]. Weather still nice.

❖ PF – May means FP for Fairplay, which is sometimes written as Fair Play.

Wed. [Jan.] 21

Weather lovely. Sold C.P.C. five head of cattle. Helped the Chucks build fence. Went over to PF [Fairplay] in the evening & signed petition for P.O. for Dad. Also made first payment. Wrote to Ida, Mary J., G.L.B., card to Amy.

❖ "petition for P.O. for Dad". It must have been successful, because the 1930 census lists [Edgar] H. Maylone, 67, as postmaster in Fair Play, employed by the U.S. Government.[16]

❖ Mary J., G.L.B. – unidentified (perhaps G.L.B. is Mr. Baxter?)

Thur [Jan] 22

Cloudy; looks very much like rain. I sincer[e]ly hope we have about three weeks of it, with lots of snow in the hills. GW set a lot of fires, I'm trying to bake bread. Hope it don't kill us all.

Later. Awful – never saw such stuff, looks like a cheap sponge and nearly as yellow. I'm disgusted. Don't look like a person could be dumb enough to forget in six or seven years how to do a thing they had done for twenty.

Rain was a fizzle, cleared off. In the evening I went with G.W. to hunt the goats, oh gee what a climb – up on Leventon Ridge. Lovely view once you get there. I'd enjoy it if I could take my time but G.W. just climbs like a goat. He is on his native heath here. Letters to Billy Erickson, Gertie & Ted.

❖ Billy Erickson- unidentified

❖ Gertie – probably George's sister Gertrude Inez, who lived with her husband and family in Alameda County. She had married Frank Hizer in 1906, in a double wedding with her brother Ferdinand and Bessie Hizer,

Frank's sister. It's quite a thought that both brides were
15 years of age! However, unlike Ferdinand and Bessie,
Gertrude and Frank Hizer had a very successful marriage
and at least six children. My grandfather Ethan Papineau
remained close to his Hizer cousins all his life.

❖ Ted – probably George's brother Theodore Roosevelt
Maylone, who was married and also lived in Alameda
County.

Fri [Jan] 23

Oh Dear I'm realy tired. I chased the goats out this morning at
eight; believe me it was a chase to[o]. How I'd love to be able to
get over the ground as they do. Washed a few pieces and outside
of my general housework that's about all I did do. Oh yes, I
forgot to mention yesterday I planted Cabbage, Lettuce, Radishes
in some tubs. Couldn't find any pepper seed, or I'd have planted
some of 'em. Diamond had a calf last night, so C.P.C. phoned up.
The two Woodchuck[s] went to PF [Fairplay] to get a tank of gas.
I'm alone with the dogs & cats.

Sat. [Jan.] 24

Rain. Chucks sawed down their first wood on the ranch. Did fine
too even if it was wet. Talked to Amy, at Plymouth. Said they
might come up. Cut out & basted Mother's dress. Had to go to
C.P.Cs after mail. Letter from Butcher, Bernice & Daisy home
from school.

❖ Amy at Plymouth. The 1920 census shows Louise and
Alexander Papineau, Amy's in-laws, living in Amador
County, Plymouth Township, East Side.[17] May later
complains about Amy being reluctant to come the 18

miles from her mother-in-law's house to visit her in Fairplay.

❖ Butcher, Bernice - unidentified

Sun. [Jan.] 25

Rain, rain, lots of it. All night, and up to noon. Chucks went to C.P.C. mining. I got a chicken dinner for the Sac' [ramento folks] but about eleven Amy phoned, they were not coming on account of rain. Our first evening alone since we moved up here. The Other Chuck went to PF [Fairplay] for the evening. We had another honeymoon. Clearing off.

Mon. [Jan.] 26

Did not waken till seven o'clock. The chucks are usually at work by that time. I wakened with the light in my eyes, clear and bright. But at ten it is again hazy. Chucks are working on the fence, think it will take three days more to finish it. Sunshine.

Tues. [Jan.] 27

Rain, just a drizzle all day – drove down after the mail. I <u>walked</u> from the Fort to the Cabin to get a few articles we needed, filled a barley sack and carried the rake, walked by to the Fort looking like a Mahalia with my load. Waited in the rain half an hour. When the Lizard came in sight, nearly passed me by but I soon saw why. The Lizard had an extra passenger, a young lady who had decided she wasn't interested in school after she saw the Lizard going over. So [I] waited in the rain for its return. Funny don't it haint it huh?

❖ the Fort – unidentified

❖ 'looking like a Mahalia' – I take this to mean that she looked like an African-American woman / former slave. The irony is that her own grandmother (who according to family legend was whisked to safety by a "Black Mammy" during the Civil War) was named Mahala.

❖ The Lizard – G.W.

Wed. [Jan.] 28

Rain. Went hunting the goats and found a Baby Kid. Darlingest thing. Guess I'll call it Leslie as today is his birthday. Another little Nannie Kid arrived later. Maybe I'd better call her Leslie for I can keep her and the little Billy will be sold or kill'd.

❖ Leslie – May's (possibly adopted) eldest child, Leslie Edward Diddy. Leslie was born in 1902, so this was his 23rd birthday. See Part Two, "May's First Marriage: from Trinity Center to the Flintlock Inn near Ingot," for family lore concerning Leslie's birth. My mother remembers that Leslie served in the Philippines in the 1920s, and that he was away in the military at this time. Three years later (30 Jan. 1928), May was to write: "There has never been a day that I have not thot of him in all the years since he left".

Thur. [Jan.] 29

Clear or rather hazy this morning. I am doing a big washing, clothes on to boil. Nine o'clock. Chucks working on fence yet: must wind it up this week. Two weeks lost when they said four or five days. One never know[s] what to count on, poor judgment. I made a realy lovely batch of bread. Twin kiddies. A billy & nannie.

Fri. [Jan.] 30

Heavens only one more day of Jan. Spring will be here befor we are ready for it. Started to rain last night. The Woodchuck & I went to Crofts after the box of vegetables Amy sent me (carrots, onions, lettuce, cabbage, oranges & steelwool. Gee but wegtables look and taste good here.) From there we drove to Fairplay after the mail. Letter from Mrs. Jurgenson & Jessie Johnson. Got the new saw, came home and tried to "wet nurse" the twin kids, poor babys their mother don't seem to take much stock in a family. Ten o'clock and raining when we went to bed. Rained hard befor daylight, but looks like clearing away at eight this A.M.

❖ Mrs. Jurgenson & Jessie Johnson - unidentified

Sat. [Jan.] 3

Drove down to the Cabin. G.W. & I got the phone which we left at Crofts for Harris, and a load of junk. G.W. sore at losing so much time. Told the Other to take the horse and be snaking [?], we got back at eight and found him by the fire reading. G.W. ready to boil over. Looks like rain. I've an earache and other ailments. G.W. says his ear aches too maybe that is why he is so cross. Look for Elwin to come over today to help sort the apples.

❖ Harris – a Harris family was listed just four entries above Edgar and Mary Esther Maylone's family in the 1920 census. Presuming that Edgar and Mary were living in Cedarville in 1920, the Harrises are now neighbors of May and George.

Feb. Sun. 1

Clear, beautiful, up fairly early for Sunday – the Other Chuck
refuses to work on Sunday no matter what the rush and I'm glad
of it, for it gives the Woodchuck and I a chance to say Howdy to
each other. I see where we would forget to love if some one is
always with us. Had a nice day. After breakfast the Other went to
see the folks. The Woodchuck and I went down to the Cabin and
moved the saw. I washed up the dishes and swept the floor, got
home by eleven. (Ray C. is ill, the effects of something he ate or
drank at the dance.) We had a lunch and fixed goatbells. Went
after the goats and found a new one, to[o] tiny to walk. I took off
part of my weaning apr' [=apron?] and wrapped his highness up
and carried him home. Nice little Billie. Another baby arrived
after dark.

❖ "refuses to work on Sundays" – I would be very interested
to know if the Maylones and Papineaus were religious.
My impression is that by the 1920s at least they were
rather flexible in terms of religious affiliation. I now have
one of the Papineau family Bibles, which is in French, as
the Papineaus were originally French-Canadian. Joseph
Papineau and Mary Esther Guerin were Catholic when
they married in Tilbury, Ontario in 1863.[18] However,
Joseph's third wife's funeral in 1897 was held in the
Episcopal church in Placerville.[19] Joseph's son Alexander,
Ethan's father and my great-grandfather, married a
woman (Louise Lehmann) whose family had been
brought over from Switzerland by the Mormon church,
but Alexander and Louise were not Mormons. My
grandparents Amy and Ethan joined the Methodist
Church and became very active members for the rest of
their lives. My mother told me that Amy said it was
simply because of her own interest that they became
involved in the church. The Maylones were of Irish origin

(May refers to George in 1926 as her "Irish husband").
Millie Hizer Cuellar told me that the Maylones were Irish
protestants, who would wear orange on St. Patrick's Day.
(If they had been Catholic, how ironic it would be if May
had at last married a Catholic boy!) May herself never
mentions church in her diaries, but according to Amy's
interview with *The Covered Wagon*, May taught Sunday
School in Ingot.[20]

Mon. [Feb.] 2

Groundhog Day: cloudy. Men went to work on fence this
morning about seven. They were hardly out of sight when I heard
a noise I thought was the car returning and as it grew louder I
walked out on the porch to see what it was. Sounded like it was
overhead. I rushed out and flames ten feet high (at least they
looked so to me) were belching from the fireplace chimney. I
yelled the "Long Yell" at the top of my lungs, grabbed a ladder
and pail of water and got on the porch roof. I saw it could not
climb the house roof so yelled and yelled thinking surely the men
would hear me but no answer so I saw it was up to me. The roof
was begin[nin]g to show fire next to the chimney. I put the ladder
in another place just in front of the chimney, pulled myself up by
a shake which was loose and let me fall. I rolled of[f] like a tub of
--- never hurt me. Made another attempt, knew it was up to me.
Of course I had to just happen to have this long blue dress on.
  I put out the fire on the porch roof, but the house roof was
still afire. I had already kicked off my shoes and was wet as a
drownded rat, but I climbed out the window and could from there
throw water on the smoldering roof. Thank heaven the roof is
realy damp. But that iron pipe chimney was red hot. I suppose the
soot hasn't been cleaned out of there in a life time. I carried
"thousands" of pails of water, I simply drown'd that old chimney.
The steam rolled clear to heaven. I can't see how it happened the
men didn't see the steam and smoke, and I realy didn't think

there was any one who could give the Long Yell as I can. Yet they didn't hear me and yesterday we heard Buddy bark when we were up on [the] ridge. Gee I'm tired. I wonder what will happen next?

After dinner, went up on the hill to get a kid & its mother. Got it home. Back after the [band?] and found another. Third one came when we got in the corral.

(Cleared up, Groundhog saw his shadow.)

Thurs [Feb.] 3

Another busy day. Clear in the morning. Rather hazy tho, no new kids till after dinner. Found two on the grade, chucks came up to help me. Little nannie I found first yesterday nearly dead. Rain'd hard after 4 P.M. Drove to C.P.[C.]s to get mail. Ray is better, is up. Got a letter from Amy dated Jan. 14. G.W. got his Homestead Right back, so I guess we get our "40" O.K.

Wed. [Feb.] 4

Rained hard all night, no new kids. Little weak one died, makes three we have lost out of fourteen. Looks like clearing away. Chucks went to work, fence nearly done.

> Two nans came in with out their babies. At least
> five lost, maybe seven.

Thur. [Feb.] 5

Ferd. went down to work on mine at C. G.W. & I worked on dam, no kids. Lots of rain.

❖ "mine at C." – on Feb. 20th May says that George "went down to C.P.C. to mine." Presumably the Crofts' land had a mine on it, probably a copper mine, but I haven't been able to identify it.

Fri. [Feb.] 6

Rained all night, clear this morning. Took goats up in pasture. G.W. & I worked on fence. Herded goats, cut down some trees in Slaughterhouse Gulch. F[erdinand] worked at C. in the evening. G.W. and I started to F[air]P[lay], mired down in Slaughterhouse G[ulch]. Dug out & went on, nearly broke a wheel going down the Hill to Freys. Never saw any one drive a car over such places as they call a road here. Bender ought to be hamstrung. It is a sin to drive over what was once good roads -- no kids.

❖ Freys – there are several branches of the Frey family listed in the 1920 census of Cosumnes Township, El Dorado County. Two Frey households are listed just above the Harris family, so they must also have lived fairly close to Cedarville. Eleanor Manning noted: "Frey's owned store in old Fairplay." I understand the Freys are still a prominent family in El Dorado County.

❖ Bender - unidentified

Sat. [Feb.] 7

Began the day with four new kids, that makes us seventeen. Eight nans. I've got poison oak on my hands – knew I'd get it sooner or later. Never saw such a working house as this is: wet kids, wet clothes, dirty clothes, dirty dishes and heaven knows what all. Dreamed last night that Leslie came home. I was so happy. I told the dream as soon as I woke to test the old saying "tell a dream before breakfast and it will come true."

Six o'clock got a message E.A.P. [Ethan Alexander Papineau], A.E.P. [Amy Emma Papineau] E.A.P. Jr. [Ethan Austin Papineau Jr.] with Cecilia D. were all on their way up here. Lord in heaven. The house goat from one end to the other. I nearly fainted, but got an extra supper going. I was so tired I thought I'd fall, but if they want to see me bad enough to dare these godblessed roads I can stand a little extra work. Storming awful hard. Eight kids, 5 B[illy goat]s, 3 N[anny goat]s.

❖ Cecilia D. – unidentified

Sun [Feb.] 8

Well it wasn't me they wanted to see so bad, they got here at eight and left at nine to go to a dance. Left Jr. here, and got home at 4 A.M., slept till nine, and left here again at 12 noon. Some visit, I'll say. The house full of new born kids, and wet goating clothes and smell. Poor Celia never ate a mouth full. I hope they fed her in Plymouth. I enjoyed Jr. tho, he had a good time. Four kids arrived, two billies & two nans. Geo. calls one billy he found in the rocks Moses, and one we found nearly dead in the corral Amy. She is the cutest little baby. Cloudy all day. ~~The male Crofts came up in the eve.~~ Hard rain in afternoon. (Sent Topsy [dog] to Mary Jane. Bud [other dog] nearly crazy – who wouldn't be?)

❖ Amy & Ethan go to a dance – Amy was 22, Ethan 24, and Ethan Jr. nearly two.

Mon. [Feb.] 9

Cloudy all day. Herded the goats till noon. Brought em in, got dinner & took em out till four. A hard way to serve my lord. But why care. Men worked on fence. Nearly done.

Tues. [Feb.] 10

Today is Austin's birthday, a warm cloudy day. Oh for a little sunshine. Twenty years ago today it was clear and sunny, a cold wind blowing hard, white cloudys flying high.

We, my woodchuck and I, finished the fence by noon. Other chuck went down to C[roft]s. The male Cs [Crofts] were all up last night and made us quite a visit. I was disapointed because Caroline didn't come too, but she said she didn't feel at all certain they'd get here so she decided to stay home. Wrote letters to R.-G.-Co., L.J. and Amy. We went after mail, not a thing of importance. Got to bed at ten, nearly worn out.

❖ Caroline – unidentified
❖ L.J. - unidentified

Wed. [Feb.] 11

Praise the powers that be, a nice warm morning. Chucks gone to work again on the wood. I hope they are able to work every day for six months. Hope it only rains on Sundays and at night.

Well the Chuck only got in a half day. After dinner was ever a dreadfull wind came up. A whirling cloud that startled us all came twisting up from the southwest, a big storm showed thru the gap. I was for rushing after the goats so they would not get wet, but the chucks were afraid a tree would fall on me. So the Chuck and I both went. It began to rain befor we got to the field gate. We met the goats coming home and rushed them in just befor the hardest rain got here. Even then we got soaked as we had to work with the little Bummers and see they had plenty of milk, not plenty, but as much as we dare steal from the others. Believe me there will be plenty of extra milk next year – I'll see these mothers of dead babies help to raise the others. F[erdinand] went to C[roft]s to mine.

The WoodChuck and I retired befor it was fairly dark. I'm so tired all the time, yet I feel fine, but don't get enough rest. I sure put my foot in it when I undertook to cook for two men. When it is clear, the Woodchuck wants to get up early to cut wood. When it is stormy, the Other Chuck wants to get up early to mine, so I don't get to sleep late at all. The Woodchuck and I made a trip to the Cabin yesterday. My plants are doing fine. I'll be glad when we can have all that stuff up here.

Thur. [Feb.] 12

Lincoln's Birthday. Cloudy this morning, was clear at midnight with a lovely moon, but raining when we got up this morning. I do so want a little sunshine. A wee kiddy arrived this morning, don't know what it is. Chucks have gone to work. F[erdinand] returned last night just after we had gone to bed. A hard rain after dinner. F[erdinand] went back down to C[rofts].

G.W. fetched in the goats and after we tended in Bummers we discover'd a bell nannie was missing. Went back up to the Papineau place and heard a most pitifull wail, looking up the hillside we saw a wee kiddy trotting down hill as big as cuffy and the rain coming down in sheets. I ran to meet the brave pitiful little thing, it had walked a long way, its feet and legs were muddy to its body but its body was clean so it hadn't tumbled in the mud. G.W. had an old woolen shirt in his pocket and wrapped the little drenched darling up. It sure had good lungs, was just yelling for Ma-a-a-h when we got there; no signs of Ma-h. We carried baby Marion home to the fireplace. I wanted to call her Nancy Hanks because she was born on Lincoln's birthday, but GW insisted on calling her Marion, as we found her near Marion's old home. Now we have Leslie, Amy, Mares [?], Curly, Bobbed Hair Bandit, and Marion. Some bunch o' bummers. There are several others but not disti[nc]tive enough to name.

❖ the Papineau place – the old Papineau homestead in Fairplay
❖ Nancy Hanks – Abraham Lincoln's mother
❖ Marion – Marion Papineau, Ethan's sister. "Marion's old home" would be the old Papineau homestead. May was to see Marion and her growing family at Amy and Ethan's for Thanksgiving dinner in 1927.

Fri. [Feb.] 13

Rain, rain, rain, oh for the sun. F[erdinand] did not come home last night. G.W. cut down a few trees in SlaughterHouse G[ulch], fixed the window in pantry and replaced broken panes in kitchen. I just gathered junk, junk, junk. Will I ever get rid of it all. No Kiddies today.

Sat. [Feb.] 14

St. Valentine. A Wonderfull beautiful Sunshiny Day – I could just yell with glee. A Baby Valentine in the Goat family, just one so far.

(Sun. 15 Chucks both went down to C[roft]s, and to Milo J.'s to see how much wood J. has cut. Came home about 1 o'c[lock] and F[erdinand] went hunting. G.W. worked around the place.)

Sat found another baby kid up in field, at least three days old, been out in all the hard storm and cold nights.

❖ Milo J. and J. - unidentified

Sun. [Feb.] 15

Got my dates mixed. G.W. went to J.'s today. A nice day and I would like to go, but don't feel any too good. Did not hear from

Amy. Got a letter from Mary, says they have a shepard pup for us for a goat dog. Worked all day. No Sunday.

Mon. [Feb.] 16

Cloudy but looks like breaking away. Chuck gone to Crofts to saw his wood, their saw a perfect whiz. Cleared off a we[e] shower about eleven, but nice and warm all day. Cleared out a lot more junk, from top of cupboard, fix[ed] the drawer in kitchen cupboard that has rested one end on the floor since I first came up here nearly five years ago.

Tues. [Feb.] 17

Oh Dear Feb is over half gone. A wonderfull clear morning. Chucks have gone across the creek to saw wood. I feel some better today, but if I do all I want to I won't feel any better by night. G.W. says "take it easy today" but he['d] pass away if he came home and found no dinner, the dishes not washed, nor floor swept. I often wonder just what he means by his "take it easy". Men are queer, even the very best ones. If I wanted him to take it easy I'd help him do what ever he had to do, but a man thinks the work in the house just does its self after he leaves.

Wed. [Feb.] 18

Good Morning, rather hazy but I think the sun will win out. Cattle came up this morning. Star, Mae & the big heifer we sold kept missing, so the Chucks have gone after them. All are due to calve soon. I hope Star has a calf, we need the milk. It would be swell for the bummers too.

Got a letter from Amy, she gave me a slap on the wrist about running around when I'm down there, so I guess we are even.

She does not stop to think that while I've gone to Mary's twice when I've been down there, I always came to see <u>her</u> <u>too</u>, and while she has been to see me twice, she has been to see her mother-in-law ever two weeks nearly and the eighteen miles up here are no more to them than the three miles down there are to me.

Well I must get all my housework done today. Have some washing & sweeping to do.

> ❖ slap on the wrist – Amy obviously felt that May didn't spend enough time with her on visits to Sacramento. But May equally felt that Amy, who often went with Ethan to visit his mother Louise in Plymouth, should have made the effort to come the extra 18 miles to Fairplay to see her more often. Presumably May walked the three miles from Amy's to Mary's house in Sacramento, while Amy and Ethan had a car and therefore, from May's point of view, the 18 miles from Louise's house to May's took the same effort.

Thur. [Feb.] 19

Clouded up last night, sprinkled this morning befor day, is not raining now 8 A.M. but looks like it would any moment. Chucks certainly cut wood yesterday, looked for all the world like a cyclone had hit the hillside. I took over some refreshments about 3 P.M. and looked the job over. Sorry they could not have started in up here last fall. Had they been allowed to do so, we'd have had at least five thousand dollars worth of wood cut. As it is we are lucky to have that many hundred. Here's hoping tho.

Got a letter from Amy, she is getting thinner, she says. I hate to doubt her word but that seems impossable. Got another copy of Bee, second one now. Wonder if some one is sending it to me.

> ❖ Bee – no doubt the newspaper the *Sacramento Bee*.

Fri. [Feb.] 20

Rain. Chucks worked a short time in for[e]noon, then F[erdinand] went down to C.P.C. [Crofts] to mine. G.W. filed saws, cut wood and did odd jobs. Late in evening just befor dark Mother phoned, she was back in F[air]P[lay] and had the puppie Robert got for us – a whale of a goat dog. G.W. went after him and of all the darling pups I ever saw, as fat as a cub bear, a funny smoky brown with black spots and white strip in his face, his mother a full blooded shepard. Don't know what his dad[d]y is, guess Robert will know. G.W. has his wish now, calls the pup Duke. I don't know why, but he's crazy over that name for a dog. Wanted to call Bud Duke, but Bud was such a wee thing I hated to tack so important a name on him. Buddie was so much more fitting. So now I had nothing to say about Duke's name. I'd like to call him Rex or Ponto, but I doubt if either of the Chucks could remember that.

Sat. [Feb.] 21

Rain again. Chucks are hunting cattle, since early morn. The sun came out for a few moments about ten and I let the kids out on green grass. Their first adventure. Just like a bunch of white cotton balls bouncing around. I laughed till I cried. Couldn't get away from the bummers to do my work, had to toll them around the shed and then run madly down the hill. Geo. found the cattle, three cows, or rather one cow & two heifers. Star, Minnie & May – each with a baby. Star has a daughter, I call her Redbud. May has a son & Geo. has named him George – Something. The something is the name of some fellow who was very bowlegged.

Got a phone from Amy. They are at Ply[mouth] and will be up tomorrow "right after lunch". I have got to hustle if I'm going to have a chicken dinner for em.

Sun. [Feb.] 21 [sic]

Everything is ready. I had my work all planned out. I'd get my apple cobbler made, dress my chickens, and while things were cooking I'd clean up the house. But about nine just when I was thru with the chores I got a phone from Daisy that she and Jim were coming over. I had counted on giving the Woodchucks a lunch, but that queered it, I had to fly around, do up the house work and get dinner, which I did as soon as dinner was over. D and J left and I fairly

❖ Daisy and Jim – unidentified

* * * * * * * * * *

Something must have happened next that May poured out her heart about and then later regretted having written down, because the next two pages are mostly ripped out with only a few words visible on what's left of p. 47/48. More than half-way down the margin of p. 47, in different ink, is written "March Tues", so May must have left off writing for at least a week after the 21st of Feb. "Other [Chuck?]" and Amy are mentioned in the bit that remains of p. 47. Page 48 was obviously filled, but there are only mentions left of "got back ... and F .. not wanted ... they all ... stayed ... we had a ... sunshine later ... turned cold .... the goats..." All that's left of p. 49/50 are the beginnings of the word "March" for two entries.

Clearly May's diaries were an outlet for her strong feelings, particularly about the treatment she received from George. She must have exercised some degree of self-restraint however, because on November 28th, 1927 she remarked: "If I wrote just what I thought, there is times the page would burn." The rest of the ledger book, pages 51- 193, is blank.

On page 194-196 May wrote family information and a quote.

"Births, Marriages & Deaths"

Born   Edgar Maylone   November 5th 1862

Born   Mary Esther Papineau French   Oct 4th 1864

Married by Jon Kohlert J[ustice of the]   Nov. 16 1884
P[eace] at Fairplay El Dorado Co., Calif.

witnesses J[oseph] N. Papineau – Estre [Esther] Papineau

          Children of E.H. & M.E.
          Maylone:

Born   Edgar Ferdinand Maylone   Nov 28, 1884

Born   George Washington Maylone   Mar 4, 1887

Born   Lewis Edwin Maylone   July 3, 1889

Born   Gertrude Inez Maylone   May 15, 1891

Born   Earl Alfred Maylone   Sep 1, 1893

Born   Elwin Albert Mayone   Sep 1, 1893

Born	Elinor Louise Maylone	July 5, 1895
Born	Theodore Roos[evelt] Maylone	Jan 11, 1902
Born	Herman Maylone	April 19, 1904
Died	Herman Maylone	April 19, 1904
Born	Marguerite Maylone	Jan 13, 1906
Died	Marguerite Maylone	Jan 13, 1906
Born	Floyd Maylone	Aug 24, 1907
Died	Floyd Maylone	Aug 24, 1907

❖ 'French' was from Mary Esther Papineau's first marriage to Kinman French.

Marriages

Edgar Ferdinand Maylone & Bessie Hizer	April 14, 1906
George Washington Maylone & Therese Schenck	July 3$^\text{d}$, 1912
Gertrude Inez Maylone & Frank Hizer	April 14, 1906
Elinor Louise Maylone & Clarence F. Nichols	Dec 20, 1914
Elwin Albert Maylone & Alta W. Nichols	Dec 20, 1914
Theodore R Maylone & Alyda Guilbert	Sept. 11, 1922
George Washington Maylone & May Ripley Diddy	Dec 2, 1922

On the bottom of the last page of the ledger book:

> The Bad Man waits for the Wicked Wind
> To blow the Girls skirts ankle high
> But the Lord is just and send[s] the Dust
> To blow in the Bad Man's eye.

(copied)

2.

May's 1926 - 1927 Diary:
Working on the Sacramento River

T his diary is written in a paperbound school exercise book that has "Compositions" printed on the front. When she began the diary, in October 1926, she and George were working on a riverboat, the Adele Hobson, that delivered goods mainly along the Sacramento River. George had been hired as the engineer, and May as the cook.

What events took May from homesteading in Cedarville (where she left off her previous diary in March 1925) to living and working on a boat a year and a half later? George's niece didn't specifically recall his and May's stint on the riverboat, however, her account emphasizes how hard it was for them to make a living:

> Mae [sic] owned a modest home in Sacramento, but George wanted to return to Fairplay and persuaded her to sell her home and back him in a mining venture. This was contrary to the wish of her family but George could be very persuasive. He at first mined the Claypool Diggins without

success, then moved on the Maylone ranch [Cedarville] for a time. They then lived at the old Croft place, but meanwhile Mae's money was dwindling.

George found the 'Belle Vista' mine, located just below the crest of Coyote Ridge, was not being worked... [21]

In her 1927-1928 diary, May mentions that after leaving Cedarville, she and George lived in a rented house where all their worldly goods were stolen – was this perhaps the Croft place? - and that from there they went to live in a tent on the banks of the San Joaquin river, before coming to work on the boat. On Nov. 1st 1926, May wrote that "five months ago yesterday", i.e. May 31st 1926, they came to work on the Adele Hobson.

May never explains quite how it came about that they were hired to work on the riverboat with no previous experience. She wrote:

Just five months ago yesterday we first went on the Feather Queen and five months ago today we came on the Adele Hobson and I never befor had step[p]ed my foot on a boat of any kind outside a ferry. And G.W. was just as green, all he knew was how to run a little powerboat. Had any one told us in five months he and I would run the boat from Stockton to a given point above Rio V[ista] and back to Stockton loaded, with only a deck hand to help us, I'd have walked off the boat right there. (1 Nov. 1926)

Her diaries show that she and George had a good deal of what we would now call "on-the-job training" working on the river.

The Adele Hobson was captained and owned by Alexander F. Johnston of Sacramento. Four years after this diary, in the 1930 census, he was 44 years old, living in Sacramento. His occupation was given as "r[iver?] freighter" and his place of work as "boat". His wife was Winnie I. Johnston, and they had four children. He must have done well for himself, for in 1930 he owned a house worth $12,000 – quite a piece of property in those days.[22] According to "The People History" website, in 1931 a new house in Oakland, California, described as an "Eight room English-style home, 3 bedrooms, electrical appliances, large basement" was worth $7,200.[23]

May's writing is much sketchier than in the 1925 diary – she must have been exhausted most of the time, apart from anything else. She seems to have written a few times a day, recording their departure and arrival times. There are several places left blank in the diary where she intended to fill in a time or a place later. The waterways that they navigated have changed quite a bit since the 1920s.[24] For instance, in 1933, Stockton became connected to San Francisco by a deepwater channel.[25] But when May and George were delivering goods to Stockton, they spent a good deal of time stuck in mud flats.

In this diary, we see the tension between May and George increasing. As always, they were both under great pressure, financially and also physically. However, it seems increasingly clear that their marriage doesn't provide them with mutual support. On October 13th 1926, the day she moved the last of her possessions from the house that she had sold to finance George's ventures, May wrote:

> I felt like I had at last become a wander[er] on the face of the earth, no place of my own to lay my head, and no hopes of ever having a home again. Once upon a time I asked the gods of fortune to grant me one wish, and promised, were it granted I'd rail no more at my unhappy lot in life. They grin'd and handed me my wish on a red hot platter, and I am holding that self heating platter yet but they won't hear me yip.

By and large, May stuck to her promise not to complain. However, she does vent her frustration with George's flirtations with other women, and his lack of care with money when it did come their way. As previously, she later tore out some of the pages in her diary – presumably regretting her ventings. Still, May made the very best of an increasingly difficult situation. As always, flowers and animals were a consolation to her, and even when she was wet, tired, hungry and dirty, she had an eye for whatever beauty was around her.

Oct. 1 1926
Friday

On our way from Stewarts Landing, loaded with corn, 1192 sks [sacks], last one overboard, for Golden Eagle Milling Co. Petaluma. Got caught on Mud Flats at 4 A.M., floated again 6 A.M. Reached Petaluma 9 A.M. Our first rain which began at 10 PM last night still falling fast. Left Petaluma 2 P.M., still raining, reached Port [Custer?] 8 P.M. Tied up till morning. Weather clearing up a little.

❖ Stewart's Landing – later May mentions two landings: Dave Stewart's Landing and Dan Stewart's Landing

Sat. 2 [October]

Started up 5 A.M., arrived Rio Vista 9 A.M. Clear. A.J. left for Sac[ramento]. We have two men on board, Pete and Slim. Engineer and Cook went to a show, very good.

❖ A.J. – Alexander F. Johnston, owner of the riverboat.
❖ Engineer and Cook – G.W. and May herself.
❖ Slim - May later (28 October) says that Slim's name is George Myers – whom I haven't identified.

Sun. 3rd [October]

The Devil built a fence of gloom around this Sabbath day
   His Imps sat on the top rail, to keep the joys away
   G.W. in the dolefull dumps, with Pete and Slim both glum and dumb
   I'm blue as sin for all my kin and wish joy didn't go by jumps

Mon. 4 [October]

A.J. arrived at 11 A.M. We start[ed] for Stewarts Landing, arrive[d] at 12 o'clock noon. Load[ed] corn only a few sacks at a time. Wrote to Mrs. Moore.

> ❖ Mrs. Moore – the first mention of an ongoing saga with Roger and Thelma Moore, involving a used car and a dog. In the 1930s census, the Moores were living in Stockton. Roger was a merchant of auto tires and batteries, listed as an employer. (His house was worth $4,500.)[26]

Tues. 5 [October]

Hot and sultry. Loaded a few more sks [sacks] – too wet to thrash. Slim painted port side upper deck – red – Adele will be Lady In Scarlet. Begun letter to Amy. Left S[tewarts] L[anding] 6:30 P.M. Loaded 1560 sks corn.

Wed. 6 [October]

Aground on Mud Flats, 4 A.M., afloat 8 A.M. Did not get clear till 9 AM, reached Petaluma at 20 to 12 noon. Finished letter to Amy. Lot of business letters. Went shopping, did not get lost, unloaded. Short 50 sks, mistake of truck men. Left Pet[aluma] 5

P.M., went aground on mud between bridge and No. 6 Beacon at 20 to 7 P.M., off again 20 to 9 P.M.

Thur 7 [October]

Reached Stewarts L[anding] at 6 to 4 A.M. Loaded 1500 sks corn, left 6:30 P.M.

Fri 8 [October]

Reached Petaluma 9 A.M., paddled mud all the way up Petaluma Creek, unloaded 2:30 P.M. Mailed letters to Nora, Mama, Maude, Mary and Austin. Left Pet[aluma] 3 P.M. Rough water. Tied up [word obscured by ink blot] grain wharf, 7:30 P.M.

- ❖ Nora – May's sister, now 42 years old. Nora and her husband Edwin Hall lived in John Day, Oregon with their son Roy.
- ❖ Mama – May's mother Olive was now 65. She was living in Portland with her daughter Lela (28) and her granddaughter Betty Lee (5).
- ❖ Maude – May's sister-in-law, married to policeman Ray Ripley (who was now 38). Ray and Maude lived in Portland and had two children, Erma Ray (5) and Guy (2 months).
- ❖ Mary – May's friend Mary in Sacramento.
- ❖ Austin – May's youngest son Austin Diddy (now 21).

Sat. 9 [October]

Left Cal Tran Grain wharf 4:30 A.M., reached S[tewarts] L[anding] at 7 A.M. No load ready for us. A.J. left for Sac[ramento] 9 AM. Looks very much like rain again. Slim

fin[ished] paint[ing] deck. Began raining 4 P.M., rained hard all
night.

Sun. 10 [October]

Still raining at daylight, clear'd of[f] at noon. Cap't returned at
noon. Letters from Amy, Mama, Mary, Mrs. Moore and R-G
saying 3067 is sold. Mama says Leo is married, he can't be very
proud of the fact as he has been wed a month or more. We pulled
out of Stewarts Landing with 835 sacks of corn; stop'd again at
Peter Cooks Landing, loading 500 sacks of onions for S[an]
F[rancisco]. Left at 6 P.M.

 ❖ letter from R-G saying 3067 is sold – R-G is Robertson-
   Govan (see 8 January 1927), who must be the agent
   involved in the sale of May's house on 6th Ave. in
   Sacramento.
 ❖ Leo – May's youngest brother (31 years old). He married
   Dorothy Nora Fay Guernsey, who like Leo was from John
   Day, Oregon. It was Dorothy's second marriage, and she
   had a son from her first marriage.[27] She must have
   divorced her first husband because Benjamin Franklin
   Bennett also went on to remarry. [28] Presumably the reason
   why Leo downplayed his marriage was because his bride,
   like May herself, was a divorcee.

Mon. 11 [October]

Reached S[an] F[rancisco] 6:30 A.M. after a night of fog. No
rough water this time, unloaded onions at Pier 23. Left S.F. at 11
A.M., reached Petaluma at 5:30. Found the Duck Pond infested
with barges, could not unload.

Tues 12 [October]

Arose this morning at 4:15 to have early breakfast in order men might get an early start. It is now 7:15 A.M. and they are still chatting about what color her hair is, or was, and where they can get the best Jackass. G.W. and I are planning on Sac[ramento] for tonight. I've still got a cold. Finished Amy's letter, she no doubt leaves for Redding today - left Pet[aluma] 8:45 A.M. Reached Rio V[ista] 5:30 P.M. Left the boat tied up under charge of Pete and Slim. A.J., G.W. and I left for Sac[ramento] 6:30, on stage to R[io] V[ista] Jt [jetty?] and from there by train to Sac[ramento]. Arrived about ten o'clock. A.J. left us to get a "Shine" and we went out to Oak Park. Got a room at the Woodruff, nearly smothered for fresh air. Good bed, good bath but no air. We are too used to the breeze from the deep waters.

- ❖ Jackass – slang for alcohol (see Jan. 18)
- ❖ Amy leaves for Redding – Amy and Ethan moved from Sacramento to Redding. I believe that they and Austin had been living in May's house in 1925, but had to move when May sold the house to Mr. and Mrs. F. C. Schofer (or Schoffer). (She later sends the Schofers the tax receipts for the house.)
- ❖ to get a "Shine" – shoe shine
- ❖ the Woodruff – the Woodruff Hotel in Oak Park, Sacramento.

Wed. 13 [October]

Arose at seven, breakfast. G.W. went to R-G to meet Schoffer; I to 3067 to sort my junk, the last dreggs of twenty-five years' gathering. Spent all day packing and sorting out things. "Toots" gave me some breakfast and gave us both dinner. After all was done we went to Mary Jane's. I felt like I had at last become a wander[er] on the face of the earth, no place of my own to lay my head, and no hopes of ever having a home again. Once upon a time I asked the gods of fortune to grant me one wish, and promised, were it granted I'd rail no more at my unhappy lot in life. They grin'd and handed me my wish on a red hot platter, and I am holding that self heating platter yet but they won't hear me yip.

- ❖ "Toots" – a friend who seems to be a close neighbor in Sacramento.
- ❖ Mary Jane – unidentified
- ❖ Junk of twenty-five years' gathering – the years since May left her parents' home in John Day, Oregon in late October 1899.
- ❖ Was the one wish that she be able to remarry? Or that she marry George? May obviously took her vow (not to complain) seriously.

Thur 14 [October]

Stored Chev[rolet] in rented garage, stored one box of Leftovers at Boon's, went to see Lon Chaney in "The Road to Mandeley" at the Calif. On returning found A.J. waiting for us, loaded up and away to Rio V[ista]. Arrived at 11 P.M., went to bed. Adele was fine. Slim's housekeep[ing] OK.

- ❖ Boon's - unidentified

Fri. 15 [October]

Left Rio at daybreak, reached Stewarts L[anding] at 6 A.M. and left at 6 P.M. loaded with 1500 sks corn. Weather very hot and close. GW's cold bad, mine better.
~~Reached the Mud F at 3 A.M.~~

Sat. 16 [October]

Heavy fog. Stuck on Mud Flat about 3 A.M., afloat at day light. Fog lifted, found our course and was in Pet[aluma] by 9:30 A.M. I went shopping, mailed letters to Amy, Mary, and also check for $59 to Standard Oil, payment in full. Treated myself to a Petaluma Special. Huh. Unloaded 1510 sks, which is ten more than we loaded, grew some I guess on the mud flats. I thought I heard something. I stood <u>watch</u> – is that what they call it – from three to six, while the rest slept, whistles bellering all around me, nothing for me to see but fog.

Left Pet[aluma] at half-past two. 2:30 P.M. ran to Riv.[?] G.W. took the wheel from the Tower L[ights] for two hours and I played "lookout" watching for light, channel buoys and listening for whistles. Reached Rio V[ista] at 10:50 P.M. Went to bed.

❖ Was a Petaluma Special a trip to the beauty parlor to have her hair done? Or something to eat? May was obviously unimpressed.

Sun. 17 [October]

Up at 6 A.M. ready to pull out and Pete asks for his time. Good-by[e] Pete. Left for Alton [?], loaded 212 sks corn, and on our way by 9:30 A.M. to Dave Stewarts Landing for bal[ance] of load, 412 sks here. Left 2 PM for Dan Stewarts Landing, where we picked up 600 sks, making a total of 1224. Left at 6 PM, nice clear moonlight night, just beyond Tower Lights our lights went out. Took some time to find [electrical] short. About [left blank] we went on the mud just a short distance from Beacon L[ights] ahead of us on our starboard. A.J. went to bed.

Mon. 18 [October]

6 A.M. still aground. A.J. and Slim still asleep. G.W. worked on engins till fifteen to six A.M. Called me to stand watch to see we do not drift on Beacon No. 2, and he lay down, is all in. Banks of fog all around us – but not very close, I can see the hills and two Beacons ahead of us and one behind us. If we camp much more on these Mud Flats, some one will have to pay rent or taxes. Sun is just rising out of the fog bank.

On our way 7:45 AM. Reach[ed] Pet[aluma] at 9:35 A.M. Unloaded 212 of load at Coullson [?] and bal[ance] at Golden Eagle. I shop[p]ed for Adele's Bread Basket, ordered a barrel of oil. Feel awful important. Got Jr. a Felix Cat, hope he enjoys it as much as I did getting it for him. Mail[ed] Amy a letter, also ins.[urance] check to R-G for 3067 6th Ave. Slim says he is going to leave us, hurt his back he say. Saw old Pete heaving on the soft end of a gangplank for Fay & Son. We left Petaluma 5:40, stop[p]ed at Port Custer for oil. Had some trouble with our lights again.

[two and a half lines rubbed out here -]

❖ Jr. – Ethan Papineau Junior, Amy and Ethan's eldest, and May's grandson. (See Part Two, "May's Life Between 1918 and 1925") Ethan Jr. was 3½ years old. Felix the Cat was a 1920s cartoon character.

Oct. 19
Tues.

Reached Rio Vista 2 PM, tied up till morning. Slim left us there on his way to Sacramento, has a lame back. Two new men just off the Sonoma came on in his place, a new Slim and our Albert, nice appearing boys but I shall miss Slim No. 1, he was a motherless mother's boy. Some woman had trained him to keep the woodbox and waterpail full and to clean up his own dirt. He was far more help than bother to me, and the first and only one who has offer'd to do anything to help me. G.W. says he is goofy and no doubt he is, for any man with common sense is not going to help a woman do her work unless he <u>has</u> <u>to</u> or is paid for it. The more heart the less brains. Some men are all Brain. Left R[io] V[ista] for Dan Stewarts [Landing], arrived there 10 A.M. Load[ed] 1500 sks, left 6 P.M. for Stockton.

Oct. 20 Weds.

Arrived Delta Warehouse No. 1, Stockton, 3:50 A.M. Went to bed, arose at 6 A.M. New man added to the family, name Walter, old-time hand of A.J.'s. G.W. went to see Rowdy – who tho glad to see G.W. still is very much in love with his new Mistress. I shall not go to see him if I can evade it. If he has not forgot[t]en me it would be bad for us both and if he has forgot[t]en me it would be bad for my vanity and self conceit. I want Moores to want to keep him and yet I don't want to be jealous of them when I'd see Rowdy cared more for them than for me, so I'd better stay away.

Left Stockton 3:20 PM, mailed a letter to Mama on our way. Somewhere near 3mile Bridge we lost poor little Polly Ann. Every time a new bunch comes on board and I'm ashamed to butt in and watch her, something happens to her: and now she's gone. Maybe we'll find her. Lacking a liveing pet, I fell back on the wee boat and she seemed to have a spirit. About the time we lost her I had a queer feeling all was not well, that I smelled smoke, so got out of bed to take a look around, but as the boat Adele was bucking and bawling against tide and wind, I had hard shift to keep my feet and did not look for Polly Ann. Reached the wheelhouse to find the Skipper and Engineer wondering how P[olly] A[nn] was standing the rough water. G.W. looked to see and she was gone; I guess my hunch was a call for help from the poor little thing. We made a circle back to the Bridge to see if we could see her and no doubt the bridge tender thought we whistled for the bridge, and the wind prevented him from hearing us, as when we had made a complete circle we found he had opened the bridge. Bet he is wondering yet if the Capt. was drunk or crazy – maybe he thinks he has seen the "Flying Dutchman," not many people of this day and age has seen her. We reached R[io] V[ista] 9:30, tied up for the night.

- ❖ Walter – unidentified
- ❖ Rowdy – a dog that May and G.W. had given to the Moores, to whom they owed $100 for a Chevrolet car. May and G.W. had understood that the Moores would cancel the debt because the dog was worth $500 (see Jan. 8 1927). May later (Nov. 2 1927) says that in exchange for the dog, Mrs. Moore had promised them the pink slip absolving them of the remainder of their debt for the car, but that she and George later searched in vain for the pink slip.
- ❖ Polly Ann – the rowboat that the Adele towed with her

Thur. 21 [October]

Tanked up with water, left at 6:50 A.M. Reached Dan Stewarts L[anding] at 8:10. My I would hate to be compelled to work for the Engineer of this boat. He came yammering in here saying we <u>must</u> have breakfast eaten befor we reached S[tewarts] L[anding] as <u>he</u> – bless you – <u>He</u> wanted the men to be ready to go to work as soon as we arrived. I told him we had plenty of time, but he said it would only take us twenty minutes. I said an hour and it realy took us one hour and twenty mins. I told him so after we got here and he laid it on to the tide. He should have been called Alibi Geo.

I've been saving scraps for either Dottie Dimple, the little stray dog that some beast in human form tied up on the levy to die, or for Royal, a wee scrubby Police pup that reminds me of Rowdy.

Left 6:30, got somewhere in about an hour and a half of Stockton and hit the fog. Was compelled to throw out the anchor, all hands went to bed 12 midnight, load 1625.

❖ The Engineer – George W. Maylone

Fri. 22 [October]

Got up at daylight, after rather an uneasy night, as I did not know how wide the river was at that point and could hear whistles blowing. Was more or less uneasy. About 2 A.M. the steamer J.F. Walker came tooting along in our direction. G.W. got up and tooted the fog horn in return. Quite exciting as it looked as tho they were headed right at us, don't know why they couldn't see our tail light as it was a bright one. I could see theirs even in the fog. And every some one called on his Maker and the boat sheer'd off from us. We did not get going till 8:30 AM and got here at 10 AM. Some delay in unloading, or rather in getting room to unload, did not get started til 11 AM. Mailed letters to Austin, Junior and Toots, left Stockton 5 P.M. Arrived Dave Stewarts L[anding] at 10 to 12, all hands went to bed.

Sat. 23 [October]

Up at 5 A.M., at least the cook was, and men at work by 7 A.M. A.J. left for Rio afoot 10:30 AM to get his car which is stored there. Mrs. J. and family around at noon. Waited till 2 PM, left to find A.J. In a short time both returned and again left for Sac[ramento]. Expect to be back sometime tomorrow. A.J. took Slim the Kentuckian with him, canned I think. I liked the Kentuckian, but he was too slow to suit the work, given to witty remarks which does not suit the Engineer who has a corner on the wit in his neighborhood, and he knocks anyone <u>he</u> does not like or anyone I happen to like – and the guy might as well ask for his time cause he will get it anyway cause the Engineer begins to earnestly poison the Skipper's mind concerning said person.

At breakfast this morning I overheard the Kentuckian say I wonder where that "pop-eyed Engineer and that ------- Captain are? Asleep? It is an Ell of a note getting us up here in the while they lay and sleep." I laughed a pain in my side, wishing the "pop-eyed – maybe he said Cockeyed – Engineer" could have heard that: take some of the conceit out of him, which I haven't been able to do in six years. Engineer and Cook took a bath, which is an event, let me tell you.

* ❖ The cook – May herself
* ❖ Mrs. J and family – probably "A.J." Johnston's wife Winnie and her children, although only his wife Winnie comes on board the next day.
* ❖ The Engineer – George W. Maylone
* ❖ The Skipper / the Captain – "A.J." Johnston

Sun. 24 [October]

Awful foggy this morning. I've quite a bunch of fish caught for today['s] dinner. No hauling to the boat to day up to 10 A.M. Too wet. Guess we will be here all day.

G.W. is having one of his Sunday grouches. I am sure I don't know what ails my husband. As long as everything goes well he is as sweet tempered as an angel, but let any piece of machinery go on the bum, let the loading be delayed or one of the men fail to do his share and he is as ugly as sin to me. Good thing Mrs. Jordon can not hear and see him. Funny part of it [is] he never realizes that he is cross, he thinks everyone else is cross. Of course when he is damning every thing and every one in sight <u>I</u> can't wear a smile and then he wants to know what <u>I</u> am cross about. I realy think what ails him is this, he sees too much of me and not enough of other women; if he could compare me with some other wives I've seen or heard tell of – maybe it would help his point of view.

Today at three o'clock P.M. Capt. A.J. returned, bringing his wife on board to make a trip with him and at once my husband was all smiles, and roaring with laughter. I nearly fainted as I did not know she was here untill I heard him laughing loudly. Maybe absence does make the heart grow fonder, if you are not absent too long.

Albert left us at Rio Vista at 7:30 PM. We left S[tewarts] L[anding] at 6 P.M., loaded 1750. Got hung up in heavy fog 11:30, all hands to bed and no disturbance till dawn. Wrote Amy a letter.

❖ "I've quite a bunch of fish caught" – May liked to fish
❖ Mrs. Jordon – unidentified (but referred to at the start of May's 1927 diary)

Mon 25 [October]

Fog hung on till 8:00 befor we could see our way clear. Then got off on the wrong foot and ran an hour out of our way befor the Skipper discovered his course. Arrived Stockton 11:30, no room to unload, had to wait till . Were unloaded by 10 to six P.M., left at 20 to seven.

Have a new man in the crew – pal of Walter's. Name is Ed Pedort or Pedart.

❖ Ed Pedort / Pedart – unidentified

Tues. 26 [October]

Reached S[tewarts] L[anding] at 2 P.M. A.J. and Mrs. A.J. left the boat, headed for Sac[ramento], supposed to return tomorrow at 2 P.M. Hope the lady makes several trips with us, it improves my husband's manners and his treatment of me. It also improves my kitchen condition. One day in the heat and flys and I have a new screen door. And I think I'll get something to cover my table with. I had to rustle my own kindling and coal this morning. Never had to build fires befor in my life till the last few years. Always swore I'd never build fires for any man to lay and sleep while I did it, but I am getting to be quite a liar, if I have to get my own kindling believe me there won't be much sleep on this boat while I'm doing it. I broke up the Capt's pet box this morning for firewood. Uh huh. I'm waiting for him to ask where it is –

❖ Broke up the Capt's pet box – I think by "Captain" she is referring to George, who was soon to take his revenge.

Weds. 27 [October]

All loaded by noon, 1750 sks. A.J. returned 1:45 PM, on our way at once. I still see results of Mrs. A.J.'s visit – a fly swatter – Got a dandy letter from Amy. All the way from the bridge below R[io] V[ista] we watched for Polly Ann. Ask[ed] the Bridge-tender had he seen a little red rowboat. Instead of answering our question, he said "Oh that is why you came back that night". So he has been suffering over that mystery ever since. About 4 A.M., G.W. spied her tied up near an old rotted row of piling. Some buildings there, but no one showed up; we were all like a pack of kids over a lost kitten, poor little thing seemed none the worse for her wild night's adventure, hadn't even tipped over, her half an oar still there.

Capt. wishes to time two ways of coming into Stockton. The river splits and goes around. This time we came the [left blank]. Entered at 25 minutes of 4 PM and reached the other end at 25 to six, so were two hours at flood tide. We reached Stockton 9:30 P.M., a very quiet trip. A.J. is not feeling well. Stomach bothers him.

Thur. 28 [October]

Men at work 20 to 8 A.M. Slim No. 1 (Geo. Myers) came back to work. Unloaded 20 to 2 P.M. Left Stockton 2 o'clock P.M. – reached Dan Stewarts L[anding] 9 P.M.

Fri. 29 [October]

A cold north wind blowing, hard to keep the boat out of the bank. Men at work by 7 AM but lots of time lost fussing with the boat. Every one very touchy. The North Wind is a trouble-maker – maybe healthy but he sure is the cause of lots of spats. I got up cross as a bear myself, cross because G.W. let me get up and build the fires. I'd lots rather build the fire than have him under my feet and the kitchen blue with smoke, but at the same time I hate to have him lie abed and let me do his work. Don't mind it if he has lost sleep or is not well, but when he's wide awake and kept me awake for an hour and then just time for the alarm to ring he gets very sleepy --

He is still smiling over the dirty trick he played on me last night. Slim is the only one who ever helps me and I guess I've published the fact, any way as soon as we got well under way, Slim began to make kindling out of all the boxes in sight. Broke up my washtub box but I thought "I'll soon get another" and I heard him say, "Geo. do you use this box" and G.W. said "Hell no, break it up." I rushed out to see what it was and behold he had smashed Junior's toybox that I gave him when he was just able to sit alone and put his toys in it. I carried it with me from 3067 over to Ross house, and down to Maritsas Camp, up to Old San J. City, on to the Feather Queen and then to the [Adele] Hobson. I wanted to cry but I thought that would give my lord and master to[o] great a kick. I guess he thinks he'll show me what a darling Slim is. Lucky I heard him tell Slim to break the box up.

A strange noise all day yesterday under the starboard propeller proved to be G.W.'s lost overalls – just the waistband and buttons left. That makes 4 pair of overall[s], 2 shirts and 2 pairs of BVDs he has forgot[t]en and let get lost on the wheel. All new ones too. He was pouty when he hung these over board and would tell me so I could watch em. They get caught when the boat lands or stops – A.J. says no more washing overboard. It's OK with me.

Loaded 1725 sks and on our way by 12:30 noon. Hard wind blowing, reached Stockton 9 A.M. On our way passed a burning island. These islands are mostly peet like the peet bogs of Ireland, and will burn for ages sometimes. Made a dreadful smoke to pass thru, worse than fog, but a beautiful sight. Am afraid it is a woefull sight to the owner of the island and buildings –

A.J. gets no better, is evidently in agony all the time. First man I ever saw who could suffer and smile, I wish he'd go home to his wife, he needs care that only a woman can give and even an old-time nurse has to step easy if she has an Irish husband.

- ❖ BVDs – a brand of men's underpants
- ❖ Ross house, Maritsas Camp – I haven't been able to find out where these places between May's house in Sacramento and the Adele Hobson are located. Maritsas is mentioned again Nov. 14, as one of the letters May has written. There is only one Maritsas family listed in the 1920s and 1930s U.S. Census, a Greek family headed up by Harry Maritsas. In 1920 he is listed as a merchant in a shoe parlor in Nebraska and in 1930 his son George Maritsas is working as a hat cleaner in Sacramento. Could "Maritsas camp" be some enterprise run by one of his other sons or relations?
- ❖ Old San J. City – elsewhere May refers to San Joaquin City. I believe this was a nickname for Stockton, the seat of San Joaquin county.

❖ Feather Queen – a boat May and G.W. seem to have travelled on for a day to get to the Adele Hobson (see Nov. 1st).

❖ old-time nurse with an Irish husband – May is referring to herself and George here. I take this reference to herself as a "nurse" as confirmation of the family story that May was a knowledgeable midwife. (And not only for goats.) Obviously May could not nurse A.J. as she felt he needed, because of George's jealousy.

Sat. 30 [October]

Twenty-odd years ago my young friends gave me a farewell party. "Surprise" – I being on the eve of flight from the home nest. Life has contained a great many surprises since then, some of them not as jolly as my farewell party from the John Day Valley.

A.J. is leaving for Sac[ramento] this morning. I hate to think of G.W. taking the responsbilaty of taking the boat to Stewarts Landing but he – G.W. – is so cocksure he can do it, far be it from me to knock the idea. A.J. is a sick man, and I can't be a wet blanket and ruin his confidence in G.W., or crack G.W.'s conceit, for they say self-confidence is half the battle, so I'll stay put and do my share.

Men worked half an hour then laid off till 10:30 to let the tide come in; load is coming off slow; unloaded 4:30, men worked just six hours. G.W. had to go on shore somewhere to get change to pay them. None of the men wanted to ship out on the boat, so we had to leave with only Slim. Got cut loose with no mishaps except the "Dammed Starboard Engin" (I believe that is the proper name as most of the time A.J. and G.W. call it that or worse) died just as we were turning around. But we got out of there with no harm done. Slim at the wheel and G.W. below.

I had started supper, it was then six o'clock, and G.W. called on me to throw the starboard engin in gear for him. I tried to "go slow" just as he told me, but how does one know how slow is "slow" when one has never tried to do a certain thing befor? Any way I believe "she died" twice or three times befor we got her going, then in about an hour and a half we hit the heavy smoke of the burning island. Slim watched the port side for the shore, and I on the starboard; we came to a place where four waters meet, a perfect cross: ---|--- While we were in the intersection of these cross streams we could of course see wide water on both side[s] and GW unknowingly bore to the starboard and I saw the brush of the point of land right in my face.

I yelled "Hard to Port – port her – hard" but it was too late and we'd ram[m]ed our starboard bow into the mud. We rushed out and down on the bow to see what we'd done. Smoke was so thick we could not see anything on the levy, but found we could not back off under our own power. While we were still debating the question of what was best to do, I heard a steamer whistle. She wanted to pass on our starboard side and as our starboard side was halfway up on the levy, I became wildly excited and yelled "That steamer is going on our starbo[a]rd side". G.W. blew several short frantic warning signals and the steamer sheared of[f] to our port side, ask[ed] us if we were O.K. and upon our telling him we had gone aground, he very calmly said, "Oh the tide is coming up and you'll soon float off".

The big liar, the tide was going out then and did not come in till two o'clock, we'd have been high and dry and in my opinion tipped over befor the tide came in, for Adele's mast was pointing to 10 o'clock instead of 12 as it should. After we gave those frantic signals for the steamer to keep off, about a thousand more or less Japs or Chinks swarmed all over the levy, very much excited, trying to tell us something "Je – le – chis pretty soon now no more water" was all we could understand and we thought we'd run in to their pumping plant and ruined their water supply. But they were trying to tell us we'd have no water for our boat when the tide went out.

About 8:30 I saw a boat's lights coming up the river and I began to clammer for aid, got the flash light and wig-wag'd a distress call. Boat slowed down – our engins were dead and we could not whistle – and ask[ed] what was wrong. We told them we were on the ground with a bad list to port and fear'd we'd tip over when the tide went out. They at once offered to help us up off the levy into deep water, but gave us such a hard pull and we came of[f] so easy it broke our head line, leaving Slim on shore.

The captain of our rescue boat – which was the Stanley Robert – said he'd take us across the river where he knew it was deep, which he did. His men, seemed to me there was at least 20 of them, were all kindness itself and did all the work needed, tied us up to their own boat and then tied us to the landing at Acker's Island where they left us, and we thanked them with all our hearts. I was just as gratefull as one person can be to another, for I was in deadly terror of Adele tipping over and being ruined. Too much responsibility. If A.J. had been on board it would not have bothered me a bit, I'd let him do the worrying, but I was sick with fear we'd stove in Adele [bust end]?

After the Stanley-Robert had pulled out I yelled to Slim in order to locate him so G.W. could go after him in the row boat. Poor Slim admit[t]ed afterward that he thought we'd deserted him and left him with a band of Japs. He had no cap, coat or money and couldn't understand what the Japs were telling him. Anyway G.W. got him back to Adele and we had examined our lady for leaks and injuries, found her O.K. and were in bed by nine P.M.

❖ Twenty-odd years ago – see Part Two (the end of "Growing Up Years: from Kansas to Oregon, 1879-1899") for an account of how May left her family home in John Day, Oregon to marry John Diddy in Trinity Center, California.

❖ Japs and Chinks – If it is true that May learned herbal remedies from Native Americans, in contrast she held prejudiced attitudes (typical of her time) towards the many Japanese and Chinese immigrants working in the western United States. She had lived in several communities where there was a strong Chinese presence. John Day, Oregon had a sizeable number of Chinese workers who came into the region beginning in the mid-1800s: John Day is now home to the Kam Wah Chung Museum. Weaverville, California, where May was first married in 1899, still has its Joss House Chinese temple dating back to the mid-19th century. And in 1900, when she lived in Trinity Centre, California, the census shows that May's neighbors were Chinese miners.

Sun 31 [October]

Up at 5 and safely on our way with both engins going by six o'clock. Reached Dave Stewarts Landing at 11:00 A.M. Starboard engin died as we were making a landing and we run our battery down. Phoned A.J. in Sac[ramento], who is in bed and he orders us back to Stockton with load. Got loaded [left blank] sks at 4:30 PM. Was just loaded when Mrs. A.J., Harvey and Mrs. L. came after the Buick. Went to bed at dark to save the batterys.

❖ Harvey – A. F. Johnston's son, age 15 in 1926.
❖ Mrs. L. - unidentified

Nov. 1
Mon.

Up at daylight and started at 7 AM. Could only get the port engin to run, battery dead. G.W. made several attempts to start it, in vain. We made good time tho with one engin. Tide was with us all the way. Arrived in Stockton at 3 P.M. and men were at work at 3:30. Three men. G.W. phoned to Moore to come get the battery to recharge it. I know G.W. has been worried, but at the same time he's awful proud of what he has done and can you blame him. Just five months ago yesterday we first went on the Feather Queen and five months ago today we came on the Adele Hobson and I never befor had step[p]ed my foot on a boat of any kind outside a ferry. And G.W. was just as green, all he knew was how to run a little powerboat. Had any one told us in five months he and I would run the boat from Stockton to a given point above Rio V[ista] and back to Stockton loaded, with only a deck hand to help us, I'd have walked off the boat right there. G.W. phoned to A.J., got orders to bring boat back to Sac[ramento].

Tue. Nov. 2

Was up at daylight. G.W. ordered oil and got his battery back. Everything in good order, and with both engins running we were on our way at 9:30, bucking the tide all the [way] to within a short distance of 3mi slough. I have become a little reconciled to G.W.'s handling the boat now and he is so stuck on himself, calls himself "Captain". I met him this morning wearing A.J.'s sweater and I said "Good Morning Captain J----" and he said "I beg your pardon, this is Captain M-----". I don't suppose we will return to Stockton soon, so I sadly bid my Delta cat goodby[e]. She wanted to go on the boat awful bad, came on two or three times and I had to put her off again. Slim wanted to keep her, but G.W. did not approve and I'm afraid A.J. wouldn't.

I wrote Amy a card but could get no one to mail it for me. So I threw it in on the warehouse floor. Now we'll see if any one is kind enough to mail it for me. This is a life not one woman in a thousand would be content to live, no home, no place to keep your clothes, no place to rest or no chair to sit in, no bath, no comfort in any way. One can't have any thing for their own pleasure. Yet I would not whimper if I could have the mail even twice a month. But no one thinks of me any more than if I were one of the handtrucks. If I were missing when needed they would hunt me up. I never know when any one is going to leave the boat untill they are gone so have no idea of when to be ready to mail a letter, and some of my mail is old enough to walk alone when I get it. I'm full of self-pity and firmly believe that every one should remember I don't set foot on land for days and days, and that they should all remember all the pleasure I get out of life beyond "looking" is what few letters I get and what I get to read. The men all get to go ashore ever stop we make but none of them think of me, unless I ask for some certain thing.

We had to buck the tide all the way from Stockton all day, had it with us a little way while in False River. We got to Rio V[ista] with no mishaps, and entered the Sac[ramento] River at 4 P.M. G.W. promised he would tie up befor dark, but I think he dreads making a landing nearly as much as I do, tho so far he has made good landings no trouble at all. We reached Ryde at good dark but he kept on going. The river is very foggy or smoky, can't see the lights ahead of us very plainly.

I was terrified at the bridges as they were slow to open, but we got thro safely, and then I began to sweat blood over those bridge abbutments that were still in the river the last time we went down. Nearly bursted my eye balls watching for them, nearly froze standing out on deck where I could see better. When my head was numb with pain and my body numb with cold, G.W. told me to come in where it was warm, and I said "I can't see those abutments from in there" and he calmly said "Oh we've passed the place long ago. I guess they've taken them out". Now wouldn't that kill you? After he ask[ed] me to watch for em, then let me stand there in the cold straining my eyes out and he knew we were by the danger point. What a queer thing man is.

We reached Georgia Deans warehouse at Courtland at 7:30 and tied up very nicely. G.W. had to go phone, insisted I go along, ask[ed] Slim if he wanted to go – and then blew poor Slim to a 95 cent treat, coffee and pie for me, coffee, pie and ice cream for them. I was as dirty as a hog, my hair atousel, hands grimy from handling the rope on Polly Ann and from the greasy rungs of the ladder and I even had a dirty apron on under my coat. It was warm in the ice cream parlor and I unbuttoned my coat, noticed my dirty apron and buttoned up again.

Got back to the boat 9:30. To bed. A.J. was in bed when we phoned but said for us to keep on coming, to pick up the barge on our way and bring it up.

❖ Ryde and Courtland – towns on the Sacramento River between Rio Vista and Sacramento.

Wed. Nov. 3

Left Courtland 7:30 and had only been on our way half an hour and Slim discovered something wrong with the oil pump on the port engin. And G.W. promptly shut her down – here we are again with only one engin and I've no faith what ever in the Starboard engin, she is as stubborn as a mule and not half as trustworthy, never know what moment she is going to balk or kick over the traces by burning out and getting hot.

We got to Freeport 10:45. Tied up to some piling across on the Yolo side. Slim and G.W. rowed across, phoned to A.J. who said "just stay there for the day" which we prepared to do, by tearing the disabled engin apart to locate trouble. Found it O.K.: some very important little do-jigger they call a "pin" has sheared off. G.W. had it nearly fixed again, when about a quarter to 4 P.M. two fellows appeared on the scene saying A.J. had sent them down to pilot the Adele in to Sac[ramento]. We cut loose and were on our way by 4 P.M. About dark we got in shoal water, even with two pilots on the job, but got back in deep water at once. After getting in sight of the M St. Bridge we gave the first whistle for it to open. Had to give the signal four times as we had only one engin. It is hard to control the boat and G.W. was afraid to slow down too much for fear that one [engine] would die and we'd be out in the middle of the stream with no control of the boat at all and boats on all sides of us. Realy if I had hold of that stubborn old nut upon that bridge I'd throw him off his perch; he is a holy fright.

We got thru safely and called for the I St. Bridge to open, which it did promptly. By that time we'd choked our starboard engin down so she was trying to die and G.W. had a time making a landing. He made the first landing fine and Slim jumped on the piling but the two men with us failed to get their rope around the bitts and we were away out in the stream. G.W. had to keep going either forward or back; didn't dare stop on the engin would die and let us back into the bridge, which would tear our mast out and maybe sink us – in backing up, the corner of the [wheel]house caught on a board some one had nailed on the piling, tearing it off and splintering it, making an awful sound. I was in the stern fighting to save Polly Ann, that some one had tied so short I could not swing her around on the safe side. Those splinters and pieces of board just rained down on me and I thought we'd torn the whole house off the boat. I tell you I nearly passed out. It was after six but not seven yet when we were safely tied up, as at 7 P.M. GW went out to see A.J. Found him in bed under Dr's orders to remain there – no better –

❖ Freeport – on the Sacramento river between Courtland and Sacramento. The Freeport Ferry "connected the Yolo shore with the town of Freeport".[29]

Thur Nov. 4

Slim helped G.W. till noon, on the port engin. Then got his time. I hate to see him go, he is more help about the boat than all the others ever on here. I feel sorry for him, he seems to be so friendless and alone, and is mentally only about ten years old and acts according, and one feels toward him just as one does to an orphan of that age. G.W. went out to see A.J. and was told to put the boat in good shape and also the barge, as there would be nothing doing till A.J. regains his health.

Fri. Nov. 5

G.W. left boat 8 A.M., to get battery for car. I started to wash as every thing on boat is filthy. Have not been where I could get even plain muddy water to wash with – all oil. Got about half of my clothes washed and partly hung out, was as wet and dirty and tired as a hog when here at 1:30 came G.W. all smiles with a lady friend – nuff sed. Could not get on boards so I climbed, dirty dress and wet sox, run over ragged shoes, out on the piling to visit. Sat there in the cool damp shade all sweaty and wet, and nearly froze, but what could I do – After an hour or so, Slim came wandering in and G.W. proposed he stay on the boat and we all go down to see the barge. Oh fine and dandy. I hadn't had a mouthfull of dinner – but no one ever asks me what I want to do, and when G.W. and M.J. get together I am no more considered than a child that has to be taken along, even if it is in the way.

Any way we went. I had to go change my clothes from the hide out and on our way G.W. insisted on chow-min. He has a check for $50.00, and now watch it fly. Up to the present time I have always got hold of the money first and promptly put the biggest part in the checking account, but I'm going to let him gang his own gait with this month's wages and see where it goes. I let him have all the money in Aug. and in two weeks we were flat broke, but as it was his vacation I said nothing. Maybe he thinks this is another vacation. We got back in time to take [name beginning with M rubbed out] our company home befor dark, and went to the Hip and to Nick Never Sleeps. I find there is $24.00 left of the $50.00.

❖ M.J. – it doesn't seem that this woman is the Mary Jane that is May's friend in Sacramento.

❖ the Hip – the Hippodrome movie house

Sat [Nov] 6

I am not a bit well, and I don't know what ails me. Sometimes I think my mind is not just right, for I seem to see the dark side of every thing. I guess I'm getting stingy too, for I am just sick when I can't pay any thing on these bills or save any money. I saw the money simply had to be spent so I insisted G.W. buy some much needed clothes, shirt, shoes and leggins, all of which I know did not amount to $15.00, yet I know the money is nearly all gone for tonight when we bought his shoes, only $4.50 and he did not have money enough to pay for them and I had to give him the last $10.00 of his $50.00. So even at the most he has not more than $8.00 or $9.00 left out of $50.00 in less than four days – and he is one who is always railing a[bout] women keeping men broke. I have not spent one cent and outside of what I've eaten, and two show tickets, none has been spent on me.

Sun. [Nov.] 7

G.W. went up after his car at 8 o'clock, did not get back till 10, said garage was not open. Alibi George.

Went out to A.J.'s. I finished my washing, which I've been laboring on for three days. After it was done, was informed any Chink would have done it for 4 bits – thank you. I myself would not admire the intel[l]ect of any animal but a Jackass that would do some of this filthy greasy washing at all. Even the deck hands won't do their own washing and theirs does not compare at all to the Engineer's dirt.

On G.W.'s return to the boat I found some of the Redding-ites had been in town, for a big box of jelly, j—k—y and fruit, also books, had been left at A.J.'s. I was just frantic to think they might be in town this very minute. I phoned to A.J.'s to find out when the box was left, but it seems no one was home who knew much about it. Irene said two young men left it Sat. We went out to Agnes's but no one home – so if Amy and the Child were here no doubt they have gone again. Met an old friend of G.W.'s who remembers meeting <u>ME</u> with G.W. a year or so befor I ever heard tell of G.W. My husband must pick on women of the same type, all the time.

- ❖ 4 bits – fifty cents
- ❖ the Redding-ites: Amy, Ethan and Ethan Jr.
- ❖ j – k – y: jerky?
- ❖ Irene – A.F. Johnston's youngest child, about 6 in 1926.
- ❖ Agnes - unidentified

Mon. [Nov.] 8

Men went down after barge, got a tug to tow them up. Paid the man $5.00 for towing. Barge in good condition, very little water in it. I don't feel any better. Have a dislike for every one including myself, in a horrid mood. Feel just as tho I want to break, bust and damage every thing in sight. Money, the root of all evil, may be the root of my ailment too. Just six days since we got $50.00 and we have 85 cents left. My husband bought <u>me</u> <u>a</u> <u>jar</u> <u>of</u> <u>cold</u> <u>cream</u> tonight, kind of him but I'm afraid the trouble with my face lies deeper than cold cream. We went to a show, "Breed of the Sea". Ralph Ince in a double role. Very good, for a while I forgot myself and felt better. But as usual G.W. wanted to leave befor the picture was over. He never yet saw the end of a show. Wrote to Amy.

Tues [Nov.] 9

Looked for Mary all day but she did not show up; we got ready in the evening to go out there but Slim did not come back to the boat, so we went to bed. Had orders from A.J. to go up the river tomorrow to the wood, and load the barge. Maybe I'll feel better when we get away from town. Too many cracks in the pavement to lose $5.00 bills in. Alibi –

Wed. [Nov.] 10

Slim returned while G.W. and young Garber were up town looking for him. We pulled out of the landing at halfpast eight A.M. but were an hour getting as far as the American river. Water very shallow, stir'ed mud all the way in spots till we hit the Feather mouth. Found the Jacinto and a barge stuck on a wing dam – I guess they called it a damn wing dam. We barely had

❖ young Garber - unidentified

* * * * * * * * * *

Here there is a page torn completely out. May was obviously upset, wrote what she thought, and later regretted it. (Alas for her nosy descendants and others!)

* * * * * * * * * *

Nov. 12

Clear again today P.M. but rained hard all night, hard hailstorm this A.M. Men loading barge between showers. Everything wet and muddy.

Nov. 13

A most wonderfull day. I feel a great deal more like my self, the weight on my brain seems to have lifted. I guess I expect too much of life and the poor wretches that inhabit this planet. Took a walk, awful muddy underfoot. Beautiful over head, millions of crows and wee brown birds flitting around among the weeds. Found red rose hips, brown grass tassles, a few yellow thistle-like blossoms and one wild aster. Saw several belated lizards that had better be making for their winter homes. G.W. and Slim went to K[nights] L[anding] but found every thing closed on account of Uncle Joe Camen's [?] death.

> ❖ Knight's Landing – According to the Yolo County Place Names of Past and Present, Knight's Landing was named after William Knight who established a ferry there.[30] It was the site of two 1920s movies: "Showboat" and "Steamboat Round the Bend".
>
> ❖ Uncle Joe Camen (or Carmen?) – unidentified

Nov. 14 Sunday

G.W. and Slim spent most of the day so far – 1 PM – trying to bag a duck – or some ducks. No success. Getting quite cloudy again, h [May was evidently interrupted here]

Jess Perry with the Solano and barge just passed up the river, they went down Thur 11. Have been to Petaluma, saw old Pete, wanted to ask him what size shoes he is wearing now – ole sticky fingers, or rather sticky toes. I mailed letters to Amy, Standard Oil and Maritsas yesterday, and started a letter to Austin.

The levy is so mud[d]y it is out of the question to haul wood just yet, and from the looks of the weather not much hopes either very soon. Hunters got 6 ducks befor dark.

> ❖ Pete must have taken a pair of G.W.'s shoes (or May believed he had), while working on the Adele Hobson.

Mon. [Nov.] 15

Nice warm clear day. Men got 12 loads on the barge, are doing fine. When we were up here befor it took them four and a half days with four men and two trucks to load the barge. If the weather holds good these two men and one truck will have it loaded tomorrow. We have been here 6 days tomorrow and it has rained more than half the time not counting Sunday as they did not work Sunday.

I am feeling "at myself" once more. Strange when I have those dreadfull blue spells, I never feel they are the same old thing and will pass away. No doubt my own moods are the cause of G.W.'s cussedness, he makes no allowance for my state of health and thinks I'm mean and ugly. And it makes him mean and ugly. If I'd tell him when I'm well what ails me, he'd think it was just an Alibi and if I was going to die I wouldn't tell him when I'm under the control of my "blue devils". Men are dumb brutes and women are contrary ones.

Tues. [Nov.] 16

Hazy again this morning, very cold. Men were at work as soon as it was good light.

Shep came down for his breakfast, cutest little tike. Talk about smart. The day we landed, I began to call him. He came rushing up to me up on the levy, could not see the boat at all. But after greeting me wildly he rushed right over the levy and on to the boat looking for Rowdy. Hunted all over the boat, out on to the bank and down to the barge and looked for him there. It is two months since he saw Rowdy but he hadn't forgot[t]en. As soon as he saw me he knew there should be a boat some where near and an old dog friend on it.

Nov. 17

Men finished loading barge at noon. Slim sawed wood in the afternoon and G.W. worked at something in the engin room. They plan to go to Sac[ramento] tomorrow and see what orders are and how A.J. is.

Thur. Nov. 18.

Men left here at 7:30 in the rain for Sac[ramento]. Rained hard all day, thank goodness I've plenty of wood. I was wet all day tho. Saving rain water, as the river is brick red yet and our tank nearly dry.

Men got back at 3:30, wet, muddy and hungry. A.J. is in the Sutter Hospital. Was operated on for adhesions of the upper stomach last Sunday Nov. 14, not out of danger yet. We are to stay here till we get Adele loaded, then when ever river is high enough we'll find some way to get to Sac[ramento].

Got 4 letters from Amy, 1 from Austin, 1 from Mary.

Nov. 19

G.W. and I went to Knight's Landing to get me a pair of shoes as I'm on the ground. Could not find a pair of high shoes or women's boots in the <u>whole</u> city and no boy's boots small enough or child's boot large enough. Surely there is some time in a boy's life when his foot is the same size of a woman's No. 4 foot. The girl clerk is a freak. She wears a men's size 7 ½ and is proud of it. Doesn't that sound fishy? Says she can't get a woman's shoe large enough for her foot and wears men's dress oxfords altogether. Her foot looked nice tho' and if she hadn't mentioned it I'd not have noticed how large they were. But my loveing 'usband had just remarked it took a <u>whole</u> <u>cow</u> hide to make <u>me</u> a pair of shoes and she says, comforting me, "never mind your feet, look at mine" and then told us about her feet. My 'usband looked a little red behind the ears, but he can get away with murder where I'd be overcome with shame at a break like that.

I finally got a very comfortable oxford that will at least keep my feet off the ground. We had an awful time coming home. The rain fell in sheets and no windshield in that old truck, I was wet as a drownded rat. Got back to Adele and Slim had let the fire die out. gee—o—mygosh

Nov. 20

Lots of traffic today. The Flora passed here four times, guess she must meet another boat a little ways down here and turn and come back. Some one on the boat ask[ed] if we had heard how "Al" was. I don't know who it was, maybe A.J.'s father-in-law – who is supposed to be on the Red Bluff.

Sun. Nov. 21

Rain-rain-rain. We three took a long walk this morning and made a sort of half moon shape trip. When we were in a stone's throw of our starting point. G.W. insisted we were lost and wanted to go on the back track. I begged to go to a certain gate in sight as I <u>knew</u> or thought I knew where we were, and sure enough when we got to the gate we could see Adele's mast. I enjoyed it even tho we got no game. We got wet, and I got a belated spray of wild peas, pretty as pinks. I saw some roses in bloom and I'm going over and get em tomorrow if it isn't raining cats and dogs.

The Red Bluff went down today, the Flora and Dover up. We got two more ducks, makes eight now. I caught 20 cats [catfish] yesterday.

Mon. [Nov.] 22

Rained hard all night but let up at daylight. G.W. and I moved the stove and cleaned out the soot oven. Men went to work at 9 till 12 – 1:30 to 4:30, got quite a lot of wood on the Hobson. River is on the rise. I baked a cake, had pretty good luck.

Tues. [Nov.] 23

Rain again, men worked till 10 A.M. then drove to K[nights] L[anding]. We got letter from Mrs. J[ohnston]. A.J. is better and says for us to stay here untill he is able to come after us. Slim was dolefull as soon as he heard that, he has had the Heebe Jeebes ever since he came back from Sac[ramento]. Guess he would [rather] starve and freeze on 2nd St. than stay here with a full belly and a dry warm place to sleep. We have treated him as we have never treated any other river-rat, just as tho he was a friend or brother. Overlooked his ill manners because we knew he had no training, or breeding. But the better one treats these poor mis-begot[t]en creatures the queerer it seems to make em. Treat them like the scum of the earth and they seem to like it and are willing to work, but as we three are alone we try to make it pleasant for Slim and he gets the big head and wants to run the whole outfit.

Wed. [Nov.] 24

Rained hard this morning but let up about daylight. The men worked from 8 to 12, then about half-past 12 to 1, and suddenly Slim came in and began to clean up. Ask[ed] for his time, and when I had it made out, took his money and never said thank you – goodbye – kiss my foot, or any thing else. G.W. said "Leaving are you Slim?" He said "I'll say I am. I've had all this mud I want" and away he went afoot for K[nights] L[anding]. Left us where he knew we'd go over the bypass if the water comes up, which it will if it rains hard enough. He knew G.W. can not start the engins alone with just myself on board. What queer things human <u>beans</u> are.

Thur. [Nov.] 25

Thanksgiving Day – the strangest one I ever spent. When we got up this morning the river had raised at least 3 feet and maybe more. Our gang planks were gone, and we were cut off from land. No way to get ashore except in the boat. G.W. went ashore and pulled up the plank and sand boards that were on the verge of floating away. Then we had some breakfast and got ready to move our outfit up the river, to where the banks are higher, and get away from this low bypass where if the water comes up as high as it does ever winter we would be out over the lowlands by morning and no way to get back. We worked from five A.M. o'clock till four in the afternoon, G.W. with block and tackle on land and I taking up the slack on the ropes on the boat. We got her up the river just an inch at a time, and I thought I was doing wonders if I got enough slack to wrap around the bit once.

After working all day with only a cold lunch and a hot cup of coffee for our Thanksgiving dinner we only moved the whole outfit about the length of the Hobson, but at least we got her up out of the low place in the bank. Yet we are not as far up as we should be, but about four an awful storm came up. It sprinkled and the wind blew a gale all day, but this storm was a humdinger. I never was so near <u>all in</u> in my whole life, but I did not want G.W. to worry about me, so just grinned and sawed wood or rather rope. The skin is all worn off my hands and I'm so lame I'm a solid ache.

Fri. [Nov.] 26

Got up at daylight, river is nearly up to where our lines are tied, if
we had anything substantial to tie to, but all there is along this
levy is little willows no thicker than my wrist, and as this soil is
only sand I'm in holy terror for fear the wind blowing against us
will tear the little weeds out by the roots. After breakfast we
worked again till two o'clock getting the barge headed in closer
to the bank as she had blown out full length of her head line and
the currant was hitting her too hard. G.W. had to do that all alone
as it had to be done on land but I helped by staying out in the rain
with him, holding the rope to Polly Ann when he got on or of[f]
the Hobson.

About noon the rain let up and sun came out and I got some
dinner, first warm meal we have had since noon the 24th,
except our breakfasts, and they was just coffee and toast. I was
too busy and too tired and too worried the rest of the time to
cook, so we just had coffee and what ever was cooked. We ate so
much dinner today we nearly comflopagaited.

Sat. [Nov.] 27

Did not sleep much. Rain, wind and the seesaw of the ropes
fretted me. We are still in danger of going on the ground if the
wind came from the North. At noon we saw the U.S.E.D. boat
The Fall taking a barge in to the old River backwater and G.W.
walked down there and told the Captain what sort of a fix we
were in. The Fall came up and nose'd us up close to the Edson
buildings where there is high banks and good "deadman"s to tie
to. We were all snug by dark and I shall sleep tonight thank
goodness and The Fall.

❖ Edson Buildings (and later, the Edson Ranch) – The 1920 census showed Lowell F. Edson living on his parents' ranch in Knight's Landing, Yolo County. Lowell married Irma Wallace in 1921. The 1930 census showed Lowell's parents living in the town of Knight's Landing, and Lowell (married and now with two children) running the "stock farm".[31]

❖ Despite my best efforts, I have not been able to find out what U.S.E.D. stands for.

Sun. [Nov.] 28

Nothing to do but watch the drift go by. I wrote to Mama, Amy and Mrs. J., also got a letter from Amy. River is still going up, will be over by night I guess. We went down and got the Ford truck up on the levy a ways out of danger and fastened all the planks, shutes, sandboards to willows with wire.

It is hard to live with a man on rainy days. Two women would read, write, sew and be quite content, but a man must be intertained every moment, don't want to do any thing them selves nor want any one else to do any thing. This one of mine wants to eat, smoke, sleep or ------- and never wants one to get any thing cooked, washed or swept up. Yet wants something to eat when he wants it and passes away if the dishes are dirty and no food cooked. Oh Hum.

Mon. [Nov.] 29

River cut thru the levy into Edson Ranch and they are out getting in their marooned livestock this morning. Ask[ed] for the boat to gather in their turkeys. I have tried for a week to make out an order for Xmas, did not want G.W. to see it, but when I got it ready by jerks I had to write to Mrs. J[ohnston?] and ask her to put in a check for me and he caught me in the act. Took the letter away from me and read it. I wonder if he realizes it takes all my joy in giveing away from me when he knows what I'm getting for him a month ahead of time.

He went to K[nights] L[anding] in the truck this morning, and I mailed my City Tax receipts. Have not got the Co[unty] tax list yet. City was $9. 04.

Tues. Nov. 30

Rain and wind, busy all day watching ropes; we moved the barge back to the starboard side of the Hobson and started in to finish up loading the Hobson from the wood on the barge. We can drop the barge back to the woodpile to finish loading easier than we can handle the Hobson and we don't want to take any chances with the Hobson.

Dec. 1

Some rain, not much, but still cloudy. River still rising. G.W. went to Knights L[anding] with the truck, got a letter from Amy. All's well. G.W. worked on Edson's rowboat which some one sawed in two pieces last summer.

Spoke for two fryers for tomorrow's dinner.

[this poem addressed to Ethan Jr. (3 and ½ years old) was written a few pages on, in the middle of what later became the Dec. 15 entry:]

Dec 1, 1926

Oh I wish I'd my Sweet Bum to love me
Oh I wish I could just hear him say
Good Morning to you my dear Granny

And what's Georgie doing today.

Oh I wish I could see him get spunky
And knock everything galley west
And I wish I could just hear him telling
A wild wooly yarn at his best.

Oh I live on a boat on the river
Its cargo is nothing but wood
Oh I wish I had what it would sell for
I'd buy Junior something real good.

Oh I wish I'd the wings of a seagull
Over these muddy waters I'd fly
I'd fly to the arms of my Junior
And no more would I sniffle and sigh.

But I think I'll be right here tomorrow
Anchored near Fremont Weir made of stone
And hark to the wind, waves and water
That whisper and sigh, wail and groan.

Now I have no sad story to tell you
But a longing deep down in my heart
That each day I might see my dear Sweet Bum
And only at night need we part.

Dec. 2

This is the anaversary of our wedding day, so we are going to
celebrate it instead of Thanksgiving Day. Have a nice little dinner
just we two. Fried chicken and gravy, mashed potatoes, green
onions, salad, sweet mixed pickles and for dessert we had Native
Sons (at least GW did) that came from Anderson and I ate cherry
perserve from the same source. I was going to make some squash

pies, but it rained so hard I would not go out and fuss with it. Finished unloading barge.

❖ Native Sons – possibly a type of grape

Dec. 3

Stiff north wind, cleared off and the Hobson fairly climbed the bank. We with the help of Mr. Edson put the barge back behind us, where when the water goes down we can reload it from the wood on the bank.

Dec. 4, Sat.

First time we have seen the sun rise since we came up here. Went for a walk. Can't go very far, just to the end of the levee.

Sun. Dec. 5

Nice day. Foggy in the early morning, river still on the rise. Cleared off and sun shone. About noon Mr. Edson came from K[nights] L[anding] bringing a box containing two snow white kittens. Mary & Robert had come as far as Knight's Landing and she was afraid of the river and would venture no farther, so sent the cats on by Mr. E[dson]. Cutest little things. I shall call the blue-eyed Jane, and the yellow-eyed Geraldine, Jerry for short. I plan'd at first sight to call em Jane and Link, but Link proved to be a lady so I didn't. Mr. and Mrs. F.C. Schofer called on us (from Sac[ramento]).

❖ Mr. and Mrs. F.C. Schofer – the buyers of May's house in Sacramento. This visit must be the conclusion of the sale, as the next day she writes: "Farewell to 3067 6th Ave."

Dec. 6 Mon

Farewell to 3067 – 6th Ave. Bright and early in the rain we drove to K[nights] L[anding] on burners. We always go in the rain. Queerest rain I ever saw: heavy thick fog with rain, hail, lightning & thunder. The river higher than it has yet been since we were here. Clear'd away while we were in K[nights] L[anding] and sun shone all day. Jane and Jerry are quite happy.

Tues. [Dec.] 7

Wind blew all day. Sun shone. G.W. worked his head off trying to keep both boat and barge off the ground. Barge has only about 14 in. of water under her port side. Got my Xmas things. No letters. Mailed letters to MJT and Amy .

❖ MJT – unidentified but perhaps May's friend Mary Jane.

Dec. Wed. 8

Same kind of weather, wind blowing us high on the bank all the time. River falling. Got barge off into deep water, nothing to spar to, hard to keep her out. G.W. complained all night about his "stomach" hurting him. Don't know if it is too much mince pie or if he hurt him self trying to spar out the barge. I yelled at him all day <u>not</u> to hold a spar against his body but he would not heed.

He's gone now with Lowel Edson to town. I had to beg him to go. He gets the Heebe Jeebes cooped up here with me. I can always find some thing to do, but he gets Cabin Fever.

Got back safe and sound but nearly frozen, awful cold wind blowing. Had a wrastle with a she-calf and hurt his finger.

Thur. [Dec.] 9

Weather still good, river falling fast. G.W. moved wood on barge and put some more on it. I spent the afternoon down there.

Fri. [Dec.] 10

One day seems just like another. G.W. worked on the barge, finished what he could alone. We are down now lower than when we came up – here in the water I mean. Went for a walk over the little concrete highway, but got in mud so we came back. Got one quail.

Sat. [Dec.] 11

Had to rush around here and get my washing done as G.W. announced he was going to Sac[ramento] tomorrow to see A.J. He has got awful restless these last few
    [this entry left unfinished]

Sun. [Dec.] 12

G.W. left at six o'clock for K[nights] L[anding] in Mr. Edson Jr.['s] Ford. From there he will go by train to Sac[ramento]. I am trying to finish my brown dress by hand. Slow work. Could do it all in ten minutes if I had my machine. No scissors and no very large glass –
    Later – G.W. got back bringing the Chev[rolet] – it has been a playhouse for somebody's kids and some one had exchanged their old tubes for our brand new ones. A.J. is better and leaves the hospital today. G.W. is to go to Kirksville and get a chap

called Jack to navigate for us down to Sac[ramento] and around the Island till we unload this wood. Take us up to the Grant line Sugar factory where we will stay put for the winter – that's the plan now. We, G.W. and I, went over to K[nights] L[anding] for supper which I enjoyed very much.

❖ The Grant Line – the Grant Line Canal runs east-west, north of Tracy and south of Stockton.

Mon. [Dec.] 13

We rushed around here like mad this for[e] noon. I swept and cleaned up the wheel house and Master's quarters and got everything ready for "Jack"'s arrival. At 11 A.M. G.W. went after him. Returned at 2:30 PM, no Jack. Had drove all over that ungodly district, broke some kind of a dojigger about his car and on arriving at the Feather Queen found "Jack" was reported on a tear in Sac[ramento]. Now we are perched on the top rail of the fence. Don't know what to do. No cash on hands. Not much grub – and no "Jack".

Tues. [Dec.] 14

Jack arrived at 9:30 A.M. We are getting ready to pull out.
    Later – men worked all day getting or trying to get started. Battery dead. At last decided to take it to K[nights] L[anding]. Maybe we'll start tomorrow.

Wed. [Dec.] 15

Got started 9 A.M. but could not turn around. Drifted sideways down to the old river. At 9:30 we got started bow end down stream, reached Sac[ramento] at 1:10, made the trip in 3 hr. 40

min. [left blank] were 7 hrs. going up there. I am glad to be away from there, the menfolks were just as kind and obliging as could be, but I was there thirty-seven days and of the three women there, not one of them ever saw me. I'm too small I guess.

One had better live in the wilderness where no one can snub you. The young woman was in a few steps of me every day, but either looked over me, by me or thru me. I suppose she thinks I'm just a river rat-ess and she is the supervisor's daughter-in-law. If that is all that ails her I can match relation with her any day. I was a supervisor's daughter and among my short-tail relation[s] I can number Bank Presidents, Railroad Presidents, [a] College President, Soldiers, cops, secret service men and better yet I'm Geo. Washington's wife. Oh Hum.

Jack and G.W. have gone to see A.J.

Returned about 6 P.M., had supper, and John of San Joaquinday arrived on the scene. All then went up town and later G.W. returned with a new man. These two are to help us unload the wood at several camps on the Islands and if he so desires John is to remain with us when we tie up on the Grant Line.

- ❖ I can match relation with her any day – May did have soldiers, cops and bankers in her family (see Part One: May's Family History), although I have not been able to locate the Railroad President, College President or – obviously – the secret service men.
- ❖ John – this seems to be J.McL, whom May also refers to as "the Virginian"
- ❖ San Joaquinday – presumably a boat?

Thur. Dec. 16

Did not get started away from the [Bear...?] till 8 A.M. as the engins are snorty for some reason. Reached the first camp about noon and unloaded 15 cord. Stayed here all night. (Fog all for[e]noon.)

Fri. Dec. 17

Rained hard all day. Moved on up to [La Monntans?] and tied up where Jack phoned to A.J. and got new orders. Moved on to Camp 8, arrived at 3 P.M. Unloaded 6 cord at one stop and 11 at the next.

Sat. Dec. 18

Unloaded 4 c[or]d at the house of ~~my~~ Mary kids, crossed over to the place where we had unloaded 6 c[or]d and unloaded 10 c[or]d more ~~at the next place we unloaded~~ Fogging all forenoon, clear in afternoon, cold wind. I washed.

❖   The house of my / Mary kids – this is a mystery to me!

Sun. Dec. 19

I am so busy I have no time nor wits to think of anything. Today is a beautiful day but cold, no fog this morning. We unloaded 5 cord at the hog pen and then moved down out of the narrow slough past Camp 14, and at the next camp unloaded 4 cord. Turned back on our track to Camp 14 and unloaded 4 cord more; moved again in the lord only knows what direction and unloaded 4 cord more. From there we moved toward Rio V[ista] and stopped at Booths Landing No. 4, which by the way is sliding into the Slough. Here we tied up for the night. Arrived at 5 o'clock P.M. Lovely moon, but cold, and off in the distance I can see huge banks of fog. I missed the twins Jane and Geraldine from their bed and began looking for them, found them curled up by the warm stacks. I suppose they thought they'd found a new kind of stove. I put them to bed as the stacks soon cool off.

Mon. Dec. 20

A cold, nasty foggy morning. I think the fog beautiful when it is draping the mountain tops in filmy veils or when I am on the mountain and see it in the valleys like silver lakes. But when you are on the river and it settles down thick as a wool blanket and the decks are slippery, the eaves drip, drip down your neck, handrails are wet and cold – say I know lots of things nicer than fog.

Men are unloading bal[ance] of load here unless they receive orders to the contrary befor they get unloaded. From here we are supposed to go to Rio V[ista] where we will get fuel oil, water, and phone to A.J. Then on to the Grant Line. Five more days till Xmas. I want to get my packages all ready and mail em in Rio tonight or tomorrow morning. Started from Booths Landing for R[io] V[ista] at 4 PM. Reached there at something to 5. I was too busy to notice.

I rushed up town all by myself, had to walk half a mile as we docked by the Union Oil dock near the bridge. Did not know just how to get to the part of town I wanted, but followed the only road till I hit a street and followed that street till I hit a street I knew, then began to hunt the P.O. Don't believe it has a sign on it any way I saw none, was right next door to it and gave up and ask[ed] a passing lady where the P.O. was. She looked at me like she thought I was drunk and said "Why right there," point[ed] to a little cubbyhole in about 10 steps of us. I felt like a fool but that's nothing new, I've often felt that way. I mailed my packages, bought some pretty handkys for men and two lovely pair of sox for my husband. The hankys will come in handy if John, Harvey or any other man is on board when Xmas comes.

After I had made all my buys I hurried back to the boat, only to find the big gate leading in to the Oil dock was locked and I'd no way to get on the Hobson. I yelled at John but he could not aid me in any way as there was no ladder long enough to reach. I finaly found a guy in the office of the Union who was busy talking on the phone to some Jane, only he called her Alice. I "beg'ed his pardon" and ask[ed] if he had the key to the gate. He turned around and gave me one dirty look. Turned his back and never looked my way again till "she" said "goodbye". I guess he did not want me to "listen in" on his conversation but I should worry. I wanted him to get sore and ring off.

Finally he did or she did, and he snap[p]ed "Now what did you want?" I asked very meekly if he'd unlock the gate and let me back on the boat. All the while I was praying fervently for strength not to lose my self control and slap his disrespectfull face. Any way he said he did not have the key, but the boy who had it was up on the tanks. When he came down I could ask him to open the gate. For which I politely thanked him, but believe me he'd been a surprised youngster could he have read my mind about then. When the lad with the key did show up, I found him as nice and obliging as one could ask. Opened the gate, gave me a hist up a two-foot step and left the gate open for G.W. and Jack, with my promise that I'd see the gate was locked as soon as they got in.

Tue. [Dec.] 21

Never slept a wink all night, constant whistling for the bridge to open, the whir and grind of the raising bridge, clang of signal bell, rush of passing boats, rocking of our own boat in their swells, whizzing of cars over the bridge. My gosh, never heard a more continuous racket all night long. I guess it kept every one else awake too for all hands were flouncing around in their bunks – oh I mean berths.

Jack phoned to A.J. last night and his – A.J.'s – orders were for Jack and G.W. to come to Sac[ramento], G.W. to bring the truck back with him and deliver this l[oad?] wood unloaded yesterday at Booth's, some 20 odd cord, to [Viners? Veneres?] camps. That will mean a wait here of four or more days. Well I don't care, only I think of how I rush around to get things done, never take half as much time as I'd like to in buying, and after

I've spent my money for some thing I don't realy like – why I've oodles of time to spare. Now all hands are gone to Sac[ramento], I'm alone till they return. We are docked here at the lumber yard, and just behind us in the barge Rio V. has two goats on it, cutest things. They walk all over it, up stairs and down, on the gangplank and decks. We hadn't been tied up 10 minutes till one was on board. I'll get a[c]quainted with em pretty soon. I want to finish the A.F.J. Xmas gift today and mail it befor we leave here.

Wed. [Dec.] 22

GW and John returned from Sac[ramento] about 4:30 P.M. nearly frozen. The truck has no windshield or cab and the wind is simply awful down here. Left this morning for Booths to haul wood. Hauled four loads and return'd as they had no lunch. Bought a windshield for $5.00 and put that on. Weather is clear but awful cold.

Thur. [Dec.] 23

Rained hard all night, and an overpowering smell of gas nearly choked us all night, an oil barge was tied up just above us at the Shell station.

Men left here early as it cleared off again, came home at noon so covered with mud I could hardly tell who they were. Awful muddy up there. Too much for wood hauling so they worked all afternoon on the engin down below, built up the lights so we can have lights once more.

Big Chief Smoke may be a good pilot and engineer, but he's sure reckless with other folks property, he has the engin room looking like a cyclone had struck it. When he lands any place if their boats are in his road he just run[s] over them. I told him of one nice little boat right behind us and he gave me a dirty look, backed right into the boat, tearing it loose from its moorings and let it go down the river. Befor we got turned around the owners were yelling their heads off and then Big Chief Smoke sent G.W. after the pesky boat in Polly and he had to paddle after it and tow it back full of water against wind and tide. I <u>was</u> <u>mad</u>.

I went up to the city of Rio V[ista], got my hair cut, and marcelled, mailed Johnston's Xmas gift, bought a roast for Xmas dinner, and got back so late my better half got uneasy and started to look for me.

- ❖ Big Chief Smoke – this must be Jack, hired by A.J. to navigate the boat.
- ❖ Marcelled – permanently waved.

[Dec.] 24
Christmas Eve

A beautiful day, clear and warm. Men got started after fighting [the] truck for an hour. Hauled altogether now 13 cord. Plan to work tomorrow if weather permits, as we are anxious to get out of here. I wrote to Amy and sent tax receipts to Schofer. At supper I gave G.W. his last gift for this Xmas, two pair silk-wool sox and a handkerchief, gave John two handkerchief.

Dec. 25
Christmas Day

I realy believe I never was so lonesome in my life. I should write letters but I am too too utterly too blue, no one would enjoy them.

Men left early this morning, tho it looked very much like rain and still looks it at 3:30. I have amused myself feeding the seagulls, little brown birds and playing with Jane and Geraldine. The latter is at present resting on the back of my neck.

Later – G.W. and J. McL. returned about 4 o'clock, are thru. G.W. phoned to A.J. and we are to start to the Grant Line tomorrow – we had our Xmas dinner at a very fashionable hour in the evening. It was good enough for River Rats, but no Xmas taste to it. Any way I had pieced all day, more for amusement than hunger.

Dec. Sun. 26

Arose early, had breakfast and helped G.W. and J.Mc[L] to get the truck on the barge. Some sweet little task to[o] as the barge was some eight or ten feet lower than the dock. We were so tightly wedged in between other barges and a lot of little launches, we had to just creep out. Got clear across the stream and the wind would turn us around in spite of all one engin could do, and as usual could not get the other engin going. When we did get headed down stream and got to Three Mile Slough Bridge, wind blew us on the wrong side of the bridge and we hit the abutment piers with all the force of the wind, crawled around the end of the bridge and finaly got through. I'll admit I was weak kneed for awhile.

Did not get the starboard engin going till we got to the end of 3-Mile, from there on G.W. does not know the way, he has just got to go by directions and what little help I can give him by landmarks. I can tell by them if we have ever been that way befor. He went out of his way about an hour, with me clammering we were wrong, as I knew we had never went in sight of the toll bridge Oakland-Antioch, and when he did decide we were wrong, turned on his tracks and after fighting with he and J.Mc, I convinced them we should take the stream where we found Polly. Got into a blind slough once for just a few moments, and had to back out.

Ask[ed] every one we saw on the river or levees if we were on the right way to Ro[o]sevelt Cut, and none of them knew sic-em, nor even ever heard of it. One very dark lady knew we were in False River, but that is all she could tell us. When we came to the pump house where A.J. tied up one night and where the Capt.

Webber overtook us next morning, I knew at once where we were, but we soon came to so many sloughs that turn in all directions, and are not shown on the map that we had to just shut our eyes and take a chance.

When we came to Queenby Island I knew I had seen those old tipsey lopsided boats, but there were four big sloughs and which one to take was a puzzle. We started up the first left hand cut, but I knew at once it was not right, for I could see a side of the picture I had never seen befor. G.W. persisted he was right and went about half a mile. We were headed N by E and he too soon saw we were wrong. Around we turned and back we went, both agreed the second slough was not the one we wanted. We passed the third and was just entering the fourth when we saw the sign Irish Camp No. 2. We had been told to turn off just befor we got to this camp, so swung of[f] to the left and took the third slough.

When we got in sight of Orewood there was two sloughs to take our choice from, both pointing toward Orewood. We thought prehaps they just ran around a small Island. We of course took the wrong one. Whistled for the bridge and when we got to in speaking distance of the bridge, found only a narrow opening. Had to turn around completely to get through it. I held my breath it was just exactly as wide as the Hobson, but plenty deep and a clean cut, for we slid through like a silk thread thro the Needle's Eye. A.J. would faint if he'd seen us, for the Bridge tender said only small boats went there. After we got around the big bend below Orewood we tied up, for we know there are lots of crooked channels between Orewood and the Borden Highway. It was just dusk. I never saw so many mud hens in all my life, counted over 50 in several bunches, and a few all the way on both sides of the slough. Hope they are that thick in the Grant Line.

Mon. [Dec.] 27

Did not get engins started till noon, all OK after that, lots of drift under boat and no one had wits to think of that. Mud hens thick as flies in May. Chink says, "shoot em, I no care. Chinaboy no eat em". We reach[ed] Bordon Highway bridge and they were so slow opening the bridge tho G.W. whistled three times that we had to poke our nose in the mud of the levee and chug away there for 20 minutes befor they got the bridge open. Then it took us ten to get turned around. We had no trouble from there on, except we turned in the Old River opening, instead of the next one. But G.W. discovered the mistake and backed around and finaly found the Needles Eye No. 2 and we made the short turn nicely, and were tied up at our first <u>dock</u> on the Grant Line again by 4 P.M.

Tues. [Dec.] 28

Awoke to find it clear and frosty, but nothing like as cold as it is at R[io] V[ista]. G.W. and the Virginian punted the barge in between Adele and the levee, drove the truck off, and after an eleven o'clock lunch went to Tracy. Saw the Mex wood choppers and they had tried to get credit at the Quality Meat Market, but it seems last summer's bill has not been paid so G.W. thot it slim chances for us and we had no money. But after waiting there for several hours the boss returned and he got his provisions and came home.

❖   Tracy – town south of Stockton.

Wed. [Dec.] 29

Men at wood all day. We had supper about 6 and at 15 to 9 [P].M., J. McL said it was a quarter to bedtime and he was going to beat it a few moments and go to bed. Just at that moment I heard a car and said "What do I hear, a car or a boat?" We listened and G.W. said I'll bet that is Johnston. I began to pick up my mess I had over the table sewing and the men step'ed out to see if the car stopped which it did, and I heard the Sweetest Voice on Earth say "Gwanny". I know my heart stopped beating. My breath hung in midair, and again I heard "Oh Gwanny". I rushed out saying "Junior, Junior, Junior, Junior is that YOU?" I had an awful feeling that he was alone out there on the levee and would fall in befor I could get to him, then I heard Amy laugh and say "Yes, it's Junior."

Talk about lovely surprises – I don't think any one could be happier than I was when I had hold of Junior and his mother. All was Babble babble babble for three hours, then we finaly subsided for the night, but I know I did not sleep, I wanted to talk so bad, and only a thin board wall between us. But G.W. said "Oh Shut UP" so I did.

Thur. [Dec.] 30

We have talked <u>my</u> throat raw – went for a walk toward Tracy. John worked all day, but G.W. took the afternoon off to go with Ethan hunting. Amy, Jr. and I with Jane and Geraldine went for a walk and befor we had gone far Geraldine had another fit. Then in a few moments Jane had one. We picked them up and carried them as they seem weak and tired after one of those spells, and while Amy was holding Geraldine she leaped out of Amy's arms and ran around and around in circles and plunged madly out in the water. Went down just like lead and never rose or made the least struggle, only a row of bubbles came to the surface.

We were just sick over it, and such an awful look on Jr.'s face, poor kid was petrefied, and in a dazed way said "Oh Ger-a-din jumped right in the water and <u>Now</u> she can't get Out" – We waited a long time for her to come up and walked back three times but no sign of her. Of course she's better off if she's going to keep on having fits and it was a merciful death. But when I told G.W. so he snorted. Geraldine was his favorite and he said "If you think that, you'd better throw this dumb one in too." Poor little Jane is deaf as a post.

Fri. [Dec.] 31

We had a great party last night. Junior was chief intertainer. He ate too much fruit and about ever hour yelled "Dada I gotta go to do toydit" and as he was sleeping in the crew's quarters with John, of course it was up to Ethan to attend to him. Ethan was sore because he had to get up. G.W. was sore because he was disturbed. Amy had to go to de-toy-det and for some unknown reason I had to go hunting gray owls, and G.W. about passed away.

He got up gravely and because I did not have the sugar bowl filled and no sack open, he made a show of himself and cut the sugar sack all to pieces, which of course shamed me and made the tears come. Why do men act that way. He would not treat any other woman that way, yet claims he loves me and can not see why I should cry over his display of uglyness. He always shows of[f] when we have some of our own people here, instead of trying to make them think he's always kind and loving – he tries to make them think he is hard boiled and mean and has me under his thumb. I don't want the kids to think he is mean to me for he is not, he is just childish and thinks it is smart.

He and Ethan went to Tracy today to telephone to Johnston about the wood. Got back by noon, worked at the wood in the afternoon. J.McL. worked all day. This is the kids' last day here. They leave tomorrow.

Sat. Jan. 1 [1927]Men did not work

We all woke at 12 last night as Ethan had set the alarm. We all said Happy New Year, and I listened to the whistles, some were at Tracy I guess. We were up at 5 and got breakfast, and the kids began to get ready to go – left here at 9 [A.]M. I was very brave, never let any one see me cry. Claimed I had a cold so no one thought anything of my red eyes and nose. After lunch I went in the rowboat with G.W. over to the Island. Second time I was ever in the Polly Ann. We tried to trim the brush, but got only berry briars and Nettle stings for our trouble. My cold realy acts like it was a cold. Mind over matter. Going to bed early.

Jan. 2

Lovely morning. I am glad, for I fear'd it would rain on the kids going home, but if it had I fancy [the rain] would be here by this time. Men worked all forenoon on the Island and in the afternoon, cut the boat and barge lo[o]se and let her drift down with the tide to the Island. She did far better alone than she would have if they had started the engin, she sidled down aways, turn'd around with the barge next to the Island just as tho she knew we wanted it that way, which we did. We tied up, or rather John did, as he went ahead in the Polly Ann and towed the head line so we would not drift on past where they were cutting wood. We were only about 20 minutes making the move. I am sorry they did not move while Jr. and his family were here. He and Amy would have got an awful kick out of it. Caught a lovely English Rock 18 in. long, and six catfish.

Jan. 3

I washed all day. At least I washed when I wasn't doing something else. Cloudy all day. Fished too, but caught nothing but a lot of drift.

Jan. 4

Still cloudy or foggy. G.W. went to T[racy] and John worked on the road up by Mex Camp. Both were back by dinner and as soon as that was over we prepared to move up to the Mex Camp as the boys have got all their wood on the barge. We were slow in getting turned around and had no more than got going when I discovered the water was not pumping on the Port Engin. That delayed us while fixing it. Pump had lost its prime.

We reached our new port at 3 P.M., all's well. Men have gone after their truck now.

I heard a strange sound like one step at a time. I looked all around the upper deck but could see no one, was standing at the head of the stairs and looking upstream when a soft Spanish voice said "Lady where is the Cap-itan". I nearly fell down on the speaker, a very dandyfied Mexican just the color of my darkest suitcase. I told him the Cap-i-tain would soon return, and he walked away.

After the boys got back they went duck hunting up the slough. I never saw such a mob of winged creatures in my life as I could see thro the glasses. They only got four and did not get back till dark and after.

Wed. [Jan.] 5

A week ago tonight since the kids came. Time flies. Men are loading the Hobson over the bow. Put on about 5 cords.

Has been cloudy or foggy all day. I washed some, but have no place to hang many things. Roasted the four ducks. I never tasted a lov[e]lier roast. They were so fat I threw away half of the fat and put no fat in the dressing at all yet. The fat ran out of the pan and I drained it out several times. Boys voted them beyond compair.

❖ Fifty years later, Amy told Elouise Shuffleton that "May cooked sumptuous meals".[32]

Thur. [Jan.] 6

Rained hard all night and my washing is ruined. Hanging under the eves all the soot that blew out of the stacks coming up here ran down on my clothes, my pink panties look as tho I'd played Santa and slid down the inside of a chimney. Boys finished loading what wood they had on the bank onto the Hobson, but I don't believe they can haul any today.

It is clearing now but I helped heave on the old mud [covered?] Ford up the bank and it took all four of us, Lizzie herself pulling, G.W. steering and J.McL and I heaving against the stern of the poor ole thing. She slipped and slid, slickered and skid, but we finally all got up. I was mud to my ears, and the mud is just like barnyard mayonnaise. Men hauled and loaded about five cord today.

❖ Lizzie – Model T Ford,"Tin Lizzy"

Fri. [Jan.] 7

Lovely all day, bright and clear when we got up. Fog rose for a few hours, sun came out and was warm and nice. The Ellen passed on her way down loaded with sand. She went up night befor last. The Elaine has been up twice since we came in here.

Passed yesterday on her way back. I have four letters to mail: Mama, Amy, Mary & P.M. at K[nights] L[anding].

❖ P.M. - unidentified

Sat. [Jan.] 8

Nice sunny day. Men loaded [left blank] cord of wood making altogether on boat and barge [left blank] up to date.

Got the mail by the Mexican – just the Sac[ramento] mail. Letter from Mrs. J., card from Jessie J., last statement from Robertson-Govan containing check for $13.99 my tax money back, a dun from Moore. I inclosed my poor check to him, maybe hold him for a while. He duns us every month now – has lots of nerve. We gave him a dog worth any man's five hundred and he duns us for a payment on an old second hand car that only cost $150 in the first place. G.W. was so sure Moore would give him the pink slip for the car when we turned Rowdy over to him. I would not be surprised to get a board bill for the dog next.

❖ Jessie J. – unidentified

Jan 1927
Sunday 9

Seven letters – Nora – Ida – Maude – Moore – Jessie – Amy and Austin. Men worked all day and stacked up a lot of wood on the levee so John can work while we are gone to Tracy tomorrow. I as usual had one of my clearing up spells as it is Sunday.

Jan. 10
Monday

We were up and away as soon after light as we could see. Rained hard all night and oh such a road I never saw, holes you could bury Irving Cobb in I know – belly and all. Amy said the road was bad. I wonder what she would say could she see it now – half the time we were crosswise on the levee. The hind wheels would just slip around sideways and I was at all times prepared to jump.

We got two men to help load the boat and I guess they will go with us to the Island: Joe Firkins and Thornly Firkins, brothers.

I got no letters but a gift apron from Maude. Geo. got a nice handkerchief. Austin sen[t] us $20.00 and three beautiful cards, I laugh[ed] and laugh[ed]. The card to me has a beautiful verse to Mother and I was so pleased to think I was and am such a wonderfull mother, never once thinking of the power of blarney. When I glanced over to my darling husband and see he too is swelling up with pride because <u>his</u> verse is telling him too what a wonderful Dad he is, and then I laugh and laugh all inside of me. And I'm so proud that my baby has turned out to be just as smart as I have always thought myself to be. I also got a surprise package, two lovely pair of silk hose, from Amy. I can't think why she sent em. Of course I need em but that's no reason. I need a thousand things. I treated myself to a 15 cent bulb bowl, a pretty glass one to put my narcises in.

About four o'clock Joe sprained his foot, don't know how it is going to pan out. Too bad too, for he seems to be a good worker.

- ❖ Irving Cobb – Irvin S. Cobb, a writer and humorist who had a very large belly.
- ❖ Joe and Thornly Firkins – Joseph and Thornley Firkins, who in 1930 were living with their parents and 6 brothers

and sisters in Tracy.[33] In 1927 Joe was 23 and Thornley 20.

Tues. Jan. 11

A lovely day, the anaversary of the day six years ago that G.W. and I met. A lot of water has run under our bridges since then, we've taken a lot of bumps and hard falls, but so far we've got up again smiling.

Men all at work loading wood to beat the band.

Later – today has made me very happy. I have seen my baby son. He arrived at 11:30 and found me fishing, my housework not done and dinner only partly cooked. He is what Luther Burbank would call a "sport" for he is so different from what he came from, a real gentleman and "class" all over him. I am so afraid he is ashamed of us, and no one could blame him. I surely will never do any thing to shame him, for I am so proud of him. He stayed till dinner was ready, took a flying trip back to Tracy to "get me some things" and was back by one o'clock. He and I ate, or rather went thru the motions and then he had to leave. He had a big box of fruit, lots of magazines, Laddie cigars and gum. It was a treat. Now if I could only see the "other one," my prodigal son.

Austin gave me a gold 2 ½ piece. I shall have a charm made of it.

❖ Luther Burbank – a famous breeder of flowers and plants. (One of Ethan Papineau's favorite jokes was "Did you hear about the time Luther Burbank tried to cross a street with a pram?") A "sport" in horticulture is a plant that has new characteristics, different from either of its parents.

❖ prodigal son – Leslie, who was serving in the military in the Philippines at this time, my mother believes.

Wed. [Jan.] 12

Still good weather. Wood nearly all loaded, guess it will be by tomorrow, then I suppose we will pull out of here. I caught 19 fish yesterday and today – nearly all large ones.

Thur. [Jan.] 13

Were all loaded, gang planks in and G.W. was just ready to leave for Tracy with the two Firkins and to talk to [sic] A.J. arrived with two men, one is a friend of John's, the other took the two Firkins to Tracy and we prepared to pull out as soon as he returned. But at dark he had not arrived. After supper G.W., John and his friend walked down the levee to see what the trouble was, met him on his way. He had ruined his timer some way and they had walked to Tracy. There the Firkins had brought him back to his car with a new timer.

In the meantime, A.J. had ask[ed] for the accounts of the months he had been gone, Nov-Dec, and after a lot of figuring we came to no real understanding. I am sadly disappointed in him. I realize he's been a sick man and may have a lot of bills unknown to me, but why he should expect us to share his debt I don't understand. We have debts of our own that I'm going half clothed and depriving my self of every comfort and pleasure to pay them, and he says G.W. told him and his wife that we would ask for no wages while the boat was tied up. G.W. says he did not say that, but instead said he would do right by them and not ask for full wages, so he told A.J. on his return from his walk, that he'd only ask $50.00 for the month of Nov. A.J. did not want to pay any thing for Nov. as for the first 15 days of Dec. and to cap the climax said the groceries bill was far too much.

Austin Ivan Diddy in the 1920s.
Austin was always elegant, even in his late 80s.

That settled it with me. I'll never forgive him as long as I live. I've worked on this boat for nearly eight months with only two weeks vacation, for my board and standing room. I've cooked in a truly little hot kitchen with the flies so thick I dared not open my mouth to talk, cooked for from one to half a dozen people; helped sack coal, cut my own wood half the time, pulled and tug[g]ed on gang planks, row boat and ropes, been wet and cold and hungry a whole day at a time in order to keep [sic] take good care of his outfit when no one else thought enough of it or him to care.

I've done what he wouldn't think of asking any woman in his family to do – and a lot he would not ask himself to do even were he well. I've given up my own pleasure any time for the sake of the boat, gave up my dog because I thought his mischief might cause trouble for A.J. and I knew the dog was a bother on the boat. Gave up my pets at San Joaquin City to go help or rather let G.W. help on the two boats when A.J.'s other help quit him. I've sat on an old hard bench for eight months, slept in a narrow uncomfortable bed, went without a bath till I stunk, for lack of a chance with men on all sides of me, cut myself off from friends, news of the world and most of the time from even letters.

I could write all day and not tell half of it all. And he tells me I've bought too much grub, when he knows all I eat in a month would not feed any one of the half starved hungry 2nd street bums he brings here for a crew, one week. He seldom has the same man twice, and when they come they haven't had any thing to eat for a month. And none of them seem to have had any decent cooking since they left their mother's table, so of course they eat three times as much as an ordinary person. And I get the blame for it. Realy the word gratefullness, and [left blank] was left out of his [left blank].

G.W. wanted to leave the boat there, I wanted to wait till we got to Rio Vista, and I again got ready to go. There must be some fate that holds us to this boat, maybe I am destined to end my life here yet. I've thought several times I was close to it, but John talked to me to coax G.W. to stay, said if I left he J. McL. would leave too, for he was not going to ruin his stomach again eating cold canned stuff and not half enough of it at that. So I told him to talk to G.W. and if G.W. wanted to let things slid, I would, so we are here yet.

Fri. [Jan.] 14

We left Grant Line as soon as we could see for the fog. A.J. took us out as far as the river and found his strength was not what he had expected, so turned the wheel over to G.W. who held it till we got past Rio V[ista] into Leach [?] Slough and near Camp G where we tied up just at dusk.

I forgot to mention letters that came and letters I mailed the 13th. I got a lovely letter from Ida, two from Amy, one from Toots and Thelma Moore. Amy lost her suitcase. Toots has had an operation. I mailed letters to Amy, Mrs. J., Montgomery Ward, United Trust, Prudential – think that's all.

A.J. says he did not intend to hurt my feelings. Maybe he didn't mean to but he sure did. When you are expecting a word of praise and thanks for all your hard work and get your wrist slapped instead it sure hurts.

Sat. [Jan.] 15

We reached Camp G last night just befor dark, and began unloading wood there. It is almost a rain, cold and nasty. A.J. gave me a check for $75.00 and left for Sac[ramento] in somebody's car. Men had only unloaded about 15 cord when Mr. Cahill and his man came, to saw. Have six now to cook for, how joyfull. A. Bernoni gave G.W. a check for $50.00 for A.J. I am mailing it to him, also a check to Boon for $10.50 storage, sent the $75 to the bank. Unloaded 30 cord here.

❖ Mr. Cahill and A. Bernoni – unidentified.

❖ Boon – on October 14 when clearing her house on 6th Ave. in Sacramento, she wrote she had stored "one box of leftovers at Boon's" (though she may have stored more than that, and just added one last box).

Sunday. [Jan. 16]

Rain, rain I never slept a wink last night. G.W. and four of the men in the crew's quarters snore in as many different keys and John groans and sighs and turns over because he can't sleep. I've manage[d] to live with less sleep on this fleet than I ever had to even when nursing, one at least had a few hours off then.

Both John and G.W. got up fretty. John from lack of sleep and G.W. from a headache and sick-at-de-belly as little Toni says. After breakfast tried to start the engins, but it was such a downpour of rain that every one got cross and G.W. gave it up, came in and sat down by the stove. I ask[ed] him what was wrong. He said "Everyone was crabbing. He wanted to move while it was raining and be ready to go to work when it did clear up but the men said they would not work in the rain so what could he do."

I saw his gloomy gus glasses perched on his nose, so gave him an extra large dose of Nyal and Asprin, put him to bed. I think all hands went to bed. Mr. Cahill and man went back to town till it clear[ed] up.

Sun came out in the afternoon. Ever one seems to feel better and we moved up to F and got tied up befor dark.

❖ little Toni – unidentified
❖ F - Camp F?

Mon. [Jan.] 17

A lovely morning. Men out bright and early at work. Fog came in about nine A.M. and hung on till noon. Fed a poor old hungry cat here. We were thru here at three o'clock, unloaded 20 cord and got orders to go to Camp D and unload 25, then leave the balance of load at Camp A. Hasting R[an]ch. We moved up here in half an hour.

G.W. made a slick get away, turned around in a small place for so wide a contraption as the boat and barge side by side. He's no pilot but at least he's carefull and don't smash in to small boats or run up on the bank as Big Chief Smoke did. Nor does he bang the boat up against the pilings as A.J. does. Had just got our gangplank out at Camp D when Mr. Cahill returned with the saw – it is now five o'clock and they are very busy.

G.W. nearly broke his finger around the saw. I'm afraid he is in for a bad sprain.

Tues. [Jan.] 18, 1927

Sawed 25 cord of wood at Camp D, were thru at halfpast 3 P.M. Seems to be a quarrelsom[e] bunch. I think there is some jackass in the Sawman's car. I notice the men making frequent trip[s] up to the car. One of the boys is crabbing about such a haywire outfit and cussing the owner for being so d--- stingy he won't fix things so the men can work to an advantage. G.W. stood it for just so long and then told the young man if he was disatisfied to work under the same conditions the others were working there was just one thing for him to do.

It is queer but the men never say much till A.J. is gone and then they find fault with every thing and dam[n] A.J. to a fareyouwell. G.W. stands it as long as he can for if he fires them A.J. thinks he should try to get along with the men, and any way it delays the work so much. The saw man swore he was sawing more than 25 cord, said he sawed that much befor dinner and that he got the same deal from A.J. last year. G.W. told him if he felt that way he'd better quit and go home.

We pulled out from Camp D at halfpast three, slid out as fine as silk. John says G.W. is a far better navagator than either A.J. or Capt. Jack. As John has worked with both I guess he knows. We are at Camp A waiting for the woodsaw. I have gathered a whole barley sack of the loveliest mustard greens, so fresh and tender. The men poked fun at me, and ask[ed] if I was trying to help A.J. E-con-E-mizer. I don't care, I love mustard greens, I'll cook em and I'll wager I won't be the only one to eat em. John will, for he helped gather em. Sawmen did not get here till eight o'clock. All mad as hatters. Had all kinds of trouble with mud. Left the saw some where on the road. G.W.'s finger in a bad way, all swol[l]en and black.

Jan. 19

Oh what a merry life, this lad Ede must be a walking delegate, agitator or something. In plain words he is a trouble breeder. I never saw John cross till this guy came on the boat. He damns ever thing, the wood gang planks, the boat, trucks, the way Johnston runs his business and hires a chuckle head to run it for him. He and G.W. has had a run in all day. He says G.W. can't fire him, says he can make trouble for Johnston for letting a man without "any papers" run the outfit. Any way G.W. did fire him and he refused to take a check and said he gets pay for every day he is on the boat. That lets me in a nice mess, as A.J. told me the men got pay for the days they worked, so there you are.

A.J. says G.W. is not consistent. I would like to know what he calls himself. He has us differing with the men all the time as he tells us one thing and the men another. He wrote us a letter telling us to receive the wood from the Mex at 4 ft and 4 in. in height, yet signed a contract for 4 ft. 3 in. with the Mex; now there you are. Had G.W. and the Mex Boss both up in the air. Consistency thou art a jewel, but not for any man's crown. Any way, we finaly had to pay E.J. Ede his money $5.00 in cash and the bal[ance] with a check. I'm tired of being a buffer between these river hogs and their employer and told G.W. today to Give A.J. notice we were leaving and to get some one to take our place.

❖ E. J. Ede / Edes – unidentified.

Jan. 20

After Mr. Cahill left yesterday at noon the other three worked like troopers. It rain'd but they got along pretty good at that the with trouble breeder gone; I've a hunch A.J. planned to put Edes in G.W.'s place for Edes bragged that <u>he</u> Ede had a pilot's papers and that G.W. did not. Edes also said that A.J. intended to can us as soon as he had some one to take our place, that the reason he A.J. came down was to see why things did not move any faster.

Dear Lord in heaven. I don't wish A.J. any harm but I hope he lives to be an old man and every day gets smaller in his own estimation. When I think of the ungodly hours G.W. and I have put in on this old haywired and hamstrung outfit, the mud we've wallowed thru, rain and cold winds, hot sun, dirt, dust, thistles, nettles and heat, and this is the result, I could damage some one. All in vain the $20 or $30 worth of grub we donated to the outfit when we first came on here, the use of a $50 set of tools that are now ruined, the use of our tires to haul wood. In vain have I saved scraps of food for pudding, dressings, salads, and hash. I am a wastefull cook. I vain have I bought fruit and pies and cookies with my own money to keep the men satisfied to stay with Soupbone Johnston. It is good enough for us. No one ever got or held a job yet by being a toady and I guess that is what we have been.

I have saved the cost of a man every day he's had a crew on here. I've stayed up night and day in order to help him and G.W. when running at night and working daytimes. I've laid on my face in the thistles and dust to help fix his old truck, when his hired men laid down on the job. I've worked under all kinds of conditions, in all kinds of weather, at any thing and every thing that would help any one on the boat, and all I've got for it was standing room, for God knows I've not eaten as much grub as I brought on here myself at no cost to A.J.

Jan. 20 [sic]

We got up at four o'clock this A.M. and G.W. and John trucked wood off the boat till six when I called breakfast. Poor fools they will get lots of thanks for it. The other guy got up in time for breakfast, and we were thru unloading, tho it rain'd some, by 11 A.M. Was underway at 11:30, and at the Mexican camp on the Grant line at 6 P.M. 6 and a half hours; of course even tho the boat has never made the run in less than eight or nine hours at least since I've been on it, I don't suppose we were speedy enough then.

Jan. 21 [sic]

G.W. went to Tracy this A.M. and gave A.J. notice we wanted to leave. He says A.J. seemed only too glad to get rid of us. I reckon he thinks he'd better get a cook that won't feed the men all they want.

A new adventure looms on my horizon. We plan to leave tomorrow either by the Mex truck or some other way.

Poem near the end of the book:

A Haunted House and Its Many Ghosts
Since Junior's Gone Back Home

A sleepy wee brown Teddybear, hid underneath Gran's
   bed.
A dirty pair of rompers is the pillow for his head
A rubber clown, half buried beneath the old peach tree
And in the sandbox shines a thing Gran use'd to strain her
   tea
Three unsightly swollen tears floats in this Old Gray Owl
And Granny sits down on the floor and lets out an awful
   howl

An empty red Paprica can, not empty full of sand
And marbles seem to grow on every foot of land
A wooden Ryzon box that once held many a well worn
   toy
Hold only happy memories of Gran's dear truant boy
And Granny find[s] her long lost pearls behind the
   bathtub hid
While underneath the couch she finds a Don't-give-a-dam
   straw Lid

A Hasbeen watch, that does not run, nor never never will
But its grinding-winding still will give its owner many a
   thrill
A plain white muslin bandage, with a streamer floating
   wide
An[d] Gran can hear His cheerfull voice: "See my new
   At" in pride
A dented battered silver cup, found in a buffet drawer,
now hangs with Granny's blue-bird cups behind the buffet
   door

An outgrown shoe, some two years old, and Granny
    seems to hear
"ATs my shoe" in shouted accents, no faint whisper in her
    ear
And underneath the bed she finds a can of Libby's meat,
A new jar rubber and wee sox makes the day's find
    complete
And every step that Granny takes both in the house and
    out
Is haunted by a wee brown form that flees with laugh and
    shout

And while Granny hoards these treasures
Both smiles and tears will come
For Granny['s] lonesome, lonesome for her darling little
    Bum.

3.

May's 1927-1928 Diary:
Homesteading in Shasta County

M ay once again wrote her diary in a used ledger book. This book had much less room to write in than the ledger book she used for her poems and diary in 1908 and 1925. Her 1927-1928 diary had first been used as an accounts book during 1910, and May wrote around the unused areas of the pages. There are listings of payments to a number of businesses, mostly in and around Redding. Some examples are: Standard Oil Co. – Marysville Cal., Redding Lumber Yard, Redding Iron Works, Gambrainies Mine, Sky Blue – Profit and Loss Prospecting, Sky Blue Boarding House, Northern California Eng. Works, Joshua Hardy Iron Works, Varnie Real Estate, C. Boyd – French Gulch, Cal., Chas. Litsch Agt. – Shasta Cal., and George Baker. There are many notations for Mine Supplies, Mill Labor and Mill Repairs. The ledger book must already have been well used by 1927 when she began to keep her diary in it, and it is now literally falling apart at the seams.

On Dec. 1st, 1927 May gave a brief account of her five years of marriage to George Maylone and all the moves they had made:

> A mousy cabin in a cow pasture [Woodchucks],
> and an old loghouse on a hill [Cedarville], a rented
> house where in we lost all of our worldly good[s]
> by theft, a tent on the San Joaquin, the tiny
> quarters of a river boat, another rented shack,
> again a tent in the tall, tall pines at Martin's Mill,
> two rooms in another, a boarding house, the next a
> whole house more an still [Whit. George house],
> and now a 2 x 4 cabin and tent at Trail's End.
> Please Heaven be kind and let us stay here.

May and George left the Adele Hobson in January 1927, unhappy due to the treatment they received from A.F. Johnston, the owner of the boat. At the very back of this diary May wrote a penciled draft of an undated letter to Johnston. On Nov. 2nd, 1927 she remarked that George had only had four months' work in ten months (the amount of time since they had left the Adele Hobson). She wrote to her brother on Nov. 22nd that they were homesteading at Trail's End because of a mining claim – George and a Mr. Lehman were both working at the Copper Queen mine.

At the start of the diary, G.W. and May had just moved to Trail's End from the "Whit. George" house, and they had a month to stake their claim. Trail's End was located between Igo and Redding, on or near Mule Mountain. Mule Mountain lies east of Igo, and north of what is now called the Placer Road (A16) and was formerly referred to as the Centerville Road. May wrote that she could see the Igo Bridge from "the point west of the house" (25 Oct. 1927).

May and George's closest neighbors were Charlie George and John Doeblin, both listed in the 1930 census as living in Mule Mountain, Igo. May got water from Mr. Doeblin while their own well was being dug. The Doeblins had been in Igo for over 30 years: in 1894, the Doebleine claim had been 200 acres, two miles east of Igo.[34] John Doeblin was listed in the 1930 census as John D. Doebelin, widowed and a miner in a gold mine.[35] In 1927 he was 72 years old.

May's other neighbor, Charles Whittington George, came from a family that had been in Igo since at least 1870. Charles's grandfather, John George, had been a market gardener in Igo in 1870.[36] Charley George, as May calls her neighbor, was listed in the 1930 census as single and miner in a gold mine.[37] In 1927, he was 42 years old.

At the start of this diary, May had just turned 48 (her birthday was September 24th), and George was 40. May's daughter Amy and her husband Ethan lived in nearby Redding. May's cherished grandchild, Ethan Junior, was now 4 ½ years old.

The diaries make it clear that May and George's marriage continued to be affected by George's flirtations with other women. Less than a week after they had arrived in their new homestead in Igo, the shopkeeper in Redding told May that "my husband is so interested in <u>two</u> <u>married</u> chickens that he met there last Saturday, when <u>I</u> was not with him that he – G.W. – says he will have to stay out of Redding if he is going to remain a decent married man." (17 Oct. 1927)

As always, May vented her frustrations in her diary. But even in her diary she exercised some self-censorship: "If I wrote just what I thought, there is times the page would burn. Often I've wished I dared say what I think, there is often a lot of thunks I've thought that would take out or put in a few kinks in this world." (28 Nov. 1927) She was mortified when Amy found and read her 1925 Cedarville diary, and wrote: "I'll will it to her." (28 Nov. 1927) Sadly for me and for others interested in May's life, she later edited her diaries by tearing out certain pages altogether.

While her diaries were a relatively safe place for May to express her feelings, she was equally determined not to feel sorry for herself. Her day-to-day existence was rudimentary to say the least, but May was philosophical and even saw the humor in her situation. Before they had dug their well, she wrote: "Gee it is a dirty world. I am so dirty I wrote my name on my thigh in the dust." (19 Oct. 1927) Despite her living conditions, the uncertainty of her and George's life, and George's behavior, May was determined to enjoy life. Nature was a solace, and a friend to

May. She loved her pets, and wrote about the trees and the plants as if they were alive to her. I find her relationship to nature very compelling – she is almost animistic in her belief that the old pine tree, and the willow tree, know her. She feels for the trees that must be cut down: "I fairly shrink in to my skin when I feel the ax cut into a beautiful pine." (18 Oct. 1927) And when they finally struck water after digging the well for nearly a week, May wrote: "I just yelled, and I patted the Ole Feller Willow and told him not to care, I'd take care of him and he could have his share [of water] first." (23 Oct. 1927)

She always took a great interest in her surroundings, and was intrepid in her explorations: "After lunch I walked down the Igo Trail to the Bridge. Lovely walk, if you don't mind walking on a three in[ch] plank a mile up in the air. I discover'd the old tunnel on the copper ledge. Bounce [the dog] went with me." (18 Nov. 1927) Even with the hard physical labor of homesteading (yet again), May's sense of curiosity and adventure remained undiminished.

10

Profit & Loss

1910   1910

June 4	Labor	24	599	75	June 7	Discount	111		91
	mill Labor	24	46	-					
	Spence		380	24					
	Livery + Barn		118	87					
	Engine Supplies		178	46					
	mine Supplies		62	40					
	Salary acc		1572	-					
	Freight		101	75					
	Legal Expense		144	60					
	mill Repair		158	01					
	assay office		878	75					
	Shy blue prospecting		2535	15					
			1132500						

Fri
Nov 11

I can hear yet the Old Western Pacific shops
whistle ed its endless screaming and not till the
rest of Sacramentos cometless whistles joined in
did any of us dream what was wrong until
Addie Coley yelled at me "Oh its Peace
its Peace" a mad mad town it was until
a might ed day had passed. certain things
stand out in my memory. Austins woe ed
wrath because he could not go with Jessie who
left the house then. I think it was one oclock A.M.
and did not return till sometime in the fore
noon. ate some breakfast and was gone again
for another ten or twelve hours - two days later
when Addie ed I came from work we saw
a band of urchins out in the Jessie field
still beating in old wash tubs.
One other thing I remember a girl whose lover
was Over there. beating up a perfectly good wash
tub, ed an old gray haired woman walking

**Page from May's 1927-1928 diary
written in a ledger book from 1910**

Inside the fly leaf of this diary, May wrote:

History of a 1927 Pioneer
Trail's End

Friday Oct. 14 – 1927

"<u>We</u>" are just 88 years old and starting a new home. By that I mean of course we are one Forty and the other Forty eight. When I think it is late in our Summer to start a new home I just think of Mr. and Mrs. Jordon in Sac[ramento]. They were in their sixty and seventyth years, yet I saw them build a new home on an empty barren lot, and in less than five years it was a beauty. So I take heart and plan on liveing here for forty years more. If I don't it won't be my fault. I'll do my darndest. Any way this morning we moved from the Whit. George place – where I had hoped to make my home – and came bag and baggage, cats and dog, which means six months old Bounce, the dog, Micky a full-grown Tom, and Lindy Lou a kitten miss of only a few months, maybe two not more than three.

When I got here Mr. Lehman had the little cabin ten x fourteen done, all but the window in, and he and G.W. put down the floor and walls for the ten by fourteen tent, and I've moved in every thing I can get in, but we have household good[s] all over the hill side. Trail['s] End is mine, and I pray I may be allowed to make a home here for I have been uprooted so often that I am slowly withering from the many transplantings. The new people, the Geo. Woods, moved in the George House this morning as we moved our last things out.

We never make a move unless it is on either Friday, or the 13th. I remember I met my husband's people on Friday the 11th and it sure did not bring me any luck – maybe <u>it</u> <u>did</u> <u>now</u>, maybe if I had never met them I'd never seen Trail's End. I've cooked for six people and pack[ed] a load of things in the car for four days now and only the Lord Himself knows how tired I am, but He sees so many tired women this wide world over, and no doubt some who are both tired and unhappy and I'm just tired. G.W. went to town this afternoon without me.

- ❖ Mr. & Mrs. Jordon – unidentified. May refers to them in her earlier diaries.
- ❖ Whit. George place / George house – this must have been a house belonging to Charles Whittington George
- ❖ the George Woods – unidentified
- ❖ Mr. Lehman – Leer Lehman (no relation of Louise Lehman Papineau, Ethan's mother). In the 1930s census he was listed as divorced and living on Centerville Road towards Redding.[38] In 1927 he was 67 years old.

Oct. 1927
Sat. 15

Last night after supper we made a bedstead and three benches to sit on. Oh such a good bed. We have been sleeping in a "one-man-and-no-woman" bed and had to give a signal when we wanted to turn over, but this is a wide bed and I could hardly sleep, tired as I was. I had to stay awake to enjoy turning over.

Sun. [Oct] 16

We did a little of every thing today, worked on the well, which we started befor we moved down here. No sign of water, but as there are three willow trees near it and one is an old tree, some say forty years and some say it is sixty, so I am confident we will get water.

This old majestic pine which stands leaning over my house, is my greatest worry. I was so in hopes the men would fall it befor the house was started, as I fear it will not fall as they think it will. G.W. went up to John Doebelin after water, and the Kids came out to see our Trail's End. Amy said she hoped to Heaven it was our trail's end. Ethan helped on the well.

❖ the Kids – Amy, Ethan and Ethan Jr. Papineau, who live 10 miles away in Redding.

Mon [Oct] 17

G.W. started to work afoot this morning. The old Chevy would not mesh for some reason. Too cold I guess and the chuffer too hot. He went to work very much perturbed. I think it hurt his dignity as much as any thing, he hates to walk. – Me – if I could walk as far in the same time it takes a car, I'd never ride in one. I bid myself and my possessions good by every time I start out in a car, but it's being done so I must follow suit.

G.W. said be ready to go to town by five o'clock and at noon he was here. Still sore at the car and with a "whoop hip and hurry up, now let's get in town in time to do something" we rushed to town and made Amy sore because we wouldn't stay to supper. I am never going to let her get supper for us again. We rushed away up town and got 10 cents worth of groceries and five of that was for tobbaco and talked <u>half</u> an <u>hour</u>, <u>and</u> Mr. Sousa tells me my husband is so interested in <u>two</u> <u>married</u> chickens that he met there last Saturday, when <u>I</u> was not with him that he – G.W. – says he will have to stay out of Redding if he is going to remain a decent married man. He need not worry about being a "decent married man". I'll attend to just how decent he remains.

Mr. Sousa did not see me in the car when he began to josh G.W. about his "pretty little chickens" and G.W. looked like less than thirty cents. When Mr. Sousa spied me he jokingly said "Oh it was not a scandal it was just a romance." I was very quiet all the way home and my Romantic husband was so interested about my wellfare, "was I cold?" was I tired? Altho I'll admit he did not ask if I was hungry. We arrived home befor dark and G.W. took Mr. L[ehman] home and I got supper.

❖ Mr. Sousa – unidentified

Tues. [Oct] 18

Mr. L[ehman] worked on the windows; got in the big double window. The Kids came out in the evening and G.W. & Ethan worked till ten o'clock on the well. No sign of water, down about 8 ft. I thought the Old Willow had a funny learing [leering] look, phst. We will take care of him and not let him die. G.W. will no doubt want to cut him down, but I'll stop that. Man is a queer distructive animal. I fairly shrink in to my skin when I feel the ax cut into a beautiful pine. G.W. hates the pines and delights to plan how he will cut down all on His land, but when it come[s] time to cut some of the ones I love to look at and listen to, he will be reminded Trail's End is not his land and I am very glad that thousands of these beauties are not on Our land and he can't cut em all. I enjoy clearing the land we need, but hate to distroy the beauty of the land one does not use by strip[p]ing it bare. That['s] why I fear this old tree near the house. Maybe it will feel G.W.'s hatred for pines and revenge its self and its children and kin by wrecking our wee hut when it is laid low.

Wed. [Oct] 19

Gee it is a dirty world. I am so dirty I wrote my name on my thigh in the dust. No water but what we had in a jug and that has to do for cooking, drinking and washing one's hands and face. I wish it would rain.

Thurs. [Oct] 20

Mr. L[ehman] finished his work on the house today. I am deeply gratefull to him, for I'd be in a tent alone and no floor prehaps, but for him, for G.W. simply has not the time to do any carpentery. He is up befor good light and puts on battens over the cracks, or cuts wood, and at night digs on the well by candle light.

Fri. [Oct] 21

Worked all morning cleaning up my yard, which means all this little point. I raked grass leaves and small rocks about halfway down the slope east and west of the house. I shall make a terrace there and gradualy build up my yard so it will not be so steep. I have cut all the unwanted limbs from two manzanitas and one chapperel that I wish to keep. If I trim them up, G.W. will leave them. Trimmed up several white oak too. Wrote a lot of letters and card[s] for catalogs and seed.

Children came out to help on the well. June [Junior] still asks if we have a "Pantry" (Panther) out here. I'm sure going to have him, Jr., here with me as soon as we can fix a bed for him.

What a life liveing in two room[s]. Everything stacked two deep. But I dare not complain for G.W. is so easy discourage[d]. That's why I hoped we could keep the George Place. Even if it was old there was shelter for all our junk. Now I'll have to be out in the rain and mud half the time, and as it is here we sleep with can[n]ed fruit at our feet, carpenter and blacksmith's and mine tools under the bed and among the clean clothes and suitcases. Boxes, cans, shoes, medicine, flowers and books all in a jumble. If you want one thing it is sure to be at the bottom. As Ethan tactfully said, "A Junk Room".

Sat. [Oct.] 22

Nothing startling today. I puttered around outside and in. We drove to Redding in the evening. I wanted to go to the show awful bad. But <u>we</u> <u>did</u> <u>not</u> <u>have</u> <u>time</u>, instead G.W. rushed up town and met the same guys he sees every day, F.Z. and his bunch, and did not get back to Amy's till half past seven. Then we left town about 9 o'clock, just when the show was out. AIN'T men odd. I often wonder if they are that dumb – or if it is just a way of getting their own way. If I should do that – garamighty.

❖ F.Z. – must be Zimmerman (see Oct 24th), whom I haven't identified.

Sunday [Oct] 23

The kids said they would be out right after lunch. We got up early and cut brush and started a dam [in] the garden gulch. The place we picked for a garden is a little hump between the upper forks of a Y made by two little dry gulches but they won't be dry this winter, so we are going to make a dam at or below the joining of the forks that will catch all the leaves and earth that washes down this winter and make a dandy garden.

I got a nice lunch, for I thought after their ride they could eat, even if they had eaten befor they left. We waited till after 1:30 then ate and went to work on the well. I am sick, have had a cold sever[a]l day[s] and I can't get my breath. The last few days have been hot and muggy.

We worked at the well till seven o'clock, and no one came. G.W. was all in, so he came in, washed up and went right to bed. At a quarter after seven here came the kids hellbent-for-leather. G.W. got up and they went at the well and Glory be by 10 o'clock they struck water. I just yelled, and I patted the Ole Feller Willow and told him not to care, I'd take care of him and he could have his share first.

Mon. [Oct.] 24

I was so tired and felt so rotten I told myself I'd let the work slid[e] and I'd rest. Just as I'd got nicely started on a letter to Mama I heard Bounce saying "Hello there ol kid, how are you". I looked out and there was Mr. L[ehman]. He had seen G.W. who told him about the water in the well. So as he intends to move his cabin down near here he is anxious for water to[o], and put in from 8:30 to about 2:30 mucking out the last shots that G.W. and Ethan put in last night.

As I had not even washed the breakfast dishes I sure had to hustle, get my house work done and rustle wood to cook the man some dinner. I had some letters writ[t]en and saw Mr. Z[immerman] stop to look at the well, so rushed out there to ask him to mail 'em. When I got back in the house I noticed my dress was on wrong side out. I'd dressed in the dark and had on an apron so had not seen my dress. Oh heck. I'll bet G.W. would have noticed his Redding chicken's dress if it was wrong side out and I'll bet Zimmerman saw my dress too.

After Mr. L[ehman] had gone home I walked over to the HomeStake to see if I could find some stove lids that would fit my stove, as one of my stove lids fell and broke. John said the old stove at Homestake was the same size. I found five lids scattered around over the hillside, also picked some oleander blossoms, and walked back as far as the main road where G.W. was to stop for me on his way home. Waited an hour or more, and when he came he looked right ahead and drove to beat his usual time. No doubt he was so anxious to see his wife he forgot where she was. I yelled Bloody Murder and had to walk down the hill to catch up. He said he was "thinking and forgot I was to be there". And I'd stood there in the cold for more than an hour rather than walk home in ten minutes and disapoint him. And at that the stove lids were to[o] big. But any way I enjoyed the walk and the oleander are lovely. Looks like rain, cold and windy.

Tues. [Oct] 25

Lined out early this morning and hunted Pine nuts. Discovered a wonderfull view from the point west of the house, can see the Igo Bridge and a long view of the road on both sides. Bounce and I spent all for[e]noon gathering pine cones, had a barley sack full over by Sterns camp and Mr. Rowlee, the truck man, came along, so I loaded the sack full on his truck and ask[ed] him to dump em off at the house. I spent the rest of the day picking up old cones to burn, they made a fire that keeps the house purely warm and saves G.W. cutting wood when he gets home tired at night. I also carried up all the limbed out wood G.W. had down in the gulch. If it is here handy he can cut a few sticks while I'm getting breakfast. Jackassin I know, and I'm a fool for doing it, but I hate to see him have to work after a day in the mine and it don't hurt me any.

The children got out here about six and the well is done now. E[than] and G.W. worked till after ten and we have plenty of water. Oh isn't it a grand and glorious feeling to use all you want to.

Began to rain about 9 o'clock. Just sprinkled.

- ❖ Sterns camp – she refers to this later as Stern's old camp. I haven't been able to find out who Stern or the Sterns were.
- ❖ Mr. Rowlee – In the 1930 census, Clark A. Rowlee, age 55, was an expressman who owned his own truck and was living in Redding.[39]

Wed. [Oct] 26

Began to rain about nine o'clock this A.M., rain'd hard for an hour.

G.W. was a little late going to work, as he waited for a Mr. Davison who lives at Igo. Mrs. D. is a schoolteacher and drives to work, so brings her husband this far and he is to go with G.W. from here to the mine. Anyway he was late. About 1:30 it began to pour down, I rushed into a rain coat and grab[b]ed the hoe. A perfect sheet of water was pouring of[f] the hillside into Prince Albert gulch and headed toward the well. I ditched around it on the jump and just in time to[o]. I only had on a dress and step-ins and below my raincoat which hit me just below my belt. I was as wet as water will make you – and here came F. Z[immerman]. He stopped and I suppose was going to offer his help but I told him to beat it. I saw no use in his getting wet and my ditch was dug, any way when I do my husband's work I don't want some other man helping me.

At that I got a free bath, came in and stripped, rub[b]ed my self dry with a towel, put on dry clothes and felt like I was as young as most people wish to be. I would not mind being thirty but no younger. Even at that age I did not have right good sense, I had to be forty years old to realize my mother is a wiser woman than I. Still it is a good thing children are Cocksure, this world would be awful hard on them if they didn't think they knew it all. I have a hard time some times to remember to play dumb, while children by nature and by law tell me how it is done and why.

- ❖ Mr. and Mrs. Davison – This was probably Louis Davison who lived in Igo in 1920 and 1930. (On Nov. 21st May says George and Louie Davison went to work.) Although May refers to her as a schoolteacher, his wife Lulu was not listed as having any profession in either the 1920 or 1930 census.[40] In 1927 they had two children.

- ❖ had to be forty years old to realize my mother is a wiser woman than I – I wish May had explained her thoughts a bit more here. When she was 30, May was running the roadhouse and had three children. The poems she wrote between the ages of 28 (August 1908) and 35 (July 1915) express unhappiness with her lot in life, but she had not yet taken the step of divorcing John Diddy. When May turned 40, she had left Diddy and had moved herself and the children to Sacramento. Did May regret leaving her first husband once she was on her own? Did she mean that she later realized that her mother – who presumably had been party to marrying May off to John Diddy – was right that it was better to have a bad husband than no husband at all?

Thurs. [Oct] 27

G.W. came home last night and found he had nothing to do; except eat his supper and rest, which he did. I had the chores all done and he seemed to enjoy it. After we were in bed about an hour I heard a car go down the hill and then heard some one yelling. I called G.W. and after listen[ing] to sever[a]l yells, I got up to see if I could locate the calls. It is impossible to tell where a sound comes from if you are in a tent. We both dressed and after going outside we could hear voices west of us. As there is no road in that direction we wondered if some one was lost. G.W. yelled asking "what's the matter?" No answer. We both called. Then blew the Police whistle and the voice stopped and answered us. G.W. ask[ed] them if they were lost, the[y] said "Hell no, come on over".

But we decided to go back to bed. We heard at least two of them singing for an hour, and I got uneasy and got up again to listen. We had guessed it was some one drunk, or bootlegging, stealing, or some one who had killed a deer, calf or hog. But the singing didn't fit any of those ideas. Then I hear a bell jingle like an animal at rest had shook the rain off. So we decided it was cattle men or sheep men, watching their livestock, camped across the creek. It is miles over there by land and water but only next door by air. I'll wager they laughed at our int[e]rest, because of course all the natives know we are "Newcomer's" "Squatters" Nesters [space left blank] are the only ones here and no doubt got a kick out of it. I'll tell the world they seemed happy singing in the rain, maybe a little Jackass along with it.

I raked the yard and cut brush till 10 this A.M., then some car parked just across E[d]geworth gulch and a man walked by going up toward Muletown, so I came in to do my housework. Of course I sang as I always do at my work, and after an hour or so I heard a child's voice over where the car was, saying "Why don't you quit yer yel-pin?" Believe me I quit and I stayed quiet. No child is going to make a remark of that kind unless some older person has made some comment on the "yel-pin".

Weather clear'd up in the night, it is lovely today. As soon as G.W. got home we worked on the "Dam Gulch". He cut trees and brush and I raked down leaves and trash to fill in. I think it will be a dandy garden spot.

❖ I sang as I always do at my work - Over fifty years later, May's daughter Amy recalled that "May had a good voice and often sang or whistled as she worked."[41]

Fri. [Oct] 28

Looked cloudy this A.M., so G.W. put the fly over the tent, which leaks in several places where something was spilled on it befor it left the store.

I took G.W. over on Lookdown Point to show him the view. I think he saw it. But while I was raving over it I found he was looking for a corner stake Section Corner. I reckon that is realy more important than the view as I've only till the 3d of Nov. to get my claim staked out.

We plan on going to town if G.W. gets home in time, but I'll bet he is late, that is usualy the case. I walked all over the hillside below Lookdown Point this forenoon but I could not find a stake or monument. I found a large White Oak deeply blazed, it may be the section corner. Tho the last word G.W. said to me this morning was "Be ready when I get home and we will go to town" yet when he got home and found me already he said in a weary tone "Oh you wanted to go to town didn't you?" --- can you beat it. If I had not been ready he'd have said "Hurry now or we won't be in time to get in the stores". Yet he is the kindest man in the world and will do any unreasonable thing for me <u>some</u> times. But he gets my Nanny just the same with his funny man way.

I know I'm still queer'er for I don't care for woman at all. I think a woman in general is the cruelest thing in the world – to other women – and I've had a father, several brothers, husbands, sons and "he friends", still I let their funny ways rile me at times. Shame on me. I know better but I think I like to be riled at times.

We drove to town, got here in time for G.W. to get his rubber boots. I flew around to Sousa's and Meuzels and got something to eat. We then drove down to the Kids and found no one home. Ernest at the Station. I hunted around and found some underwear for G.W., got my quilt out of the box which contains some of my junk, and after getting gas we lined out. Stop[p]ed at Ferguson's to get a battery. Left ours to be recharged. Ethan hunted us up, having returned home and found we had been there. He put in the battery for us, as the man in charge seemed to know nothing about it. We returned to the house just to say Hello to Amy and Junior, then on our way home I swiped two little geranium and one rare geranium slip at Ferguson's, his flowers need pruning anyway. We got home at nine o'clock. Too tired to get any thing to eat so went to bed. Raining again. Set out my Iris today.

- ❖ Lookdown Point – this could be a name that May has given this "point west of the house".
- ❖ "my claim staked out" – this implies that the homesteading claim, or part of it, was in May's name.
- ❖ Gets my Nanny – gets my goat
- ❖ Ernest at the Station – Ethan Papineau was by now running a Shell service station in Redding, and his younger brother Ernest (16 years old) was helping him. I believe May's youngest, Austin Diddy (22), had moved to Dunsmuir by this time, to run the Shell service station there.
- ❖ Ferguson's – unidentified

❖ quilt – May was a gifted needlewoman.

Sat [Oct] 29

Still cloudy. G.W. went to work with Mr. Davison, who drove his car today. Mr. D. brought us his surveying instrument and tomorrow we plan on running out these lines on the "Trail's End" and put in our stakes. Mr. L[ehman] came by on his way to meet the stage and get his mail, said if it was not raining he'd come down in the morning and help us run the lines out.

Yesterday while hunting for that corner stake I saw rings of old land slides. Those hillsides are steeper than a house roof, so steep I am sure a person could not walk there were it not for the little trails animals have made every few feet. These trails run around the sides of the hills [like] the hoops on a barrel. Any way I thought how easy it would be for those hills to slide right down into Clear Creek. I think this point on which the house stands has one time slid out of these high hill[s] north of us – any way it looks so and today I got the thrill of a lifetime.

I heard a terrible cracking rushing sound. The dog yelped crazyly and I rushed from the house to see a huge yellow dust billowing down those north hills, a roaring grinding snapping wave of Something. To[o] scared and amazed to run I just stood there and I was in the direct path – or so it looked to me – of the thing had it kept coming – but it stopped on a sort of bump on the hillside and the dust settled and I could see it was a huge Oak that had fallen down and rolled over and over down the steep side of the hill taking several other trees with it. I walked up there and saw it is a tree I walked under last week and peered up its half hollow trunk. How near we walk by Death and brush against its skirts unheeding. The earth was fairly plowed for two hundred feet, and broken limbs thrown many yards away.

Saw Mr. Kingsbury going down the trail today, not to speak to. He has never stopped here. Used to alway[s] up at the other house. I wonder if the actions of the new tenants concerning his livestock has anything to do with it. Should not as we were always good to them.

Wrote to Mary Jane today – I've said I must get one certain job done each day, but it is hard work to not take Bounce and climb a new hill each day.

- ❖ Mr. Kingsbury - probably William Kingsbury, who in 1920 was listed as the owner of a ranch in the Igo-Ono Township.
- ❖ the other house – the Whit. George place
- ❖ Mary Jane – friend from Sacramento

Sun. [Oct] 30

Wakened to find it raining hard, much to both our disgust as we wished to run out the lines in Trail's End. But we got up "betimes" and after an eight o'clock breakfast put up some paper and my little "office," the box of pigeonholes where I keep letters, papers and so forth.

About one o'clock we started to town, rain regardless, to get our own battery and return the rented one. Found all O.K. at the children's, and after having lunch we came home early to get home befor dark, as the roads are wet and slippery. I brough[t] home some plants to set out. Today is Ernest['s] birthday – Seventeen. I don't know how boy[s] are but it is a wonderfull day for a girl. I remember on that day I wrote – "Seventeen years of sunshine and shadow. Seventeen years of pain and woe" – Grin now Forty, and Twenty-four thinks "Silly" but to Seventeen, it was just as solomn as Forty years is to Forty and Twenty four is to Twenty four.

Monday [Oct] 31

Tonight is Halloween, the anaversary of the night I left my
father's care to intrust myself to the care of another man; a thing I
regretted in less than a year and continued to regrett untill I grew
old enough to understand it was only a kind of school where in I
received needed training in order to make me a good mother; and
a better wife to the one whose name I now bear.

There came a strange brown dog to this house this A.M. just
after G.W. went to work. Seemed tired, footsore and half starved.
I think he may be a cattle dog and has lost his master. I fed him –
he was very hungry and lies out in the sun.

Clear'd up in the night and is a beautiful clear but windy day.

About 11 A.M. Charley George and Mr. Lehman drove down
from the mine and one look at their faces scared me sick. I
thought I was a widow for I am in terror of that mine. It was bad
enough tho. G.W. had hurt him self and C[harles] W[hittington]
G[eorge] said he had come after me. When we got half way there,
I saw our car coming and sure enough they were bringing him
down. We followed them back and put him to bed. Mr. Jinierson
[?] had gone for a Dr. and we waited till half-past twelve befor
we did any thing for him. The onery doctor Dr. Dozier, sent a
stretcher out for them to bring him in town, but he is better off
here. I can take just as good care of him as any of those sap
nurses he's got.

- ❖ Charley George / C.W.G. – Charles Whittington George
- ❖ Mr. Jinierson – unidentified. It is difficult to read May's
  writing of the middle of this man's name but it seems to
  have two dotted 'i's each time she writes it.
- ❖ Dr. Dozier – Earnest Dozier, who along with his wife
  Irene Chinery Dozier, ran the Dozier Sanitarium in
  Redding. Irene C. Dozier was a pioneering nurse, who
  had served with the American Expeditionary Force in

Paris. Ruth Dozier O'Donnell wrote that "[t]here was, for some years, a large 'Compensation Ward' on the first floor where the injured and ill from the mines were cared for." She also described her father as a man of "an individuality that was unquenchable, distinguished in its pride, [and] in its absolute inability to accept second best of himself or anyone around him. He was often difficult and controversial. But no one could deny that he was brilliant and courageous..."[42] May writes more about Dr. Dozier on November 20th.

Nov. 1 1927
Tues.

I am not sure I know yet what I'm doing, my brain seems addled yet. There were so many men here yesterday, I counted up to ten or eleven and then lost count. The children were out in the evening, brought out a new Big Ben and two pair of nice blankets, part of Austin's Birthday Gift to me. I thank him and them.

G.W. is doing nicely this A.M., is very lame and sore but in no pain for which I'm thankful.

I think I feel worse than he does. Last night my back hurt me so bad I could hardly tell what I was doing. Amy said the scare made her sick at her stomach. Had a bad effect on all of us. Poor Jr. was sore because he missed Halloween and because I had no rice cooked. I promised to cook him some next time. The kids came out and got the Chev[rolet] this P.M.

❖ Austin's Birthday Gift – May's birthday was Sept. 24th. A new Big Ben is presumably a clock?

Wed. [Nov.] 2

We walked around a little today, as I think G.W. better off if he moves around and does not allow him self to get stiff. We run out the lines in the Trail's End. I did the running and my husband follows slow-slow. I hate to see him walk like an old man.

I'd love to give some one a piece of my mind but don't know just who. Any way I'm afraid the "Chevy" is gone. When we let the Rodger Moore[s] take Rowdy, Mrs. Moore promised us the pink slip for the car as we only owed a hundred dollars on it and we'd been offered $500 for the dog. I did not want to sell him, but prefer'd to let some one have the dog who would be good to him. We have looked in vain for the pink slip and now some one in town is asking about us and the Chev. So we fancy it must be Moore's men. It never rains but it pours. G.W. has had only four month's work in ten months, and and... I wrote Moore our circumstance and ask[ed] for time, he does not answer my letter.

G.W. looks so bad and worried, I'm just sick over it. If he were well it would not be so bad. We sent the old brown dog into town by Mr. Jinierson [?] to see if he belonged to Mayel or Hoff. The dog chases cats and would soon teach Bounce to chase and kill them.

❖ Mr. & Mrs. Moore and Rowdy the dog – the continuation of difficulties which had begun the year before. (See May's entry for 20 October, 1926.)
❖ Mayel or Hoff – unidentified

Thur. [Nov.] 3

G.W. went up to the mine this morning, rode up with Mr. Jinierson [?] and Mr. Davison. I am afraid for him to try to drive the Ford which the kids left here. I am also afraid to leave the house for fear Moore's men will come and go on up to the mine. I shall try to head them off and not worry him.

Several prospectors came this way today so rather alarmed I rushed around and put up temp[or]ary stakes. I have some real ones painted for that purpose, Northeast Corner of Trail's End, Southeast Corner of Trail's End, Northwest Corner of Trail's End and Southwest Corner of Trail's End, but I need 4 x 4 posts to nail them to and G.W. wishes to do that. But as Trail's End is a month old today I dare not wait untill he G.W. is able to fix the stakes.

Fri. [Nov.] 4

G.W. had to go to Redding after caps – grantpowder – for the mine. We arose befor daylight and worked till broad day getting Ethan's Lizzie to start. She was strange to us and we were strange to her so we didn't connect some way. Of course G.W. raved, hit, but I have grown callus'd to that only it is realy tiresome as we both grow older. It is rather amusing to be childish when one is young, but in later years it seems rather embarrassing. Finaly I guess his conduct shocked the Ford into life and we headed for Redding.

Found inquiry parties was not Moore but that filthy old Livingston. Any way we brought the Chevy back and I realy enjoyed my husband's quiet happiness over driving his own car. Poor man, if only these things would teach him a lesson, but his mind is like a slate, he can wipe out all past experience with a gesture. I alas must have an ivory or granit brain, for all that's carved there stays there, for me to read and ponder over thru the endless hours of many a sleepless night.

We found the kids all well. Drove down to the ranch with Amy and June [Junior]. We got some tools that Ethan said we could borrow. That ranch and its contents makes me smile. It and all on it I bought and paid for with hours of work, pain, misery, shame and grief. The money paid out there should have been paid for a home for I and my children, should have raised, clothed and educated them, should have made me a sheltered and protected wife, should have saved me from insults that are the lot of an unloved wife.

When I think of <u>All</u> I paid for that ranch, what is on it and what was on it before its present tenants scattered things to the four winds of heaven, I go a little mad sometimes, but I regain my sanity when I see my now-husband's boyish delight over a load of rusty junk for my now-ranch. The irony of fate. I kicked it all from my path once – trash – on any frantic way to freedom, and here it is – Is my brain warped, or why do I see things so – and none of my kin do. I am sure if my people knew the things that hammer in my brain and urge my tongue to turn them loose – sure ah too sure[l]y I'd have a home in Napa. I pat myself for having power to hold my tongue.

I dug up some plants for I know some stranger put them there and I'm beholden to none for them. We got home – to Amy's – about noon. Amy gave Ethan a Grab-it lunch and came on up here with us. G.W. went to the mine with his g.p. [gunpowder or 'grantpowder'] caps, and after Amy, June [Ethan Junior] and I ate another Grab-it lunch, wash'd the dishes and visited awhile, we walked up to the Copper Queen. June kept up "Whos[e] mine is it?" "Whose road is it?" and everything we saw he ask[ed] the same questions. I'd say "Georgie's and Mr. Lehman's" which was fine in a way. Jr. knows anything that's G.W.'s is also his. But he don't just [savys?] Mr. L.'s intrest in things here.

As soon as G.W. got back from work we took the kids home, and after dinner came back to Trail's End. Got a letter from Mama dated Oct. 30, saying Nora was operated on for tumor, Oct 27, was in the Prairie City Hospital, Dr. Lawson operating. Says Nora as well as can be expected. I am as much worried over Mama as I am Nora. Poor Mama. I think in some life Mama and I must have failed to do our duty, but we have sure paid for our sins in the life we are now liveing.

❖   Ethan's Lizzie – Ethan's Ford

- filthy old Livingston – unidentified
- the ranch, and May's bitterness – it seems May is referring to the roadhouse at Ingot ("Flintlock Inn") which she and John Diddy ran for about 15 years. I don't know why Ethan would be giving May permission to take "a load of rusty junk" from the former roadhouse.
- Napa – large state mental hospital
- Nora – May's sister, who was 43 years old and living with her son and husband in John Day, Oregon.
- Prairie City Hospital – Prairie City is about 7 miles east of John Day, Oregon
- Dr. Lawson - unidentified

Sat. [Nov.] 5

Work, work, work. Some times I wonder why I work so hard, work till the pounding of my forty-year-old heart flies the red danger signal, work untill I wonder if I won't drop dead some day and <u>they</u> will <u>wonder</u> what killed me. No one ever has realized in all my life how much harder I work than any human of my size and lifting power should. As a child I did the work of a grown person from the time I could stand on a box and bend over a washtub of dirty didys, as a woman I did the work of two women and one man most of the time.

The deadly terrors of childbirth was dimmed by the ten days rest I'd have and no one could drag me out of bed.

Now after forty years of hard labor, labor that would make a prison term seem like a vacation, I find myself dragging in whole manzanita bushes so that we can have dry wood. I commented on the fact that we had nearly two months this summer that we could have cut wood in, and my lord says "yes but if we'd moved any what good would it have done." Now can you beat that. An hour a day for two weeks and he'd have cut as much wood as I can drag in if I work all day for two weeks. Men are so [vainy?] with labor – for themselves. It looked like rain today so I dragged in wood all day.

* * * * * * * * * *

The next page has been torn out – another occasion when she wrote frankly about events (or her reaction to events) and later didn't want anyone else to read what she had written.

* * * * * * * * * *

Tues. [Nov.] 8

Rain yet. I wrote to Mama, Austin and Ray, did not get done till 1 o'clock. Five hr. with a pen. Mrs. Davison came just as G.W. started to work, said Mr. D. was ill.

Rested this evening, didn't do a thing all day but write letters to Mama, Ray and Austin.

❖ Ray – May's brother, who was 38 years old and living in Portland, Oregon with his wife and children.

Wed. [Nov.] 9

G.W. worked till noon. The men put it up to him "no pay day, no work" so we drove to town to find Zee and learn the reason why pay day is ten days late. Zee paid up to the 1 of Nov, and laid the men off, for a <u>short</u> <u>time</u>, that's the way he laid off the Potosi crew and it is still "off". All well in town. Letter from Austin to Amy. Rain all day.

❖ Zee – this must be Zimmerman
❖ Potosi crew – the Potosi mine was between Mule Mountain and Igo.
❖ All well in town – all was well with Amy and her family.

Thurs. [Nov.] 10 in margin: Ernest got his arm broke

Cleared off about midnight. Cold of course, pulled covers the rest of the night, arose at the usual time and began to clear land as soon as we had a bite to eat. Cut manzanita from where we want to make a garden, killing two birds with one <u>axe</u>. Made a lot of good wood and cleared a spot of land, also clear'd off the South Point below the house, can get a glimpse of the creek. About 1 P.M. started to Redding, found all well there. No mail.

On our way home saw a man and woman camped at Sterns old camp. G.W. spent the evening up at the boarding house. Heard some queer things about Zee.

❖ Ernest – Ethan Papineau's younger brother Ernest, who lived with Ethan and Amy and worked at the Shell station. Poor Ernest had just turned 17.

Fri. Nov. 11

I can hear yet the Old Western Pacific Shop whistle and its endless screaming, and not till the rest of Sacramento's countless whistles joined in did any of us dream what was wrong untill Addie Colby yelled at me "Oh it's Peace, it's Peace". A mad mad town it was untill a night and day had passed. Certain things stand out in my memory. Austin's woe and wrath because he could not go with Leslie who left the house then, I think it was one o'clock A.M., and did not return till sometime in the forenoon. Ate some breakfast and was gone again for another ten or twelve hours. Two days later when Addie and I came from work we saw a band of urchins out in the Gerber fiel[d] still beating an old washtub.

One other thing I remember, a girl whose lover was Over There, beating up a perfectly good was[h] tub, and an old grayhair'd woman walking down the street, sobbing wildly and dragging a cowbell on a rope. Where any one in Sac[ramento] could find a cow bell. I've wondered why she wept. It wasn't joy. Prehaps Peace came too late for her. All the woe of the world was in her face and sobs.

This Armistice Day my Ex-Service man and I played out in the rain all day. We cut wood, cleaned ditch[es], made bonfires and enjoyed ourselves to the fullest extent. So did Bounce, he is never so happy as when we are one or both tramping around. Also set the stakes on the Copper Queen again and put in the new stakes on Trail End and that's done.

People are still camped up on Sterns old camp.

❖ May's recollections of Armistice Day, Nov. 11th, 1918 (9 years earlier) are very vivid. 1918 was the year that May left John Diddy and moved to Sacramento with Leslie, Amy and Austin. On November 11th, Leslie was 16 years old, and Austin only 13. George had registered for the draft in May 1917, the year that the United States entered the First World War. His niece wrote that he was sent overseas and that his throat was damaged by mustard gas.[43]

❖ Addie Colby – I believe this was a young neighbor of May's in Ingot, who moved to Sacramento at about the same time (or possibly along with) May and her children. Addie Ruth Colby was born and brought up in Ingot. She was not listed as living with her parents in the 1920 census.[44] In 1918, Addie R. Colby was 19 years old. Addie Ruth Colby Connelly died in 1990, age 94, in Sacramento.[45]

Sat [Nov.] 12

Rained all day. We grounds sluiced above the garden, had lots of fun. That is just about all we did do too.

This is Nell's and Earl's wedding day. I wish them all the happiness tha[t] can be found in married life. I hope they never regrett the loss of their freedom.

❖ Nell and Earl – unidentified

Sun. [Nov.] 13

G.W. made a wood box this A.M., about noon we drove to town. Still raining. Found the kids had not breakfasted yet, so helped them do it. About 1 P.M. we started out. G.W. and Jr. in the front seat, Amy, Peter and I in the back seat, to find the old Olive orchard we have been hearing of for ages. Following Amy's directions we made a complete circle of about ten miles and found the orchard just three miles off the highway, some joke on us. But a dandy trip. I think we will make a raid on it some day. The orchard I mean.

We got back to Redding about three P.M. and on home. The people up at Sterns have gone. A bunch are in the old shack on the road. But if it is the same I do not know.

In the evening we drove up to John Doeblin's and had a nice visit. Mr. L[ehman] gave me some new Sat. Eve. Post[s] and G.W. made so many unkindly remarks that I think Mr. L[ehman] was sorry he gave them to me. Isn't a man queer. If some one gave him a "smoke" and I said nasty cutting words, he'd think me crazy and I would be too.

❖ Peter – a dog, presumably Amy and Ethan's (see 24 Nov.)

Mon. [Nov.] 14

G.W. drove up to J[ohn] Doeblin's after Mr. L[ehman] and they two, went surveying again. It began to rain befor they returned. Chas. G[eorge] passed on his way to John's. Poor old John failed to knock on wood when he said he was glad to get a rest. Drizzl'd all day. A month to the day since we moved in our Home Sweet Home.

Tues. [Nov.] 15

Thirtytwo nights have I slept under the swaying arms of a majestic old pine that stood One Hundred and Fifteen feet in the air. Was nine feet around and it[s] long arms reached [left blank] feet on each side of it. I say slept but it was a troubled sleep that found me wide awake at every blast of the wind. I had begged that the tree be cut down befor the house was put up, but men are queer. For the sake of twenty minutes work they took a chance on smashing the house and leaving us homeless.

This morning G.W. and I went up to the mine Copper Q[ueen] and about nine A.M. Mr. L[ehman] came so I returned home to do my work. We worked up there awhile yesterday aft. Both men came down for lunch and as it was a very quiet windless day they decided to cut the old pine, which leans over the house. After moving some of my treasures, I took Bounce, Linda Lou and Micky, went up on the hill. After planning and measuring in order to lay the tree "just so" at the fall crack, both men exclaimed "she's going over the house" and in the time it takes a tree to fall halfway, my heart fairly broke, as I saw the tree waver.

But as the words were hardly out of his mouth G.W. grab[b]ed a sledge hammer and began to maul the wedges on the underside of the tree. Madly for a second the old tree waver'd in the air as the wedges lifted. She began a whirling movement and fell – clear of the house and tent. I know I did not draw a breath from the time they said "She['s] going over the house" untill the jar of the earth said safe. I cried after it was all over much to my husband's amusement and Mr. L[ehman's] astonishment.

Wed. [Nov.] 16

Clear. A little hazy in the east. G.W. and L[ehman] working in Copper Q[ueen]. I air'd all the bedding and tried to clean out some dirt. I walk up to the C[opper] Q[ueen] every morning and stay untill L[ehman] comes as I do not want G.W. up there alone. Zee went up and back with some Sac[ramento] men. Rowlee took up a truck load of lumber, said when he saw the big tree down "I call that plum foolishness." Had he slept under it for a month as I have, and had it worried him as much as it did me, I fancy he'd "peachy wisdom" to remove the cause of worry. I am so glad it is down, and I love a tree beyond telling. I shall if I live plant two trees for every one we cut down. I have transplanted any number of ferns, several vines and one tree, the kind I'm uncertain as yet.

In the evening G.W. went up to the boarding house and spent the evening. I stayed home and read some magazines. Bunch of cattle passed this P.M. Adam K. was helping drive.

A pretty black cat came to us today. I fancy Marcel [?] Machado dropped it here, or near here, as he is the only one who has been in today.

- ❖ Adam K. – possibly Adam Kingsbury of Igo, who in 1920 was the owner of a ranch.[46]
- ❖ Marcel Machado – unidentified. There were several Machados living in and around Redding at this time.

Thur. [Nov.] 17

Lovely this A.M., just like spring altho the wind is from the North.

Walked up to C[opper] Q[ueen] with G.W. He says we will go to R[edding] this aft[ernoon].

Mr. L[ehman] went to town with us, lovely day. Got a letter from Mama, Nora doing fine. Am so relieved.

Fri. [Nov.] 18

Looks like rain again. Walked up to C[opper] Q[ueen] with G.W. and tuned [?] the blower till Mr. L[ehman] arrived. Mr. L[ehman] is fixing up his cabin at the C.Q. and intends to move down as soon as he has a roof on it. Too much poison tongue gossip up the line for his peace of mind.

Mr. Zee dashes up and down the road, but nothing seems to happen. Says North [Star – May has drawn a star here] will start up again Monday. I hope so. This should be a rich county there is so much corral dust floating around.

Big band of cattle. Driver said – 1700 past by this aft[ernoon].

G.W. saws a cut from the old pine every evening. Makes good wood. After lunch I walked down the Igo Trail to the Bridge. Lovely walk, if you don't mind walking on a three in[ch] plank a mile up in the air. I discover'd the old tunnel on the copper ledge. Bounce went with me.

❖ The North Star mine – May is referring to a local mine rather than the famous North Star mine in Nevada County. She goes to see the North Star mine somewhere near Redding at the end of November, and writes of George working there in December.

Sat. [Nov.] 19

Rain began about eight this A.M. and a slow quiet drizzel all day so far, 2:30. Yesterday, G.W. said he had a "missed hole" when he shot in the mine. I ask[ed] him this morning to attend to that missed hole befor he drilled any more and he hooted at the very idea. Said the tunnel would be full of smoke and he [would] lose the whole day for one shot – so when in about 20 minutes after he had gone to work I heard the dull <u>boom</u> of a blast my knees turned to water. I <u>knew</u> that missed hole had gone off and killed him, so I ran and fell, stumbled and staggered up the hill to the trail, my heart began to pound and choke me befor I had got to the ditch. When I got half way up there I heard voices, and yelled to them if "All was all right" and my witty husband Ha'h Ha'h-ed his fool head off because he'd scared me. I wish I could scare him as badly as he does me, but I don't think it would be possible. **** [presumably this is May "swearing"!]

Bounce and his two lady-cat chums are cur[l]ed up here so snugly you can['t] tell which is cat and which dog. He's as rough as sixty but good as gold to them two. Made friends with the Blackcat at once. Men only worked till ten A.M. Mr. L[ehman] went after his mail, and G.W. took him home. On arriving there found he'd lost a letter, so both came back and are now on their way back. He got the returns from the Copper Queen assay. Very good. Better in gold than in Copper.

Sun. [Nov.] 20

New ink, at last. [All the preceding was written in red ink, now May has blue ink.]

Still raining. Left for Redding about 10 A.M. Had the strangest experience, found an old man lieing unconscious under a tree, had no doubt lain there all night in the rain. G.W. was pop-eyed and yet when I cried in pity, he was very grown-up, said "No use being childish over it. We will get him to help as soon as we can."

We loaded the poor old creature in the back of the car, with his head and shoulders in my lap, and G.W. drove as fast as we dared. As the day was cold and rain falling we thought we'd try the first hospital, which is Dozier's Sanitarium. A nurse – I am inclined to think it was the Dr.'s wife – came to our call. She shook her head and said she hardly thought they could take him in <u>there</u>. I said "sur[e]ly they will take him in long enough to revive him". She called the Dr. and after one look at the poor old shabby creature he fairly raved "What did you bring a <u>man</u> <u>like</u> <u>that</u> here for" and "man use a little common sense". I was so astonished I could not speak.

Not so very long ago Dr. Dozier's son died from exposure and lay out in the weather for a whole year. At least the newspapers say he died from exposure to the weather, and one would naturaly think that the father of one who died as that boy did would not turn away a sick cat. I used to feel sorry for Dr. Dozier, but now after this I shall wonder if he wanted to find his boy as much as he pretended when he ran ads in the newspapers for a year.

We took the old man to the county hospital where it seems he was already an inmate but had wandered away.

I brought home some walnuts I picked at the County H[ospital] and shall plant in the memory of poor old waif. Also brought home three Heaven Trees and an unknown tree, some bulbs from Amy's and some hops. Planted some English walnuts.

❖ Dr. Dozier's unfortunate son Tilford (from his first marriage; his first wife died in the influenza epidemic after the First World War) would have been about 21 when he died. Earnest Dozier's daughter does not elaborate on the details of Tilford's death: "Earnest lost his son in January 1924."[47]

❖ Heaven trees – *ailanthus altissima*, known as the "Tree of Heaven".

❖ hops – I was surprised to discover that hops (*humulus lupulus*) do grow wild in North America. In one of May's poems ("Waiting and Watching") she mentions "wild hop blooms".

Mon. [Nov.] 21

G.W. and Louie Davison went to work this morning. The North [Star - drawing] is running again. Don't know how short winded it will be this time. Here's hoping it runs all winter. I do want a fence and some trees so bad, so very much I mean. Mr. L[ehman] is working on his house. I washed some, finished my corner cupboard and hung a curtain. Wrote to Mary Jane. Lovely day, clear and warm.

Tues. [Nov.] 22

Another sunny day. Mr. L[ehman] moved down. Wrote to Austin. Nothing doing that amounts to much. G.W. spent the evening at the Copper Q[ueen]. I wrote to Dot thus –

> Dear Leo and Dot,
>
> I can plainly see where I shall spend the rest of my days and evenings alone. My husband works all day and spends his evenings with a yellow hussy they call the Copper Queen. When we first came to this country she belonged to a man named Lehman, but I guess he grew tired of her and so got my husband interested in her, and now as soon as he swallows his supper, he['s] off to Lehman's cabin to see the Copper Queen. An Indian, did you ask? Oh no just a mining claim.

- -

I'll wager both Leo and Dot sat up in amazement for well they know, at least Leo does, that I'd never whimper if my husband was chasing a dozen yellow, black or red hussys.

❖ Leo and Dot – May's youngest brother was now 32. He had married Dorothy Nora Fay Guernsey in September the year before. (See notes to the diary entry of 10 Oct. 1926).

Thur. [Nov.] 23

Sunny today but gathering haze. Hard frost last night, and ice in the well bucket. I wrote to Mama, now I've four letters to mail. Cut out Junior's "jammers" one pair which I'll try on him befor I do any more.

G.W. got paid $40, a big check to divide between store, Lumberyard, truckers and a lot I'll have for Xmas I can see.

❖ "jammers" - pajamas

Nov. 24
Thur.

Thanksgiving day. Looks rather like rain, but still cold. G.W. went up to C[opper] Q[ueen] after breakfast, said we would go in town after lunch, but that we'd go to city dumps after some tin first and he did not want to hurry so we'd be late getting to the kids. We spent 15 minutes at the dumps and he said "Well are you ready" as tho he had gone there just for my pleasure.

We arrived at Amy's with the back of the car full of empty oil cans, music free. And imagine my feelings to find the house full of company, only sixteen people there, and they had not yet eaten. I tried to get out of it by saying we had just eaten, befor leaving home, which was not altogether a lie as G.W. had devoured a plate of beans, several hunks of bread, some fruit and a gal[lon] or two of coffee. But pride never interfered with a man eating, at least none of the men I've ever know[n], except Austin. Food does not interest him any, but he is like a girl, he's thinking of his "figger".

Amy had a lovely dinner, which I'd have enjoyed if I had not felt as tho I was butting in to a family party to which I did not belong – to be sure, they were my husband's people, but I never feel as tho I belonged to any one any more. I've lost all my old friends, have made no new ones, and my blood relation[s] have all married into other familys; except the boys and they are weaned away till they are strangers to me. "Aunt Louise," "Uncle Alex," Tony, Marion, Ernest, Elmer, Melvin, Ethan, Amy, Junior, Clarence, Everett, Leslie, Francis, Tessie Lou and baby Chester – I think that's all but Peter the dog. All went to the ranch about 4 P.M. I waited till G.W. returned and we came home. G.W. had been up to town having the Chev fixed. He was rather inclined to feel snubbed because no one ask[ed] him to go, or told him they were going.

❖ except the boys – her sons Austin and Leslie.
❖ my husband's people - "Aunt Louise" "Uncle Alex" – Ethan Papineau's mother Louise Lehman Papineau (49) was G.W.'s aunt, and Ethan's father Alexander Papineau (58) was G.W.'s maternal uncle.
❖ Tony – Antony Vaira (34), who was married to Ethan's sister Marion.
❖ Marion – Ethan's older sister Marion Papineau Vaira (Louise and Alexander's daughter), 27 years old.
❖ Ernest – Ethan's brother, 17 years old
❖ Elmer – Ethan's brother, 15 years old
❖ Melvin – Ethan's brother, 13 years old
❖ Clarence – Clarence Vaira, Tony and Marion's 7-year-old son
❖ Everett – Tony and Marion's 9-year-old son
❖ Leslie – Tony and Marion's 6-year-old son. I knew "Cousin Leslie" as a girl. He was extremely kind and

always let my Grampa (Ethan) take me and my sister to use his pool when we were visiting our grandparents in the scorching Redding summers.

❖ Francis – Tony and Marion's 2-year-old son
❖ Tessie Lou – Tony and Marion's 1-year-old daughter
❖ baby Chester – Tony and Marion's son
❖ All went to the ranch – my mother believes this might have been a property in Anderson. Louise and Alexander Papineau, Ernest, Elmer and Melvin lived there but lost the ranch through not paying the property tax.

* * * * * * * * * *

The next page of the diary is torn out. All that's visible is the start of "Nov. [25] Fri." and "Sat. 26" on one side, and on the other "letter – ex-wife – all I – any one – G.W. – noon ..." Clearly May was making some less-than-complimentary reflections about her own family. The diary continues:

* * * * * * * * * *

family that have not a festering sore somewhere. There was Uncle John and his lies and gambling, his fly-by-nights and stealing. He may be too old to be sinfull now – but he was a cancer on the happiness of one generation of Ripleys, and our generation has not escaped. Some of the family bow their heads and pretend to not see, some grin and shake their heads, and I? I wonder, I look at my mother and Nora, and think, I've seen a lily spring from a dunghill, but never saw a dunghill spring from a lily. Some old ungodly ancestor of ours looks on and laughs when he sees how his spawn can raise hell here on earth to the consternation of a bunch of sober sided women and men who at least keep their dirty laundry out of sight. I'm glad I'm not God for he must have his hands woefully full of the slime that oozes out on some of his flowers sometimes. I heard a certain little 1927 puritan say it would be a good thing if a certain animal ["creature" written above in pencil] would break its fool neck; the whole family would be happier and more at peace, and a certain ~~baby~~ little child might grow up to be better for the loss; but alas if all the seed of Satan should break its neck, there'd be a lot of vacant houses to rent. No new jobs tho for they don't do any of the world's work that amounts to anything.

- ❖ Uncle John – John Henry Ripley, May's paternal uncle. John Henry and Jehu Ripley, May's father, followed each other to French Gulch, California and from there to John Day, Oregon, so the two families would have known each other well (see Part One, "Ripleys in Illinois, Nebraska and Beyond"). John Henry married Ann Armitage in Nebraska in 1888. They had 13 children, of whom at least eight survived childhood. They emigrated to Penticton, British Columbia, Canada, in 1909.[48]
- ❖ Our generation has not escaped – I don't know whom May was referring to.
- ❖ Mama and Nora / lily sprung from a dunghill – I presume May is comparing her mother and her sister Nora to the lilies!
- ❖ certain little 1927 puritan say... – I don't know whom May was referring to.

Mon. [Nov.] 28

Still it rains. Amy says "who cares what the weather was". I think I shall write her name in here every other line, for why? because she found my old diary written when we – G.W. and I – were at the old home at Fairplay, or rather at old Cedarville, and she promptly began to devour it. I did not realize how very personal it was untill she began to read it aloud, and she just skipped around where ever she saw her own name – I shall not let her see this one. I'll will it to her. She says I write just what I think.

Beggar the thought. If I wrote just what I thought, there is times the page would burn. Often I've wished I dared say what I think, there is often a lot of thunks I've thought that would take out or put in a few kinks in this world. If we dared be as honest as June [Ethan Junior] for instance: yesterday Amy had roast duck and we were all saying how very good it was and June looked at me with the most sinfull twinkle in his eyes and said "Granny ther[e] <u>was</u> 'karka' inside this duck once". My in[n]ards turned a summersault, but I calmed myself rather than be horrified and get Jr. punished. Oh yes I know he needs it, but I'm not going to be the cause.

I planted G.W.'s walnuts today, thirty of them. I hope he and others will remember when eating nuts from these trees that I planted them in the rain and was wet to the hide when finished. I wonder if I'm planting nuts for G.W.'s third wife. If I thought so I'd go dig em up right now. Lot of cattle passed today. I dug up some ground for onions.

❖ old diary – May's 1925 diary. The very fact that we still have these three diaries after all of the upheaval in May's life is an indication of how important they were to her, and the fact that she speaks of willing them to Amy indicates that she did think they might have a value to generations to come. In addition to her "editing" certain passages by ripping out pages, there are also a few penciled corrections here and there, so she obviously went back and read them over.

29 – 30 – Dec 1 – 2

Don't know if I can go back and think of what happened those days or not. I'll try. I've sure been a sick man, and my brain does not mesh just right yet.

On Tues. 29 we went to town in the evening to get the powder and some paper for C[opper] Q[ueen]. On Wed. 30 the kids came out about noon. I had looked for them early, but it was noon when they arrived. I had lunch ready. Amy brought out weenies and kraut, which I put on to cook for supper. After lunch Ethan sawed on the old pine log. Jr. worked on his farm with his farm tools. We "girls" gossiped. Not knowing any one here to gossip about we talked out our relation[s] and we have a fruitfull subject there.

Later we went up to the North [Star – drawing] and saw the new mill, and went in one tun[n]ell where G.W. was. Jr. got a wonderfull kick out of that. I suggested we go see John Doeblin, which was all Amy needed to start her and we did not have to ask but once, both Jr. and Sr. were wil[l]ing. We found John pecking around where his garden used to be. He was as pleased as Punch to see us and gave me his only rose blossom and his hat full of quinces.

We came home and had supper as soon as G.W. got home, or rather as soon as Ethan got back from the C[opper] Queen where he had gone befor G.W. got home. As soon as they had eaten they both went up to the mine again, shooting five holes. About nine the kids went home. I enjoyed their visit, and more than enjoyed the youngest generation's conversation. He talked continualy about movie shows he has seen and broke off his movie yarn to remark thoughtfully "Mama, why haven't you nice big rimples like my granny?"

A question we could not answer.

On Thur. Dec. 1 there is nothing to state except I was dreadfuly sick all day and night. High fever and aching head, was rather alarmed as my spine from my neck halfway down hurt me. I had G.W. rub enough horse linament on me for a span of mules. He was sick all day too so we wondered if it could have been the weenies – but I think I'm just bilious or a touch of malaria. This is Fri. the 2d of Dec, and I am feeling better this evening. G.W. was scared I think for he drove home at noon to see if I was O.K. We all think in terms of Infantile Paralysis these days.

Nine cowboys and fourteen dogs passed up the trail today.

My husband did not think of Our Anaversary so I did not mention it.

I remember five years ago I walked up the long flight of step[s] at the Woodland Yolo Co. Court House and each step I said – Martha says to May – Bein a fool again, didn't have slavery enough with your first Master, bein' a fool again, and May said to Martha, "Oh leave me be you sour old maid".

With each step I said Will I be sorry? Will I be glad?

And I'm glad – what would life be if I had not married. I'd [have] been just like Mama and Aunt Julia, at every one's beck and call, no home of my own and oh so unhappy. Even tho our several homes together have been humble, we have been together and that makes Home. A mousy cabin in a cow pasture, and an old loghouse on a hill, a rented house where in we lost all of our worldly good[s] by theft, a tent on the San Joaquin, the tiny quarters of a river boat, another rented shack, again a tent in the tall, tall pines at Martin's Mill, two rooms in another, a boarding house, the next a whole house more an still, and now a 2 x 4 cabin and tent at Trail's End. Please Heaven be kind and let us stay here.

- ❖ Infantile Paralysis – polio
- ❖ Martha said to May – This conversation between Martha and May (her two forenames) is May's dramatization of her own inner debate about marrying George in 1922.
- ❖ Mama and Aunt Julia – "Aunt Julia" was Julia Holloway Adkins, Ray Ripley's mother-in-law. Julia, like May's mother Olive, was from western Missouri. I don't believe they were related but they were close friends. Julia was widowed in 1920, and in the 1930 census, she was 65 years old and living with Ray and Maude Ripley and their two children in Portland, Oregon.[49] We have a photo of Olive and Julia taken in Portland in 1930.
- ❖ Martin's Mill – unidentified

Sat. [Dec.] 3

Am able to navagate once more, but awful weak on my pins. Done no work, just lay around. Weather is still clear, high N[orth] wind rings in our head.

Sun. [Dec.] 4

Had a wonderfull day. G.W. as per usual rushed me around as fast as my weakened state would al[l]ow me, said we'd rush right to town and right back again. I wanted to ask him what we were going for, and had a notion to tell him if he was in such a rush there was no use in me going, but I was afraid he might take me up on it and leave me at home. So I looked wise and said nothing, which is the wisest thing to say.

We left here at eleven A.M. and the first thing Amy said after she had fed G.W. was would he take her for a ride – and he never batted an eye but told her to get ready. She [coming?] up was ready and we drove up the highway to the new Harlan Miller bridge over Dog Creek. Today is the opening day. A wonderful bridge, wonderfull ride and a wonderfull day. I am not jealous. I enjoyed the ride and I know very well that my husband loves me better than he does my daughter – but if I'd ask[ed] to take a whole day for a ride he'd have simply roared and we would not have gone. Now why? I'm glad she does know how to handle him. I'm sure I don't know how to get him to do any thing I want and he don't care for. I never ask to go any where or do any thing, it is easier to go where he says we will go and do what he says we will do. When I want any thing I ask Amy to suggest it to him, and it is most usualy O.K. She knows how to handle these he-animals an[d] I either don't, or am too independent to beg for my pleasure. But then I have to live with him and she don't.

We had lunch at the Savoy Grill on our return from our ride. Jr. winked at the waitress and brought down the house. I'm sure I don't know why he did such a thing but she smiled at him and he winked at her just in a flash. She and I both exploded and startled Amy as she did not see it. G.W. looked too astonished, I guess he thinks his grandson is encroaching on his preserves.

Mon [Dec.] 5

Thot I'd go fishing this A.M., left my house work and Bounce and I lined out for Clear Creek. Found a dandy place to fish and hadn't any more than got settled when I saw a smok[e] bellow up the creek. Scared me wit-less and I fled home but all O.K. here, the smoke was down by the bridge I guess.

Had not been home ten minutes, was just making a fire to wash my dishes when here came the kids, wanted me to go home and do the washing as Amy has lost her voice and Dr. says she must not dapple in cold water. Ethan drove on up to tell G.W. at the North [Star – drawing] and we drove our car to town leaving the small car for G.W. to come after me in. He came to town from work. Ethan took us to see "A Town Gone Wild". I enjoyed it. We brough[t] Jr. home with us.

Mon. [Dec.] 12

A week has passed – Reason – the baby has been with us, and I found amus[e]ment enough in him. I'm so lonesome today I'm sick. We took him home yesterday and I feel like a traitor. He did plead so hard to stay here, when we told him we were going to town he begged to be left here alone rather than take a chance on not coming back with us. Said, Oh I won't be afraid, I'll stay right here with Bounce. And when we did come away and leave him my heart cracked and so did his. I left him crying oh so bitterly.

There is no earthly reason why he couldn't stay here till he's tired of us and wanted to go home. None but motherly and fatherly jealousy. He's never in the house, only to eat and sleep so I can't see how they miss his company. They leave him with just any one to go to a dance and I hate to even trust him with them, in fact I don't trust them, but I can't help myself. I'd take him away from them in a holy second if I thought I could do it. He does not worry them or cause them as much care [as] a pet dog does me. And I fret myself about him all the time.

He is smarter than any one among his forebears, in fact I think he has more brains than all of them put together. Nothing goes over his head. I could fill this book with his doings and saying[s] in one week. We considered the possability of an angle worm devouring me in case he was not here to take care of me and I said "and then the angle worm would crawl in bed and what would Georgie say when he found an angle worm in his bed?" Jr. said calmly, "Oh he'd say 'What in hell is that dammed angle worm doing in my bed'" – which is just what G.W. would have said.

Dec. 24

Went to Redding for Junior's Tree, had a good time.

❖ Junior's Tree – Ethan Junior's Christmas tree

[Dec.] 25

Merry Xmas. Came home about 2 PM, after having lunch at the Oyster Grotto, Ethan, Amy, Junior, Ernest, G.W. and I. Snow fell last night here in Redding, none at Trail's End.

1928
Jan 1

Came to Redding New Year's Eve. Went to a show, play'd cards till after 12. Happy New Year to All.

Came home to Trail's End, awful storm while we were gone.

Jan. 12

Children went to see Austin yesterday. To be gone two weeks. North [Star – drawing] closed down.

❖ I believe Austin was running the Shell station in Dunsmuir, on the slopes of Mount Shasta, at this time.

Jan. 22

Went to Redding to get the house warm for the kids. Found they had been home since Fri 20. Baby has chicken pox. We have our fence up around the place.

Jan. 25

Leased gravel claim from Wm Hill.

❖ The 1930 census lists William L. Hill, owner of a gold mine.[50]

[Jan.] 28 [in margin:] LESLIE BIRTHDAY

I went with G.W. to help work, as Lehman says work to[o] hard
for him. Queer place, haunted with the ghosts of chinks and other
old timers.

❖ Lehman says work too hard for him – this is hardly
  surprising, since Leer Lehman was now nearly seventy
  and had just finished building two cabins.
❖ Queer place, haunted with ghosts of chinks - there had
  been many Chinese working in the mines around Igo in
  the 19th century. One study says that the Hardscrabble
  Mine in Igo / Piety Hill used 600 Chinese workers in the
  1860s.[51] By the 1920s these old mines were worked out,
  but had by then turned into something like gravel pits. No
  Chinese are listed in the 1930 census of Township 1,
  Shasta County, the area around Igo.
❖ Leslie was 26 years old on this day.

[Jan.] 29

We worked all day. I'm nearly dead I'm so tired. No gold so far.
Found the hard rain of last night had washed the dam out and the
boxes helter skelter.

Mon.
Jan. 30

Had I dreamed yesterday that it would prove to be the happiest
day of my life, I wonder if I'd have grown tired regardless of
work.

    The last month I have felt Leslie's presence all around me.
And I've dreamed of him every night. There has never been a day

that I have not thot of him in all the years since he left, but the last few weeks he has been so constan[t]ly in my mind that it has been a worry to me as I feared some thing ill had befallen him.

Last night after we had gone to bed, we heard a car and soon Amy's and the baby's voice. I grew frightened and could find no clothes to put on so put on my coat. Amy kept saying "guess who we have got here." My heart kept saying "Is it Leslie?" but I dared not trust my voice.

At last my endless prayer has been answered. It was Leslie.

He has not changed as much as my more sheltered children, tho he has aged more than they. Now if fortune and fate will only make it possible to keep him with us.

The kids took him home with them and we drove down today and brought him back. He is going to help G.W. in the mine.

- ❖ the baby – Ethan Junior (who was not really a baby, soon to be five years old)
- ❖ he has not changed as much as my more sheltered children – Leslie had been serving in the military, in the Philippines.

[Jan.] 31

I stayed home and the boys mined. No gold yet.

Feb.
Wed. 1

Boys worked till about 3 P.M. We drove in to town to see the kids, came home after dark. Raining.

Thur [Feb.] 2

Hard Storm. Boys worked. I mended clothes.

Fri. [Feb.] 3

A dreadfull storm. I've fought to keep the tent from blowing down all day.

This is the end of May's diary.

At the back of the ledger book is penciled an undated draft letter to A.F. Johnston, owner of the Adele Hobson:
Thank You A.J. for your good opinion of my honesty, for you are well aware that G.W. Maylone is like A.F. Johnston, he leaves his writing as well as thinking to some one else. If G.W. Maylone and A.F. Johnston had not both married more Brains than they already had, they would as Will Rogers might say be in a Helluvafix.
Hence when you say you do not owe the charge for the battery and that G.W.M's OK does not change your opinion, you are saying I am a liar, as you know it was I who kept account of all the things bough[t] for the Adele when I was on the boat. That is twice you have given an opinion of my honesty.
I still have the log of Adele Hobson from May 30 1926 to Jan. 1927 and when Mr. Moore sent me the bill to OK, I ask[ed] G.W. to do so – as I knew it was a just bill and supposed you had paid it. When this bill came in to [ex ?] you were at home sick in bed near death['s] door; and I had shed tears of pity at your suffering when you left us to take care of your boat.[52] We G.W. and I and no one but we two gave a whoop in Hades what became of your boat, your grain contract or any thing else. And we begged Slim to stay with us. We had made the trip out of

~~Stockton and loaded grain and made the trip back with only one engin.~~

had to have the battery recharged in order to make the trips as you wished and we did make them to[o], and when I stop to [think] how easy that sounds, and just what those trips were on two of us at least, I think as I told you once befor you are lacking in gratatude and fail to appreciate when one does try to do more tha[n] the 8 hr. law call[s] for – I am mailing Mr. Moore a check for the amount due him. Not that I think I have to, but because that battery was worth that much to me. And I'm not doing it for you but for the love I bear the Hobson. To you she is just a means to an end and to me she is some body and I love every rotten old board in her – and regardless of all the work, worry, loss of sleep, hide and hair, bruises, bumps, rips and tears, I would not change the eight month[s] I lived on the Hobson for any other year of my life. I never expected to leave the boat alive but I took a chance and loved it. G.W. does not know of this bills many trips back and forth and I do not care to lessen his opinion of you or have him think you have doubted his honesty so he has not seen these letters. And <u>maybe</u> you won't see this one. Just the same this [is] not the first time I've paid a bill for Adele and you can tell her for me she's welcome[e]. I've paid more than that to help her go. With kindest regards to your wife and Mrs. Johnston Sr., my sincere affection to Harvey, the finest fellow I know; and regardless of this letter my esteem for you is as high as ever.

I remain a friend,
May R. Maylone

Part Four:

May's poems (1908-1915)

A lthough I have put them after the diaries, these poems are the earliest writings of May that we have. They come at the front of the black ledger book in which she later kept her 1925 diary. Inside the front cover is written "May Ripley-Diddy" with "-Maylone" added later, and the date (in the earlier script) is "Aug 18 1908"

Flyleaf: "Thoughts"

p. 1:

Roses

Roses, roses pure and white
Bow to me a sweet Good-night
Fragrant is your wafted breath
Far away seems sin or death
Oh that I a rose might be
In unstained spotless purity

You thro' life seem quite content
Grateful for the blessings sent
Be it sunshine, wind or rain
What care you for others pain

When my work on earth is done
When my life its course has run
Lay me in my narrow bed
Plant a white rose at my head
It will guard my slumbers deep
When my friends have ceased to weep.

M.R.D.

The poet sings of a day in June
When all the world's with songs a-tune
But let the clouds be dull and gray
Or blue skies gleam above
All days are fair
Beyond compare
When I chance to meet my love

M.R.D.
[a tiny cross is next to this poem, and very small 'EM' in
    margin]

p.2

Wishes

Last night I bowed to the moon nine times
I wished to it nine times too
And what do you think my wishes were, love
My wishes were all of you

I wished that I soon might stand by your side
And gaze in those eyes so blue
And read the sweet story they've told me oft
A story I know to be true

I wished that our path would grow plainer
That the thornes into roses would bloom
That day-light take place of the darkness
And sun-light would follow the gloom

I wished that the time would come when we might
Cast away sorrow and care
I wished that this storm of darkness and pain
Would burst into morning so fair

M.R.D.
[tiny 'EM' in margin]

Waiting, waiting, waiting.
For the sun-rise gleam
Watching, watching, watching
For the ripples in the stream
Following forever the rain-bow's lure
Searching for the waters that's a sick heart's cure
Poor bleeding feet, that have lost the trail
Pity the striveing that is bound to fail
Crying forever for the silver moon
Weary wandering lost one
May your rest come soon.

M.R.D.
[tiny 'JF' in margin]

p. 3

Ask me not what makes me weary
Ask not why this long drawn sigh
Only take me in your arms, love
There I'd be content to die

Life to me is a weary burden
One I dare not cast aside
Galling is the chains I'm wearing
Tho' for patience I have cried

Patience, strong to do my dudy [duty]
Patience, yet this yoke to bear
Yet there is a dearer boon, love
One I've craved in constant prayer

That you never know the sorrow
That has searched and seared my heart
That you never know what anguish
I shall feel when we must part

M.R.D.
[tiny 'EM' in margin]

I wish you all things well
And all your dear desires
Joy no tongue can tell
And all your heart aspires
May each day in its train
Bring rain to lay the dust
Bring sun to dry the rain
And wealth no time can rust

M.R.D.
[tiny 'EM' in margin]

p. 4

As you follow the train by the river
Do you think of your love on the hill
The path that leads you from me
Do you tread against your will

As your work leads onward and upward
Do you think of the one left behind
When friends and loved ones surround you
Will your thought of me still be kind

You will have all that life can give you
And you'll think this a mid-summer dream
While to me gropeing thro the dark storm-clouds
T'will be like the lightning bright gleam

So bright it lights my pathway
But to leave me in deeper gloom
And my hopes are dieing, dieing
For me the flowers will ne'er bloom.

M.R.D.
[tiny 'JF' in margin]

The same sun shines on us both each day
The stars light our way by night
I think of you so far and hope your path is bright
This world is fine if we make it so
We may weave our lives as we will
Tho' we may not choose the color you know
As the shuttle we empty and fill.

MRD
[tiny 'JF' in margin]

p. 5

I want you my darling, my darling
The wind softly sobs thro' the vine
I can hear the quick sound of your footstep
In each throb of this sad heart of mine

With each sound that the breezes come laden
I can hear the sweet tones of your voice
Tho' I know that my ears are unfaithfull
For the moment I've cause to rejoice

Tho' wild with the joy of our meeting
Knowing well t'will be followed by pain
I comfort myself with believeing
You will come to your love once again

So with heart everburdened with longing
To your voice in the breezes I'll hark
My tears will be loveingly hidden
By Night's tender curtains of dark.

M.R.D.
[tiny 'JF' in margin]

p. 6

Smile tho' your heart be breaking
Cover your woes with a smile
To tell all the world your sorrows
Surely is not worth while

Smile tho' grief's keen dagger
Pierces some vital spot
Smile tho' the world is unfriendly
And no matter what is your lot

Smile when you battle with slander
Smile when you war with sin
Smile at the finish of each task
Smile when the next you begin

The world will declare you are happy
If you face it each day with a smile
And to hide your heart from prying eyes
Is surely a task worth while

M.R.D.
[tiny 'JF' in margin]

p. 7

Only a scrap of Eden, drop[p]ed by the hand of fate
Just a ray of sunlight, only it came too late
Like a flower on a pool of still water
Like a gem in a tarnished ring
Like bread to a starveing creature
To me is this wonderful thing.

It has passed thro my life like a flurry
Of rain, and sunshine, and song
Has freshened the parching desert
Of my heart, that has thirsted long

And when it has left me in darkness
I must weave with life's old gray thread
And go gropeing in vain for the glory
Whose light made me lift my head
Never more to list to the story
That to some hearts is daily bread.

It maybe my heart will famish
And mayhap my soul wither up
Yet I know of the wonderful wine of love
My lips have at least touched the cup.

M.R.D.
[tiny 'JF' in margin]

p. 8

I send to you a clover, Dear
Tis not the four leaf kind
But the three are full of tender thoughts
From a heart where you are inshrined

One leaf is for Hope, Dear
When the clover blooms again
We together may search for the four-leaf
May the hope be not in vain

One leaf is for Faith, Dear
Faith that may never fail
For Faith is harder to find, Dear
Than the long lost Holy Grail

The third leaf is for Love, Dear
A Love we grant to few
Which our absence One from Another
Will strengthen and renew.

M.R.D.
['JF' in margin. Also: 'Sent S.W.S. Printed']

p. 9

Down in a bare little valley
Where the burning sun shone hot
Lived a lonely, fading Bluebell
Unhappy was her lot

She longed for the Frost King's coming
To end her life of pain
But lo, e'er the Frost King's coming
Came the beautiful Prince of the Rain

And her drooping form he lifted
With a strong and gentle arm
And words of loveing promise
To shield her from all harm

And no more does she long for the Frost King
No more does she fear Death's pain
Tho' deep be her dreamless slumber
She will wake at the kiss of the Rain

I have passed thro' my life's young Spring time
I have toiled thro' the Summer's sun
I have felt the kiss of my Prince of Rain
And I feel that my life is done

Yet no more would I greive o'er Life's sorrows
No more would I fear Death's pain
If I knew beyond Lifes Winter
I would wake at the kiss of the Rain

M.R.D.
['JF' in margin]

p. 10

Here in the shade of the locust
I've waited and watched in vain
My eyes have grown dim with watching
My heart has grown heavy with pain

Tho' somehow I've not found the path-way
That leads to a Heaven on earth
I've found a few flowers on the hill-side
And heard the birds singing with mirth

The sweet scented flowers on the hill-side
The little birds singing in glee
I'll try to not think of the time past
And may-hap learn a lesson from thee

I've a nest if I only would line it
And birdlings to feed every day
And while I am fretting and wishing
My birdlings may soon fly away

I've a garden that['s] filled with sweet flowers
Each day growing fairer of face
My Master has traced out my pathway
But alas, have I walked it with grace?

My eyes have been watching the glory
That tints the bright clouds from a-far
And have longed in vain for the silver beams
That falls from a radiant star

I must bring my gaze to the earth again
And search for the flowers at my feet
And I hope I may find
Some Rosemary among the Bitter-sweet

M.R.D.
['JF' in margin]

p. 11

Dont hitch your wagon to a Star
For you'll find when your ride is over
There are safer steeds on earth by far
Try one that lives near the clover

I hitched my wagon to a Star
And I found e'er my ride was ended
That I came back to the earth with a jar
And the Star went his way unattended

My child, don't try to fly to[o] high
When you know to the earth you['re] shackled
If you try to follow the style of the Stars
You'll be sick of the job you've tackled

The Tail of a Comet once called on me
Oh he told me a wonderful story
He ask[ed] me to go for a spin with him
Said he lived next door to Glory

I went far aways but I soon came back
From the earth no more I'll roam
The Star may follow the Milkmaid's track
I'll stay with my steed at home

M.R.D.
['JF' in margin]

When you pillow your head on these butterflies white
May your slumber be peacefull thro' out the night
And the dreams that come in the silent hours
Like butterflies flitting 'mong summer flowers
Be only of those whom you hold most dear
With never a shadow of pain or fear
For with every stitch my needle wrought
I wove in for you a loveing thought

p. 12

Oh sweet Gray-bell why do you hang your head?
Your beautys hid, rude gaze you need not dread
Each spring I've fondly searched the Plains for you
Found my reward, a brimming cup of dew

Your home's a damp, cold, dreary spot
And yet you seem contented with your lot
Oh freckled child of Shasta's sun and soil
You live your life with neither fret nor toil

And when your sweet and sunny hour is past
You surely know it will not be your last
For when the winter's chill has flown again
I'll search and find you on the Rocky Plain

M.R.D.

Twas only a little blue wild flower
Plucked on the plains
Gently twas kissed by the sunshine
Softly twas washed by the rain

Laughingly tossed to a maiden
Loveingly worn in her hair
When withered, twas lain away sacred
With a hope that was almost a prayer

Alas for the hope that was riven
Alas for the heart that was torn
Alas for the love freely given
That met in return nought but scorn

M.R.D.
['EM' in margin]

p. 13

As the rain comes patter patter
With its dainty soft refrain
Tis freight'd with sweetest music
Songs full of Love and Pain

Songs that fills my eyes with tears
Then my heart with joy and mirth
Thoughts of days agone Love
When Heaven seemed near to Earth

List to its soft sweet patter
Hark! There's a change in its song
Me-thinks tis a whispered promise
Of happier days e'er long

Who knows where those laughing rain-drops
Have been in their world-wide flight
Who knows what they've heard among the stars
That the clouds hid away from our sight

Prehap they heard our wishes
That unknown from us have flown
Prehaps they know that Someday
We all shall come to [our?] Own

MRD
['JF' in margin]

p. 14

First in ever waking thought
Rare the reward my love has brought
Always a joy with every grief
Never a woe but it sent relief
Known to none but my Other-soul
Just ahead is the long sought goal
Dearer then aught else neath the sky
Ever I smother its pleading cry
Always onward, and never back
Ready to blaze out an unknown track
Braveing the perils unseen ahead
Only to know that the path I tread
Rough and steep, o'ergrown with thorn
Now smoother made by my feet so worn

M.R.D.
['JF' in margin]

The white snow mantles Willowvale
The trees look ghostly and gray
The hills you loved look wan and pale
They have changed since you went away

The pines up here on the little Flat Hill
Seem like sentinels tall and brave
Seem to know full well they've a place to fill
And the charge makes them stern and grave

The beautiful snow like charity's dress
Covers many a mark and scar
A cloak of dainty white lovelyness
Drapeing the hills near and far.

M.R.D.
['JF' in margin]

p. 15

The rain-drops are winging their way to the earth
My needles gleam in the firelight bright
My children's voices ring with mirth
For my many blessing[s] I thank Thee tonight

The wind blows cold over hill and dale
The rainladen clouds hang heavy and low
But all's snug and cheery at Willowvale
As we cluster around the fire's bright glow

Tho Winter reigns we are well content
And have found full many a task to do
And feel at eve, that this day's well spent
The night will bring rest and our strength renew

The birds must build a nest each spring
And each summer their nestling[s] all flit away
While we build for life as we work and sing
May we keep our nestling[s] for many a day

Oh Guardian of All watch over our home
And grant us sun with the wind and rain
Oh grant our nestlings may never roam
And our labor of love be not in vain.

M.R.D.

A note in another hand is inserted between p. 16 and 17 –
presumably from an editor. It says: "p. 2 – 5 – 16 – 19 = Rosary
Page 16 is the most true – more of the simple expression of the
author's own thought in words more her own. Quite a literary
bent – but of course too artificial in its choice of words."

p. 16

Dear Heart, I know that you doubt me
And it makes my sorrow complete
Tho' my head may lie upon the breast
My heart lies at thy feet
The flame of ill-will has scorched us
And you lay the blame on me
Like Eve I must bear the burden
For you say I tempted thee
Poor Eve I often wonder
Did you ever regret the cost
Of the pitiful thing you paid for
Was it worth your innocence lost
There is nothing worth the striveing
For virtue is nought but a show
And the deeper the sin the more honor
As long as the world don't know.

M.R.D.
['EM' in margin]

Say do you know, my darling
That the light of your loveing eyes
Is fairer far than any I find
In the sunny summer skys

And do you know, my loved one
That the sound of your cheery voice
Is sweeter than any music
And makes my heart rejoice

And do you know my sweetheart
That the sound of your step on the stair
Fills my weary heart with gladness
And drives away my care

Oh the bar so strong and steadfast
Still keeps me and thee apart
But dear you know you are always
Shrined deep in this loveing heart

M.R.D.
['EM' in margin]

p. 17

Tis said that Love doth come·
Like a flame of lovely light
But tis not always so
For days and days Thou passed befor my sight
I saw Thee come and go

And yet I knew Thee not
Untill within thine eye
I saw thy soul look forth
And greet mine own
I heard Love's welcome cry

These chains that we have forged
We dare not sever
Altho' Love's pleading voice
Will haunt us ever

The bitter with the sweet
Our Love we must deny
Prehaps we'll know Someday
Dear heart the reason why.

M.R.D.

p.18

Under the ruby-trimmed Yew-trees
We rest with a laugh and a sigh
The laugh for the days that are comeing
The sigh for the days going by,
Days over-flowing with sunshine
Days we will see no more
We hope the days that are comeing
Will hold such a golden store

Till again we camp neath the Yewtrees
Hushed to sleep by their whispering song
To one of the happy campers,
I fear the days will be long

Prehaps ne'er again in the comeing days
Will we rest in the Yewtrees shade
Nor list to their gentle whispers
Keeping time to the stream in the glade
Yet still we will have a memory
That time cannot take away
With all of life's work and worry
Came a pleasant day of play.

    Written at Yew Tree Rest Camp
        Hatchet Creek
        August Sunday 9th
            1908
        By M.R.D.

[In the margin: 'JF,' and in a fainter hand, 'sent SWS']

❖ Hatchet Creek is near Round Mountain, Shasta County,
    not far from the roadhouse at Ingot.

Last night I bowed to the moon nine times
And I wished to it nine times too
What think you those wishes were, Heart-o-Gold
I'll tell you – if they come true

[In the margin: 'M' and 'June 7 – 13']

p. 19

<u>My</u> Rosary

My rosary, my rosary, each pearl is stolen ev'ry one
And yet I love and cling to them, as day clings to the
    dieing sun
I hide my treasures from the world, and tell them o'er in
    sobbing
    prayer
A prayer with you in every thought, to keep you from
    each worldly
    snare

Each pearl to me a holy thing, to sacred keep from pagan
    eyes
Beneath my dull life's garments gray, upon my heart it
    hidden lies
A cross I find with every bead, a cross I kiss and yearn to
    bear
If only I might ever shield my darling from all pain and
    care

And yet I know my prayer is vain, for in your life I bring
    no light
My beads I tell and pray, for grace to help me bear
    perpetual night
We've had our night befor our day, for us no "radiant
    morn" has
    passed
May He grant us our "glorious noon" and lead us safely
    home at
    last

M.R.D.
Written June 20, 1912
After readin[g] "The Rosary"
by C.L. Barclay

['M' in margin]

Rare is a love that will last
Always a friend have I sought
Loveing me true and steadfast
Priceless, this love can't be bought
Haveing this friend for my own
Many's the storm I can brave
All tho I face them alone
Ready to meet wind or wave
I with Love for my anchor feel sure
On life's harbor or open sea
Nought I'll fear, but bravely endure
        all that fortune send[s] to me

        Sept. 8, 1912
        M.R.D.

['M' in margin]

p. 20

Oh! to be clasp[ed] in your arms, my darling
To feel your heart beat fast
To meet the press of your loveing lips
Oh! to know it would always last

Today you have left me in sadness
Another now sits by your side
When she took the place I call my own
It seemed that my soul had died

But when your arms are clasp[ed] around me
Then I feel that your heart is mine
But, now you are with another
And I tast[e] deep the dregs of the wine.

M.R.D.
[symbol of merged backwards E and K in margin]

Out here alone in the starlight
Where the Pitt rushes by with a roar
It[s] thundering voices all saying
My darling is here no more

The North Star looks down pale and stately
There is naught to break its calm
Yet to know we have watched it together
To my bleeding heart is balm

The pines sob and sigh and tremble
The wind moans like a wounded dove
My soul like the pines all aquiver
My heart longing for you, love

M.R.D.
[symbol of merged backwards E and K in margin]

❖   The Pitt river runs east of Burney, which is east of Ingot.

I think of the message you sent me
"Any place in the world with you"
And the Pansies bring me heartsease
They whisper your love is true

p. 21

Sweetheart, I'm so sad and lonely
You have gone so far away
All my thoughts are of you only
Thinking of you night and day
Come and comfort your poor Baby
That you left to grieve alone
For your kisses and carress's
All her sorrows will atone
Since you've gone away and left me
Life is like an empty vase
Tho' the roses long have perished
Naught their fragrance can erase

M.R.D.
[symbol of merged backwards E and K in margin]

I am sitting here by my window
Watching the rain patter down
Thinking of one that I love best
Away in that far off town

The meadow-larks singing so gayly
The rain has made cooler the air
But warm is my love for you, darling
And to see you my unending prayer

I am hidden away from the others
Their talk nearly drives me wild
If only you were here, sweetheart
To comfort your lonely child

When night veils the hills in darkness
And the stars shed light
My empty arms ache with longing
To enfold you throughout the night

M.R.D.
[symbol of merged backwards E and K in margin]

p. 22

Waiting and Watching

Off o'er the billows of pine trees, and scrub oak
Waves of live oak, and wild hop blooms
Kissed by the sunshine, and swept by the north winds
Afar like an isle, snowcrowned Shasta looms
Green are the mountains, and brown are the valleys
Perished the flowers that were sown by the spring
Breathless the land lies, till cooled by the evening
Then hark! to the joy bells the song birdies ring

Far lies the trail, where the changing hued mountains
Merge as they meet with the constant blue sky
Then will my rover lad fondly remember
To send back a thought where the dun valleys lie
And when "Our Star" in the south sky is gleaming
Shining o'er valley and mountain and plain
Then will he think of her who is watching
Watching and waiting his coming again

Cloud veiled old Shasta, as you I am lonely
Missing and wanting the lad of my heart
Pine trees do whisper a soft word of comfort
Tell of a day when we no more shall part
North wind and south wind caress him so softly
Bear him my love as he rides on his way
Tell him my heart is his only, and ever
And its throbbing keeps time to his steps thro the day

Knight o' the Rodeo, where e'er you are riding
Down where Pitt River is lashed to a foam
Or up on the hills where death hides with the rattler
There follow my prayers for your safe return home
And may you know in the long lonely hours
When you would follow your rover heart here
Down in the valley is one who is waiting
Watching and waiting your homecoming, Dear.

M.R.D.

[in margin at top: 'M']
[in margin at bottom: Aug 21 1913]

p. 23

I watch you, lad, ride down the road
As far as I can see you
I see you turn and wave your hand
And ride away alone
I try to call you with my eyes
So loath am I to lose you
The trees bend low and loveingly
And hide from me my own

How lonely all my world has grown
You've gone, how can I bear it
Here lies your gloves and clinking spurs
Forgot[t]en by the door
A wrapper from your "spearmint kind"
So willingly you share it
How I long to hear your whistle
And your step outside my door

The days pass by, they're all alike
I can cross them out no more
The bright beads on my rosary
Still number just the same
Those woodland spots that we have named
In happy days of yore
Have lost their mystic charm for me
And you'r[e] alone to blame

x xxx xxx xxx
<u>Then</u> when I hear a whistle, faint, far away and sweet
My heart most stops its beating
And I fairly hold my breath
As I catch the "pitty patter"
Of a pony's flying feet
Then I tast[e] the joys o'Heaven
E'er I pay the Toll o'Death

M.R.D.
July 7 1915

[in margin at top: 'M']

[p. 24 is blank, and on p. 25 begins the 1925 diary]

Part Five:

Postscript

A s far as we know, May didn't keep any more diaries after January of 1928. I haven't been able to find out how long May and George stayed in Igo. They aren't listed as living there in the 1930 census, but then I have not been able to unearth May and George anywhere in the 1930 census. Perhaps they were up a hill somewhere when the census taker came by.

Although we don't know where May was when the census taker came to call in 1930, her mother Olive on the other hand appears twice in that census: on April 8th she was in Redding visiting Amy, Ethan, Ethan Jr. age 7, and baby Ruth Ann (my mother), who was not yet a month old. She was listed as Olive A. Rippley, age 68, "gr. mother-in-law".[1] A week later (April 14th) she was in Portland with Lela and 9-year-old Betty Lee.[2] As May's diaries suggest ("I'd [have] been just like Mama ... at every one's beck and call, no home of my own" 29 Nov.- 2 Dec. 1927) Olive went back and forth between her children. Olive's obituary says that after Jehu's death (in 1915) "she had been in Portland and in California a considerable part of the time."[3] In Portland, we know she stayed with Lela, and presumably also with Ray; and in California she stayed with her grand-daughter Amy and perhaps also May.

Olive had already lost her son Perryman as an infant in 1901, and her 16-year-old daughter Maggie in 1902. If her obituary is correct in stating she and Jehu had nine children, then she had lost another two in earlier years as well. In 1929, her son Leo died in Portland at the age of 34 (I haven't been able find out why he died so young). The next year, Leo's widow Dorothy was working as a waitress in Portland, bringing up her 11-year-old son. Living with them was her 60-year-old mother, who was working as a chambermaid.[4] Life was not easy for them either.

In November 1931 there was a family reunion in Eastern Oregon. This may have been the first time May had returned to John Day since leaving in 1899. We have two photographs of that visit, one showing four generations (my mother Ruth born in 1930, Amy, May and Olive), and one of Olive with her four surviving children (May, Nora, Ray and Lela), her grandchildren and great-grandchildren.

The next year, in June 1932, Olive passed away. The circumstances of her death somehow caused a rift in the Ripley family. Her obituary states "She had but recently returned from California, where she spent the winter with a daughter." This daughter can only be May, as Nora and Lela were in John Day and Portland. But it also states that "Mrs. Ripley died the day following her arrival from Portland." Therefore Olive must have travelled from near Redding to Portland, and from there to John Day, where she died. My mother Ruth remembers a story about my grandfather Ethan having to drive the 550 miles from Redding to John Day when there was some kind of emergency – she thinks because Great Grandma Olive was visiting and became ill. It may well have been this trip that remained in the family's oral history and thus in my mother's memory.

My grandmother Amy told my mother that after Olive's death, Nora never answered any of her correspondence. Amy said that some of the Ripleys had disapproved of how she and Ethan had treated Olive. Amy found it so painful that she didn't elaborate, and so we don't know any more about what actually happened, or the reasons behind this family division.

In 1932, May and George were living in Lewiston, California, between French Gulch and Weaverville. They were living in a shack called "Hummingbird Hut," (this cheerful name must have surely have been May's invention!). George was listed in the November 1932 voters' register as a miner.[5] The photograph of Ethan and Ruth Ann on a visit to their Granny that August shows two very happy children. We know from her diaries that May would have loved having them with her. My mother remembers May and George visiting them in Redding in 1932, at a house on South Street, when she was about 2 ½ years old. It was during these visits that May made the miniature doll quilt, and Ruth remembers helping to piece some of the larger squares. Ruth told me: "I loved her. I remember doing cut-out dolls, and lots of hand-work. She was very clever and lots of fun."

George died very suddenly in the summer of 1933, at the age of 46, of appendicitis. His niece's recollections are that he was then working in the "'Belle Vista' mine, located just below the crest of Coyote Ridge." As far as I can determine, this mine was near Coyote Ridge in El Dorado County, near Fairplay (and isn't the locality of Bella Vista near Ingot in Shasta County). Therefore May and George must have gone back to El Dorado County sometime between August 1932 and July 1933. Eleanor Manning's account reads:

> Mae's money was gone so George found a couple of backers in San Francisco. He first built a miner's shack with two rooms, no comforts, no running water and with an outside toilet. But, Mae did the best she could with what they had. ...

> When [George] was but forty-six years old he had an appendicitis attack at the mine. The family didn't know where to go for help, so put him in a

car and travelled all the way to the home of his sister Gertrude in Hayward. Gertrude and Frank, with much difficulty, got him admitted to the county hospital in Oakland. When the doctors tried to operate they found the poison had spread throughout his body. He died within hours.

Mae had accompanied him on his journey to Hayward. She was in frail health and stayed with Gertrude and Frank for a short time.[6]

George died on the 27th of July, 1933.

May did not survive George for long. The circumstances, and even cause, of her death are shrouded in some mystery. My mother remembers May coming to stay with her family on Cypress Street in Redding, where Amy and Ethan had moved in 1933. May shared a room with 3-year-old Ruth Ann. But May was so changed that my mother didn't recognize her beloved grandmother. She concluded that this must be some other Granny. Ruth was afraid of this new Granny, who was out of control and mean to Amy. My uncle Ethan (who was then ten years old) also remembers her as being crazed during this time. May had a goiter (caused by lack of iodine in the water of Northern California) and little Ruth Ann was told that Granny was sick because of her goiter. Eleanor Manning also recollected how changed May was at the end of her life: "When George met Mae she was a little 5 X 5, quite heavy and very short. A couple of years before her death she developed a huge goiter in her throat, and as it grew it seemed to gradually choke the life from her. She couldn't eat and weighed only 95 pounds when she died."[7]

**Ethan Austin Papineau (age 9) and Ruth Ann Papineau (age 2)
visiting their Granny May at George & May's house
"Hummingbird Hut"
Lewiston, California, summer of 1932**

When my mother was older, Amy and Ethan told her more about how her Granny May had come to stay with them. They said that they had discovered that May had been put in an insane asylum in Sacramento. (This story sadly reminds me of May's own ironic remark "I am sure if my people knew the things that hammer in my brain and urge my tongue to turn them loose – sure ah too sure[l]y I'd have a home in Napa." [4 Nov. 1927.) My grandparents told my mother that Ethan went to a hearing in a court-room and found May in a hospital gown without any clothes on, very disheveled and confused. He told the judge he was taking her home. He wrapped her up in a blanket and brought her back to Redding to live with them.

May died only six weeks after George, on September 7th, 1933. She was just two weeks short of her 54th birthday. She didn't die in Redding, but in the University of California Hospital in San Francisco, where she had been admitted on August 26th (a month after George's death). How it was that she came to be there my mother doesn't know. Her memorable stay in Redding, and Ethan's rescue of her, took place only within a space of weeks. May's death certificate states that she died of "cerebral thrombosis – date of onset Aug 12 1933" and "Broncho pneumonia – date of onset Sept 5 1933".[8] She was buried in Fairplay cemetery next to George W. Maylone.[9] Eleanor Manning recollected the tributes paid to May by her former neighbors and friends in El Dorado County: "A casket was purchased in Placerville and her body was laid out and viewed by friends, relatives and neighbors in the old Fairplay store."[10]

There is another family story about May's death, one that Amy told my mother years later: she said that George Maylone had given May syphilis. I have no proof that this is correct, and I do not wish to malign the memory of George Washington Maylone. However, given how many other family stories have turned out to be true, and because of the admiration and affection I have for May, I feel it is worth including as a possibility. In this, I am taking the heartfelt advice of the late Millie Hizer Cuellar, a very knowledgeable genealogist who believed it was important not to cover up the truth. Millie advised me to present it simply as an unconfirmed family story.

It is very sad to read May's diaries with this possibility in mind. Despite her doubts about marrying George ("Martha says to May – Bein a fool again, didn't have slavery enough with your first Master" [29 Nov. -2 Dec. 1927]), May believed in love, and she always desperately wanted a home of her own. Her diaries – as well as Eleanor Manning's recollections – testify that she always made the best of a bad situation. George Maylone, as the diaries clearly show, was to some extent a womanizer. (In this he was perhaps very like John Diddy, May's first husband - if the family story about Leslie being born to another woman is true.) Also, George had served in France during World War I, where syphilis was rife in an age before penicillin, and he could have contracted the disease then.

May wrote of her marriage to George: "Once upon a time I asked the gods of fortune to grant me one wish, and promised, were it granted I'd rail no more at my unhappy lot in life. They grin'd and handed me my wish on a red hot platter, and I am holding that self heating platter yet but they won't hear me yip." (13 Oct. 1926) If May had contracted syphilis, then she was indeed holding a "red hot platter". Syphilis is a disease that can manifest itself in many ways. Secondary syphilis is characterized by fever, aching joints and severe flu-like symptoms. I wondered, reading about the solicitous George applying "enough linament for a span of mules" when May was terribly ill with fever and aches in early December 1927, whether this was a symptom of the disease. Insanity is another symptom of advanced syphilis – was this the explanation behind the crazed Granny who so frightened my mother? Or was May driven mad by her goiter, or the impending stroke?

It is almost certain that if May believed she had contracted syphilis she would not have had absolute proof of her suspicions. As there was then no possibility of a cure, I doubt very much that May would have subjected herself to the expensive humiliation of a trip to the doctor. If it is true that George had given her syphilis, May was certainly not alone in her fate: a few brave campaigners had been raising the issue since the late 19th century, but their warnings largely fell on deaf ears. This was not a disease that nice women had, not a disease that polite society recognized. Even Thomas Parran, the Surgeon General from 1936-1948, struggled in his campaign for a recognition of syphilis as a public health concern.[11] Not only was there no cure for syphilis, but in May's lifetime there was no compassion for women who – quite possibly through no fault of their own – had contracted the disease.

We will never know if this sad family story is true or not. What we can say with certainty is that in her nearly 54 years, May had worked extremely hard to keep body and soul together, to raise her children, and to create a home for her family in the face of constant change and pennilessness. It doesn't matter so much, to me, to know the exact details of May's health in her final days. What remains shining forth from these diaries is the incredible sense of Life that was always present in May, and that was cherished in her family's memories long after she died. Although I was born nearly thirty years after May had gone, her spirit and personality were communicated to me by my mother and grandmother as I grew up. For this I am very grateful.

After May's death, Amy kept in touch with her aunt and uncle Ray and Maude Ripley. My mother Ruth remembers that when she was ten, her family drove to Portland to visit them. Ray Ripley died a few years later, in 1944, but Maude lived another 45 years. I remember going to visit Great-Aunt Maude as a child. She was kind and gentle. When our family moved to Portland, in 1967, my mother tried to contact another of May's siblings – this must have been Lela, as Nora had died in 1963. However, my mother's overture was not reciprocated. As a child I was completely unaware of any ill feeling amongst my Ripley relations – I was just quite impressed to have had a Great-Uncle Ray who was a policeman.

I hope that May would approve of what I have tried to do in bringing to light her diaries, her life, and our shared family history. My admiration for her is enormous. When I have a difficult day, I think of May battling to get water, to herd the goats, to keep the tent up, to keep clean – and I am thankful for all that I have. (I concur completely with Arlene Wright's comment after she read May's diaries: "I'll never complain about hard work again!") I believe that May's love of learning (and writing) was transmitted to me, and I am very grateful to have had the opportunities that I have had to study and teach. As I have noted, I wouldn't have been able to complete my Ph.D without financial help from my grandparents Amy and Ethan: in helping me, they were working to realize the ambitions that May had for herself and for her children.

I am so privileged to have come to know May through her diaries. She was lively and loving, she was alive to nature, and she was very funny. Her writing is fresh and compelling. I love the word she invented to describe what one does when overly-full after Thanksgiving dinner: "comflopagait". She never gave up hope, and she kept her sights on the poetry inherent in life. I'm grateful to her for writing in all sorts of conditions, and for protecting her diaries during all the upheavals in her life, so that we could someday read them.

About the Editor

C hristine Laennec grew up in Portland, Oregon although she often visited her grandparents Amy and Ethan Papineau in Redding, California. She travelled to France to study after high school, and eventually earned a Ph.D in French from Yale University in 1988. She and her husband Michael Syrotinski taught first at Illinois State University. In 1992 they moved to Aberdeen, Scotland where Christine learned Gaelic, as well as taught French and Women's Studies. They adopted their son Calum in Aberdeen and soon after were surprised by the more conventional arrival of their daughter Isabel. Christine now works helping students with academic writing. She has published poems and short stories in Scottish anthologies and literary magazines. She is also an Elder of the Church of Scotland.

For more photographs of May's family and relations, go to:

www.christinelaennec.co.uk

Endnotes

Notes to the Introduction:

All references to census forms and other records, unless otherwise indicated, are to documents found on Ancestry.com. This website requires payment of a yearly subscription for full access, but currently some access is available to non-subscribers, on a trial basis.

1. I have never quite been able to determine whether May's name was Martha May or May Martha. She is listed as May in the 1880 census, as Martha in the 1885 Iowa State Census, as May M. Ripley on her 1899 marriage certificate, and as May M. Diddy in the 1900 census. An article based on my grandmother's recollections, however, states "The family and friends of Martha May Diddy called her by her middle name". Elouise Shuffleton, "The Diddy Family of Flintlock Inn ... As Recalled by [Amy] Emma Diddy Papineau" in *The Covered Wagon* (Redding, Calif: Shasta Historical Society, 1984), p. 42. I am greatly indebted to Arlene Wright for sending me an original copy of this issue of *The Covered Wagon*.

2. My grandmother also recalled "May wrote poetry and had some published in the *Sacramento Bee*." "The Diddy Family of Flintlock Inn," p. 42.

3. Obituary of Fannie May Ripley, Harvard (Nebraska) Courier, 27 Dec 1959: "In the fall of 1887 she with her brother John and sister Mattie came to Harvard, Nebr. in a covered wagon." A copy of this obituary was kindly given to me by Dan Mitchel, another Ripley descendent. It appears on his family tree (Mitchel Tree) and on my family tree (Christine Williams Tree) in the online genealogy website, Ancestry.com.

A note about my last name: In 1988, I married for the second time. Because my husband was a fellow Ph.D student and we hoped to find jobs in the same French department at the same university, it would have been professional suicide for me to take his name, as American universities lived in terror of being accused of nepotism. I didn't wish to continue using my first husband's name, nor did I wish to go back to my maiden name, Williams. After several months of pondering what to do, a dear friend cut the Gordian knot by suggesting I change my last name to one of my own choice. At first I dismissed this as ludicrous. Then I considered becoming Christine Papineau, because I felt these (my maternal grandfather's) were the family roots I identified most with. Eventually I chose Laennec, another surname from Brittany. I have been completely happy with my own name ever since. Michael and I did indeed both land our first (and subsequent) academic jobs in the same department – a rare feat. When asked about my last name, I generally say, "I have French-Canadian roots, via Brittany," which is the truth. (My apologies to future genealogists. If they feel disapproving, I invite them to consider that I come from rather renegade stock.)

Notes to Part One:

1. 1880 U.S. Federal Census (St. Louis, St. Louis County, Missouri) lists Robert A. Goodin, age 49, as a "bank collector". In the 1900 Census (St. Louis Ward 25, St. Louis [Independent City], Missouri) his sons William G. Goodin and Harry A. Goodin were bookkeeper and

clerk, respectively, at the bank. Both William and Harry went on to have successful careers in Los Angeles.

2. Information from Dan Mitchel.

3. I have a typed note from my grandmother Amy that states: "Olive Alameda Ann Perryman, born Cave Spring, Green Co Misouria". Since the Mulanaxes and Perrymans were living in Cave Spring in the 1850s, I believe my grandmother's note of her birthplace to be correct. (I think Alameda was a mis-spelling based on a confusion with the town Alameda, as the name is usually spelled Almeda. Also, this is the only indication I have found of her having a second middle name, Ann.) One of my mother's family history notes lists her birth date as 29 August 1861. This is borne out by the 1900 U.S. Federal Census (Marysville, Grant County, Oregon), which lists her as born in Missouri in Aug 1861.

4. Missouri Marriages, 1766-1983. William A. Perriman and Josephine M. Mullinax, married 21 October 1860, Greene, Missouri.

5. Family Data Collection – Individual Records. Mary Louise Perryman married Joseph Riley Mullinix, 29 Jan 1861, Greene Co., Missouri

6. 1860 U.S. Federal Census (Cass, Greene County, Missouri). Mahaly J. Mullenax, age 18, born Missouri, is living with her parents, 9 siblings and 2 cousins.

7. 1860 U.S. Federal Census (Cass, Greene County, Missouri). Joseph Mullenax, head of the family and a farmer (value of personal estate $500), is listed as age 65, born in Virginia. Many family trees on Ancestry.com list Joseph Mullenax as born in Circleville, Pendleton County, West Virginia.

8. Mary Louise Perryman Mulanax died on 30 Dec. 1912 in Woodland, Yolo County, California. Family Data Collection – Individual Records. I don't know if there was any connection to the fact that a decade later May was married in Woodland.

9. Jacob Perryman married Margaret "Peggy" Knight in 1798. (Family Data Collection – Individual Records) He appears in the 1800 U.S. Federal Census (Salisbury, Rockingham County, North Carolina). In the 1830 census he is in Wilson County, Tennessee, and in 1840 in Greene County, Missouri. Only as of the 1850 U.S. census are family members other than the head of household listed.

10. http://thelibrary.org/lochist/history/holcombe/grch28.html (8 Feb. 2010). The entire typescript of Holcombe's 1883 History of Greene County is available online at the website of the Springfield-Greene County Library.

11. As above.

12. http://thelibrary.org/lochist/history/holcombe/grch20.html

13. 1860 U.S. Federal Census Slave Schedule for Cass Township, Greene County, Missouri.

14. 1850 U.S. Federal Census Slave Schedule for Greene County, Missouri. Sarah Perryman is slave owner of a 35-yr-old black female; 23-yr-old black female; 15-yr-old black female; 11-yr-old black female; 8-yr-old black female; 6-yr-old black female; 3-yr-old mulatto male and a 1-yr-old black male. In the 1850 Census (Cass, Greene County, Missouri) she is listed as widowed, 49 years old, and living very near her brother-in-law Thomas Knight Perryman - William Alexander Perryman's father – and his family.

15. http://thelibrary.org/lochist/history/holcombe/grch5pt1.html

16. John G. Perryman is listed on the 1890 Veterans Schedule (List of Union Veterans). Jessyphy's brother Joseph Riley Mulanax is listed in the American Civil War Soldiers as serving for the Union, enlisting in Company E, 46th Infantry Regiment, Missouri, as a corporal. Her brother Alfred Constantine is listed in Civil War Service Records as having served as a private in 2nd Missouri Light Artillery, fighting for the Union. Alexander's cousin back in Tennessee, Absalom Perryman, also fought for the Union in the 4th Tennessee Mounted Infantry (U.S. Civil War Soldiers, 1861-1865).

17. http://thelibrary.org/lochist/history/holcombe/grch6.html

18. As above.

19. William Wells Brown, *Narrative of William W. Brown, A Fugitive Slave* (1847, republished by Cosimo, Inc., 2007), p. 8. (Google Books)

20. See, for example "The Border War Rages On..." Missouri Civil War Museum website at: http://www.mcwm.org/history_mizzoukansas .html (15 Sept. 2009)

21. http://www.historynet.com/americas-civil-war-missouri-and-kansas .htm (15 Sept. 2009)

22. As above.

23 http://thelibrary.org/lochist/history/holcombe/grch6.html

24. In Holcombe's words: "Fort Sumter was fired upon April 12, 1861. On April 15th, President Lincoln issued a proclamation calling for 75,000 men, from the militia of the several States, to suppress combinations in the Southern States therein named. Simultaneously therewith, the Secretary of War sent a telegram to all the governors of the States, excepting those mentioned in the proclamation, requesting them to detail a certain number of militia to serve for three months, Missouri's quota being four regiments." (http://thelibrary.org/lochist/history/holcombe/moch8.html)

25. http://thelibrary.org/lochist/history/holcombe/grch8pt1.html

26. http://www.mcwm.org/history_facts.html (2 Oct. 2009). Given that the population of Missouri was 1,182,000 (slave and free), the number killed in the Civil War represents approximately 2 ¼% of the population. See http://www.civilwarhome.com/population1860.htm (8 Feb. 2010), which cites Randall and Donald's "Civil War and Reconstruction" and the 1860 U.S. Federal Census figures for total population by state.

27. American Civil War Regiments; The Union Army, vol. 4, p. 275.

28. Thomas J. Perryman joined the Confederate 8th Missouri Infantry Company G. He was captured at Helena, Arkansas on July 4th 1863, and was transferred to Fort Delaware on Feb 24, 1864. (Civil War Prisoner of War Records, 1861-1865, Selected Records of the War Department Relating to Confederate Prisoners of War, 1861-1865, Roll of Prisoners Received at Military Prison, Alton, Illinois, Roll M598-13, image 13392.) He does not appear in the 1870 census; his wife Nancy is on her own with their children (the 1870 census did not record marital status so she isn't listed as widowed) (1870 U.S. Federal Census [Looney, Polk County, Missouri]). In the 1880 census his wife Nancy is listed as widowed (Looney, Polk County, Missouri). Thomas and Nancy had ten children, of whom the last was born in 1867, so he must have survived the war for a few years.

Owen F. Perryman joined the Confederate 5th Missouri Infantry Company D (U.S. Civil War Soldiers, 1861-1865). After his capture he was transferred to Fort Delaware on June 22nd, 1863 (Civil War

Prisoner of War Records, 1861-1865, Selected Records of the War Department Relating to Confederate Prisoners of War, 1861-1865, Roll M598-101, image 877). He and his wife Elizabeth had only two children, the eldest born in 1860. In 1870 his wife and two children are living with her parents (1870 U.S. Federal Census [Boone, Greene County, Missouri]). Owen appears in no census after 1860.

Like his brother Owen, James M. Perryman enlisted in the Confederate 5th Missouri Infantry Company D (U.S. Civil War Soldiers, 1861-1865). Unlike his brothers, he does not appear in records of Civil War Prisoners of War. He married in 1870. He and his wife were living in Texas in 1910 and 1920 (1910 U.S. Federal Census [Mineral Wells Ward 3, Palo Pinto County, Texas] and 1920 U.S. Federal Census [Justice Precinct 3, Brazoria County, Texas]).

William enlisted in the Confederate 3rd Missouri Infantry Company G (U.S. Civil War Soldiers, 1861-1865).

29. For striking first-hand accounts of conditions at Fort Delaware, see the website of the Fort Delaware Civil War Prison at: http://www.censusdiggins.com/fort_delaware.html (28 Jan. 2010).

30. Civil War Prisoner of War Records, 1861-1865, Selected Records of the War Department Relating to Confederate Prisoners of War 1861-1865, Roll M598_39, image 29358.

31. Civil War Prisoner of War Records, 1861-1865, Selected Records of the War Department Relating to Confederate Prisoners of War, 1861-1865, Roll of Prisoners of War at Military Prison, Louisville, Ky., Roll M598-92, image 51286.

32. See the Ohio History Central website entry for Camp Chase: http://www.ohiohistorycentral.org/entry.php?rec=662 (28 Jan. 2010).

33. "Transferred to New Orleans May 2nd 1865 for exchange" from Civil War Prisoner of War Records, 1861-1865, Selected Records of the War Department Relating to Confederate Prisoners of War, 1861-1865, Roll M598-23, image 22046.

34. Lonnie R. Speer, *Portals of Hell: Military Prisons of the Civil War* (Mechanicsburg, Penn.: Stackpole Books, 1997), p. 15-16. (Google Books)

35. American Civil War Regiments; The Union Army, vol. 4, p. 275.

36. "During its service it participated in the battles at Lamar, Mo.; Van Buren, Brownsville, Little Rock, Pumpkin Bend, Prairie Grove, Chalk Bluff, Bayou Meto, Augusta, Clarendon and Long Prairie, Ark.; and in numerous scouting expeditions, etc. On every field it was always at its post of duty, and the unerring marksmanship of its men made it one of the most effective regiments of the army." American Civil War Regiments; The Union Army, vol. 4, p. 275.

37. Civil War Pension Index: General Index to Pension Files, 1861–1934. Mahala J. Perryman is listed as the widow of William A. Perryman, who served in "M 8 Mo. Cav". The date of her application for a widow's pension is difficult to read on the handwritten form. My guess is that it says "1862 Dec 20". The first three digits of the date are clearly 186, so the latest year William Alexander could have died is 1869.

38. http://thelibrary.org/lochist/history/holcombe/grch14pt1.html

39. As above.

40. Civil War Pension Index: General Index to Pension Files, 1861–1934.

41. Alfred Milton Sewell served in Company D of the 6th Regiment Missouri Cavalry, entering as a private and leaving as a corporal. U.S. Civil War Soldiers, 1861-1865.

42. Family Data Collection – Individual Family Records: Jehu Beal Ripley married Olive Perryman on 14 Sep 1876. This is confirmed by the 1900 U.S. Federal Census (Marysville, Grant County, Oregon) which states that Jehu and Olive had been married for 24 years.

43. I have taken his exact birth date from Dan Mitchel's family tree on Ancestry.com. Census records confirm that he was born in 1855. The earliest of these is the 1860 census, where he is listed as age 5, born in Illinois.

44. Their wedding certificate is posted on Dan Mitchel's family tree on Ancestry.com. It reads: "This Certifies | that the rite of | Holy Matrimony | was celebrated between | Asbury Ripley of Gurnsey Co. Ohio | and Elisabeth E Owings of Tuscarawas Co. Ohioh | on November 9th 1848 at Westchester Ohio | by Rev Harvey Bradshaw | Witness { Job Gilpen | Margaret Gilpen".

45. The information I have for Beal McKenzie Owings comes from other people's family trees on Ancestry.com.

46. Mary Ann Owings, 1825-?; Denton Owings, 1826-?; Elizabeth, 1828-1908; John Mark Owings, 1830-1911; McKenzie Owings, 1832-sometime after 1915; Jessie Owings, 1832 - ?; Minerva Owings, 1836 - ?; John Beal Owings, 1837-1917. (See Dan Mitchel's family tree and also my family tree [Christine Williams Family Tree] on Ancestry.com.

47. There are two documents regarding Maranda Young on the Ancestry databases. One (Family Data Collection – Individual Records) shows Miranda Young born 1806 in Tuscarawas, Gilmore, Ohio; she is the daughter of Denton Young and Mary McKenzie; was married in Harrison on 21 Sept 1824, and died in Gilmore, Tuscarawas in 1844.

48. Maryland Marriages, 1655-1850. Mary McKenzie married Denton Young on 7 April 1798, in Baltimore, Maryland. Dan Mitchel's family tree has Mary McKenzie born in Wales in 1777, but as the name is Scottish I wonder if she was originally of Scottish descent. Some family trees list Denton Young's father as William A. Young, born in Baltimore in 1740. Other records indicate that Denton Young was born in Ireland.

49. One World Tree on Ancestry.com.

50. "Young, an iron-man pitcher in both major leagues in his 22-year career which ended in 1911, set a number of records which still stand. ... He was the first pitcher to hurl three no-hit games... He was the only pitcher to hurl 20 straight innings without giving up a base on balls. He did this in one day, on July 4, 1905." From "Cy Young, One of Baseball's All-Time Greats, Dies Quietly in Rocking Chair," *Coshocton Tribune* (Coshocton, Ohio), 4 Nov. 1955 (available on Ancestry.com).

51. 1900 U.S. Federal Census (Perry, Tuscarawas County, Ohio) states that James E. and Ella L. Ripley were married in 1893. I discovered that Luella "Ella" Young was married to a Ripley when I read a report of Cy Young's funeral ("Baseball Greats of Past Listed Among Honorary Pallbearers for Cy Young in Peoli Service Monday" Coshocton Tribune, Coshocton, Ohio, 5 Nov. 1955 [available on Ancestry.com])

52. The names Beal and McKenzie were used as first names for generations, both preceding and following Elizabeth's lifetime. I wonder if there was some connection between the McKenzie name in the Owings family tree and Maranda Young's mother Mary McKenzie?

53. For example, Gwerfyl Verch Iorwerth, born in Anglesea, Wales, in 1375, married Howel Ap David, also born 1375, and their son, an Owings ancestor, was Howel Vain Ap Howel, born 1405. See family trees on Ancestry.com, as well as the One World Tree. Two useful websites are Following Their Footsteps (http://followingtheirfootsteps .net/index.php (14 Feb. 2007) - search for example Capt. Richard Owings) and the Owens Genealogy Page on Rootsweb: http://freepages.genealogy.rootsweb.ancestry.com/~colettesite/Genealo gy/Rector/Owens.html (14 Feb 2007). There is also a book, now difficult to find, by Addison D. Owings, *Owings and allied families, 1685-1979: Genealogy of Some of the Descendants of Richard Owings I of Maryland* (1980).

54. U.S. and International Marriage Records 1560-1900 list their marriage date as 1690. However, as their first child was born in 1683 (and Rachel continued to bear children until 1704, when she was 42) I believe their marriage date must be closer to 1680. Several online family trees list their marriage date as 1682, but I have not found a source for this.

55. I say "seems" because most family trees list her mother as Ruth Polly Moore, born 1852 and marrying Ninian Beall in 1668. As Rachel Beale was born in 1862 (when Ruth was only 10 years old), and all other children from Ninian Beall and Ruth Polly Moore's marriage were born after 1672, it seems clear that Ruth Polly Moore was her mother. Also, some family trees list Richard Owing's wife as Rachel Roberts or Rachel Roberts Beale. However, I believe that Rachel Beale was Ninian Beall's daughter (from another marriage) because of the presence of the name Beal in the Owings and Ripley families, which is documented from Beal Owings, born 1784, to May's own first-born in 1900.

56. For information on Ninian Beall – who apparently pronounced his name Bell – see for example Ruth Beall Gelders, 'Ninian Beall' 1976 (this was available online at http://www.geocities.com/Athens/ 5568/ninian1.html, which is no longer available; it seems to have been

reproduced on this website: http://tjaskren.com/family/ninianbeall.html [8 Feb. 2010]). I have drawn my portrait of Ninian Beall largely from her article, but much of it is also confirmed by information in the public domain.

57. The BBC website offers short videos on this and other chapters of Scottish history: http://www.bbc.co.uk/scotland/history/covenanters/cromwell_invades_scotland/ (26 Nov. 2009)

58. From a scanned document, "Stephen Owings son of Richard Owings Jr." on Ancestry.com, attached to the Major-Owings Allied Families family tree. The Soldiers Delight Hundred was an area of land listed in the Maryland 1810 Federal Census, available online at: http://ftp.us-census.org/pub/usgenweb/census/md/1810/index-o.txt (6 May 2009). It has now become the Soldiers Delight Natural Environment Area.

59. There is a photo of the waymarker and a map of its location on http://www.waymarking.com/waymarks/WM505T (6 May 2009).

60. Marie Forbes' short history of Owings Mills stated that "the earliest settlers arrived around 1700" and that there were several mills along the Gwynns Falls. I found this information in May 2009 at http://www.gotomytown.com/history/owingsmills/history.htm. In August 2009 this website had disappeared but I see that Marie Forbes has published a book on the history of Owings Mills.

61. Richard Owings' 1806 will is one of a number of Baltimore and Anne Arundel County wills transcribed and published online by RootsWeb: http://www.rootsweb.ancestry.com/~mdbaltim/wills/will077.htm (4 Feb. 2008)

62. http://www.rootsweb.ancestry.com/~mdbaltim/wills/will078.htm (4 Feb. 2008)

63. See family trees on Ancestry.com.

64. Mitchel family tree on Ancestry.com. The online 'Genealogical Records of James M. & Elsie Klinger Eaves' also lists Beal McKenzie Owings as born ca. 1804, and as being buried in 1839 in Gilmore Cemetery, Gilmore, Tuscarawas County, Ohio. (http://www.jmekeaves.info/p1495.htm#i46961, 8 Feb. 2010)

65. "The Ohio Constitution of 1803 prohibited slavery, honoring one of the provisions of the Northwest Ordinance." From "The Ohio

Constitution of 1803," *Ohio History Central* website, http://www.ohiohistorycentral.org/entry.php?rec=1459 (4 May 2009).

66. See Dan Mitchel's and other family trees on Ancestry.com.

67. Passenger and Immigration Lists Index, 1500s to 1900s, shows Johannes Ruppel, age 35, arriving in Pennsylvania in 1736. There is a discrepancy of three years in his birth date compared to Ancestry.com family trees and one other immigration record, but I think it is more than likely this is our Johannes.

68. Lorine McGinnis Schultz, "Palatine History," 1996, available on http://www.olivetreegenealogy.com/palatines/palatine-history.shtml (2 June 2009). This mass migration was the beginning of the Pennsylvania-Dutch (from "Deutsch" meaning German) community in Pennsylvania.

69. See "All Pennsylvania Foreign Oaths of Allegiance": Ludwig, David Ruppel. Ship: Two Brothers. Thomas Arnott. List of Foreigners Imported in the Two Brothers. Thomas Arnott. Place: Rotterdam. Date: Sept. 15, 1748. (Ancestry.com) There is a full passenger list for this sailing published on the Olive Tree Genealogy website. See: http://www.olivetreegenealogy.com/ships/palship22.shtml (2 June 2009). Ludwig David is listed as "Ruepfel", and there is no other Ruppel or Ruepfel listed as being on board.

70. Pennsylvania Census, 1772-1890: Name - Ludwig David Ruppell, State – PA, County – Philadelphia County, Township – Philadelphia, Year – 1748, Database – PA Early Census Index.

71. See family trees on Ancestry.com. There seems to be consensus that they both died in Somerset County, and that Ludwig died in 1788. However, the few family trees that indicate death dates for his father Johannes give no consistent date of death.

72. This information is from family trees on Ancestry.com.

73. U.S. and International Marriage Records, 1560-1900: in 1774, John Kasebeer, born 1744 in PA, married Catherine Dibert, born 1755.

74. *History of Bedford, Somerset and Fulton Counties, Pennsylvania: with illustrations and biographical sketches of some of its Pioneers and Prominent Men.* (Chicago: Waterman, Watkins and Co., 1884), p. 247-248. (Google books)

75. The 1800 U.S. Federal Census lists him as living in Donegal township, Washington County, Pennsylvania, along with his son John Casebeer Jr., but according to family trees, he died in Tuscawaras County, Ohio in 1813.

76. According to family trees on Ancestry.com.

77. It became the 17th state on February 19th, 1803. Ohio History Central: An Online History of Ohio History (http://www.ohiohistory central.org/time_period.php?rec=2, 8 Feb 2010).

78. Tuscarawas County website: http://www.co.tuscarawas.oh.us/ History.htm (8 Feb. 2010).

79. Charles Knisely, "The Founding of New Philadelphia" on the website of the City of New Philadelphia, Ohio: http://www.newphilaoh .com/html/history%202.htm (8 Feb. 2010)

80. The typescript of John Ripley's 1846 will was – in yet another odd twist – made by Dan Mitchel's aunt, who must have been in touch with my grandmother. I have attached photographs of it to the Christine Williams Family Tree on Ancestry.com.

81. A photograph of their calligraphed marriage certificate has been posted on Ancestry.com. It reads: "John Ripley & Unity McBride / Marriage License Issued February 19th 1821 / Certificate, State of Ohio, Harrison County / I hereby certify that on the 22nd day of February last I joined together in the Holy State of Matrimony John Ripley to Unity McBride of lawful age / Given under my hand and seal this first day of May 1821 / William Wychoff, Justice of the Peace"

82. The 1880 U.S. Federal Census for Guernsey County, Ohio, shows Unity Ripley as born in Delaware in about 1795, and both her parents as born in Ireland. Some of the family trees on Ancestry.com name her as "Eunice or Unity" McBride.

83. From American Civil War Soldiers: "Name - Ezekiel Ripley; Side Served – Union; State Served – Ohio; Service Record – Enlisted as a Corporal on 20 Sept 1861 at the age of 40. ... Died of disease, Company E, 51st Infantry Regiment Ohio on 14 February 1862 at Camp Wickliffe, KY." He left a widow and seven children.

84. From U.S. Civil War Soldier Records and Profiles: "Name – Isaiah Ripley; Age at Enlistment - 30; Enlistment Date - 20 Sep 1861; Rank at

Enlistment – Private; ... Service Record: Enlisted in Company E, 51st Infantry Regiment Ohio ... Mustered out on 20 Sep 1863."

85. John and Eunice / Unity appear in the 1850, 1860, 1870 and (Unity) in the 1880 U.S. Census. (1850, 1860, 1870 and 1880 U.S. Federal Censuses [Washington, Guernsey County, Ohio].) I have taken their death dates from Dan Mitchel's family tree.

86. In some of the records, Asbury is spelled Asberry, Ashbury or Ashberry.

87. Margaret Unity Ripley Spencer, 1849-1928; Sarah Maranda Ripley Critchlow, 1851-1943; Jehu Beal Ripley 1855-1915; Mary Ann Ripley (b. & d. 1856); Andrew Denton Ripley (1856 – 1871); John Henry Ripley, 1859 – 1939; Edith Ella Ripley Curry, 1861-1898; Clara Alice Ripley (b. & d. 1863); Martha "Mattie" Lavinia Ripley McBride 1864-1925; Fannie May Ripley, 1867-1959. This information is from Dan Mitchel's family tree on Ancestry.com. Dan has posted a family list of the birth dates of the Ripley children handwritten sometime before 1952.

88. In the 1860 census, Margaret (age 10) is listed as born in Ohio in about 1850, and Sarah (age 9) as born in Ohio in about 1851, but Jehu (age 5) as born in Illinois in about 1855 (1860 U.S. Federal Census [Cambridge, Henry County, Illinois]).

89. 1870 U.S. Federal Census (Cambridge, Henry County, Illinois).

90. This map is available on the website of the Henry County Genealogical Society: http://www.rootsweb.ancestry.com/~ilhcgs/ (8 Feb. 2010). The family is also in the 1880 U.S. Federal Census (Cambridge, Henry County, Illinois).

91. Obituary of Fannie May Ripley, Harvard (Nebraska) Courier, 27 Dec. 1959. In Dan Mitchel's family tree on Ancestry.com.

92. Her first child, Mary Elizabeth Curry, was born there in 1890. (1910 U.S. Federal Census, [Howard Ward 2, Clay County, Nebraska].)

93. From Fannie May Ripley's obituary, posted on Dan Mitchel's family tree on Ancestry.com.

94. Jehu Ripley and his family were in Eastern Oregon by 1895, as their son Leo was born there in this year (1900 U.S. Federal Census [Marysville, Grant County, Oregon]). John Henry Ripley and his

family were also in Marysville in the 1900 Census. They emigrated to Canada in 1909: the 1911 Canada Census, Yale and Cariboo District, lists the family as having arrived in 1909.

95. See "Accident Kills Retired NU Professor," *The Lincoln Star*, Lincoln, Nebraska, 27 Mar. 1965. (Available on Ancestry.com)

96. I would not have made it through college and graduate school without a monthly check from my Granny and Grampa for many of those years. I continue to be grateful to them for their love and support, and belief in me.

97. Margaret H. Hendricks married Glenn R. Leymaster. See "Bright Future for Women in Medicine... says ex-Nebraskan," *The Lincoln Star*, Lincoln, Nebraska, 24 Mar. 1964. (Available on Ancestry.com)

98. Information on their wedding date is from Dan Mitchel's family tree on Ancestry.com.

99. 1880 U.S. Federal Census (Humboldt, Allen County, Kansas).

Notes to Part Two

1. She gave the same information to Elouise Shuffleton: May "was born to Jehu and Olive Ripley in Yates Center, Kansas. Jehu had been working for the railroad..." Elouise Shuffleton, "The Diddy Family of Flintlock Inn ... As Recalled by [Amy] Emma Diddy Papineau" in *The Covered Wagon* (Redding, Calif.: Shasta Historical Society, 1984), p. 48.

2. 1860 U.S. Federal Census (Cambridge, Henry County, Illinois).

3. 1870 U.S. Federal Census (Cambridge, Henry County, Illinois).

4. Elouise Shuffleton, "The Diddy Family of Flintlock Inn ... As Recalled by [Amy] Emma Diddy Papineau" in *The Covered Wagon* (Redding, Calif.: Shasta Historical Society, 1984), p. 48.

5. From Frank W. Blackmar, ed., volume I of *Kansas: a cyclopedia of state history, embracing events, institutions, industries, counties, cities, towns, prominent persons, etc.* (Chicago: Standard Pub. Co.),

Transcribed May 2002 by Carolyn Ward. Online at: http://skyways.lib
.ks.us/genweb/archives/1912/y/yates_center.html (8 Feb. 2010).

6. Louis Reed, "Railroads in Kansas" available on the Kansas Heritage
website: http://www.kansasheritage.org/research/rr/rrhistory.html   (8
Feb. 2010).

7. From Frank W. Blackmar, ed., volume I of *Kansas: a cyclopedia of
state history, embracing events, institutions, industries, counties, cities,
towns, prominent persons, etc.* .. (See note 5).

8. Iowa State Census Collection 1836-1925: 1885 census (Sheridan,
Poweshiek County).

9. Information taken from the Poweshiek County, Iowa Historical and
Genealogical   Society   website: http://showcase.netins.net/web/
powshk/Text_Files/Townships/sheridan.htm (8 Feb. 2010). According
to their website, Poweshiek County takes its name from Chief
Poweshiek of the Sac and Fox tribes. He was nicknamed "the Peaceful
Indian" because he signed the 1842 treaty that put an end to the Black
Hawk   wars.   (http://showcase.netins.net/web/powshk/histinfo.htm).
Sheridan township does not seem have been near a railroad. From what
I can tell, it has since nearly disappeared altogether, appearing as an
intersection of two roads on Google maps.

10. "The Diddy Family of Flintlock Inn," p. 42.

11. "Mother of Mrs. Ed Hall Died Here Last Saturday" – newspaper
obituary from John Day, Oregon, June 1932. In my possession.

12. Ray stated his birth place and date on his draft registration card in
1917. World War I Draft Registration Cards, 1917-1918 (Shasta
County, California).

13.   Encyclopedia   Britannica   online: http://www.britannica.com/
EBchecked/topic/622327/Valley-City (14 Sept 2009).

14. From the Valley City, North Dakota tourist board website:
http://www.valleycitynd.com/tourism.php (14 Sept. 2009).

15. See Encyclopedia Britannica online. One of the main events in
Valley City is still the agricultural show, the North Dakota Winter
Show.

16. Source: *The Wild West: The Way the American West was Lost and Won, 1845-1893* (London: Channel Four Television Books: 1995), p. 29.

17. Shasta Historical Society, 1894 Great Register, Ra- Ri (http://shastahistorical.org/). Having looked at some of Dan Mitchel's photographs of John Henry and Jehu Beal Ripley on Ancestry.com, I wonder if their heights are not reversed on this record.

18. From Leo's 1917 draft registration form (World War I Draft Registration Cards, 1917-1918, Grant County, Oregon).

19. From the website of the French Gulch Hotel: http://www.frenchgulchhotel.com/history.htm (16 June 2009).

20. For a good article on the history of copper mining in Shasta County, with many photographs, see Dottie Smith's Shasta County History.com website. (http://shastacountyhistory.com/ [22 Mar. 2010])

21. Elouise Shuffleton, "The Diddy Family of Flintlock Inn ... As Recalled by [Amy] Emma Diddy Papineau" in *The Covered Wagon* (Redding, Calif.: Shasta Historical Society, 1984), p. 48. Curiously, when I did an online search about the Gladstone Mine in French Gulch on September 4, 2009, I found that it was up for sale! (For less than half a million dollars.) According to the advertisement, "experts suggest gold ore still remains". (California Mountain Properties, http://www.californiamountainproperties.com/CMP/gladstone_details.a sp)

22. 1900 U.S. Federal Census (French Gulch, Shasta County, California).

23. Source: "Dean of the Mountain," Oregon Historical Society article by Nick Sheedy, 2006. This is a short article about mining in Canyon City in 1900, which includes two photographs of Canyon City from that time. Available online at: www.historycooperative.org/journals/ohq/107.4/sheedy.html (4 Feb. 2007).

24. Source: *One Woman's West: Recollections of the Oregon Trail and Settling the Northwest Country by Martha Gay Masterson 1838-1916*, ed. Lois Barton (Eugene, Oregon: Spencer Butte Press, 2nd ed.), pgs. 103-105.

25. Quoted in Nick Sheedy, "Dean of the Mountain" Oregon Historical Society article, 2006. Available online at: www.historycooperative.org/journals/ohq/107.4/sheedy.html (4 Feb. 2007).

26. The Encyclopedia Britannica online says: "The city was named for the river, which had in turn been named after a heroic Virginian scout of the Astor overland expedition (1811). The present city is a trading point for a cattle and mining region and is headquarters of the Malheur National Forest, which spreads over the foothills of the Blue Mountains. Timber, beef, and tourism are John Day's economic mainstays." http://www.britannica.com/EBchecked/topic/304969/John-Day (15 Sept. 2009).

27. See the Oregon Historical Society's Oregon History Project: http://ohs.org/education/oregonhistory/historical_records/dspDocument.cfm?doc_ID=1C23D5FF-E9E1-D5F1-484DACDF311E5FA7 (13 Oct. 2009).

28. From the section on Grant County, Oregon Historical County Records Guide: "Over $20 million in gold was mined from the Canyon City and Susanville areas [in the second half of the 19th century]. Following the decline of gold and placer mining, stock raising and agriculture became the main work of county residents. Grant County contains the headwaters of the John Day River, which has more miles of wild and scenic designation than any other river in the United States. More than sixty percent of the county's land area is under public ownership, and the county contains parts of four national forests. Principal industries are agriculture, livestock, forestry, and recreation." (http://arcweb.sos.state.or.us/county/cpgranthome.html [13 Oct. 2009])

29. I am not sure of the exact date when John Henry moved his family to Oregon from French Gulch, California. Neither Jehu Beal nor John Henry is present in the Shasta County 1896 register of voters. According to my grandmother, John Henry was the first to go to John Day, and Jehu followed. Since Jehu and Olive's son Leo was born in John Day in 1895, John Henry and his family must have been there before this. In 1900 John Henry and his family are living in Marysville, and are listed on the page after Jehu ("Jay") Beal and his family. 1900 U.S. Federal Census (Marysville, Grant County, Oregon).

30. 1900 U.S. Federal Census (Marysville, Grant County, Oregon).

31. His gravestone reads "Perryman B Ripley 1901" and is in Section 11, Row 14 of Canyon City Cemetery, Grant County, Oregon. (Information given to me by my mother, Ruth Papineau Williams.)

32. Her gravestone reads "Maggie R Ripley 1886 1902" and is by her infant brother's grave in Section 11, Row 14 of Canyon City Cemetery, Grant County, Oregon.

33. The only reference to Jehu's birthplace that I have from my grandmother is on May's death certificate, which was signed by Amy. On it, May's father is listed as "John Ripley" born in Iowa. This may simply reflect Amy's distress and confusion at the time, or it may mean that she believed that Jehu was born in Iowa. Nowhere in my notes or family papers is there any indication that Amy knew that Jehu was born in, and was from, Illinois.

34. See the 1850 and 1860 U.S. Federal Censuses (Richland, Vinton County, Ohio), and 1870 and 1880 censuses (Cambridge, Henry County, Illinois)

35. My mother's handwritten family tree and my grandmother's notes list her name as "Bull". (The article "The Diddy Family of Flintlock Inn" lists her name as "Beal" but as the article was published after Amy's death, I believe this was a confusion with the many Beals on the Ripley side of the family.) Her birthplace is listed in the entry for William Diddy in the 1880 U.S. Census (Trinity Center, Trinity County, California).

36. Jehu and Eleanor Owings Ripley were in Ohio in 1850 and had come to Illinois by 1860 (1850 U.S. Federal Census [Freeport, Harrison County, Ohio] and 1860 U.S. Federal Census [Cambridge, Henry County, Illinois]); William and Mary Diddy were still in Ohio in 1860 but in Illinois by 1870 (1860 U.S. Federal Census [Richland, Vinland County, Ohio] and 1870 U.S. Federal Census [Cambridge, Henry County, Illinois]).

37. William and Margaret Diddy were in Cambridge, Illinois, in the 1880 census. (1880 U.S. Federal Census [Cambridge Township, Henry County]). The 1890 census is not currently available. Margaret died in Trinity Center in 1896 (see note 40).

38. From the Trinity County Areas and Towns website: "Established in 1851 and located 40 miles North of Weaverville, on Highway 3.... This

is the location of the original Scott Ranch. The activities support both the Lake and the Trinity Alps Trail activities, with horseback riding, pack trips, hiking, camping, lodging, licensed guides, supplies and information." (http://users.snowcrest.net/wb6fzh/tcstat1.html [31 Aug. 2009]). There is now a Scott Museum in Trinity Center.

39. Iowa State Census, 1895, Margret Diddy residing in Belridere [sic], Monona, Iowa.

40. "Pioneer Records of Trinity County, California". These records were generously provided to me by the staff at the J.J. Jackson Memorial Museum in Weaverville, California, in the summer of 2008.

41. 1880 U.S. Federal Census (Trinity Center, Trinity County, California).

42. Sam Cornwell, 28, born in Ohio. 1880 U.S. Federal Census (Trinity Center, Trinity County, California). Listed in the census just above the two Owings family are nine Chinese miners, and one Chinese woman, Ah Kim Lee, whose occupation is listed as "Prostitute".

43. 1880 U.S. Census (Redding, Shasta County, California).

44. The 1885 Trinity County directory is available online through the Shasta Historical Society website (http://shastahistorical.org/), and is viewable by township or by surname.

45. From the 1885 Trinity County directory, township listing. (http://shastahistorical.org/)

46. In the 1870 census, the Ripley family's value was listed as eight times that of the Diddy's. 1870 U.S. Federal Census (Cambridge, Henry County, Illinois).

47. 1900 U.S. Federal Census (Belvidere, Monona County, Iowa).

48 1900 U.S. Federal Census (Iowa Hospital for the Insane, Page County, Iowa).

49. Iowa State Census Collection, 1836-1925: 1905 census (Belvidere Township, Monona County, Iowa).

50. 1910 U.S. Census (Trinity Center, Trinity County, California).

51. 1920 U.S. Census (Portland, Multnomah County, Oregon). The word "inmate" most probably meant that he was simply a resident there, without implying that he had mental problems.

52. 1900 U.S. Federal Census (Trinity Center, Trinity County, California).

53. My notes from conversations with my Granny specify that Scott's Ranch is "now underwater". The reference in the Pioneer Records of Trinity County to John Mark Owings residing in "Trinity Valley" also indicate the location of the original town of Trinity Center.

54. "I was born at Flintlock Inn, on Diddy Hill... I am not sure when the house was built, but my folks bought it in 1900." Notes typewritten by Amy Papineau in 1974. I am very grateful to Arlene Wright for sending me a copy of these notes.

55. "A second son, Everett Oliver Diddy, had also died the day of his birth, April 12, 1901, at Flintlock Inn." Elouise Shuffleton, "The Diddy Family of Flintlock Inn ... As Recalled by [Amy] Emma Diddy Papineau" in *The Covered Wagon* (Redding, Calif.: Shasta Historical Society, 1984), p. 41.

56. From typewritten notes by Amy Papineau in 1974.

57. "The Diddy Family of Flintlock Inn," p. 41.

58. As above, p. 42.

59. As above, p. 42.

60. As above, p. 44 and p. 45.

61. As above, p. 44.

62. As above, p. 43.

63. 1910 U.S. Federal Census (Round Mountain, Shasta County, California).

64. The birth dates do make me feel it is unlikely that Leslie was born to May: Everett Oliver was born and died on April 12th, 1901, and Leslie Edward was born on January 28th 1902 – nine months and two weeks after Everett Oliver's birth and death. Although it seems very unlikely that May would have fallen pregnant again so very soon, it isn't impossible. Also, if Leslie was her own son, he could have been born early.

65. For example on the 1920 census, his mother is listed as having been born in Kansas, May's birthplace. However, as he is living with May as her son, this is hardly surprising. I have not been able to locate him in

the 1930 census. Also, he may not have known who his biological mother was.

66. Another family story ties in with the idea that John Diddy was known to be a philanderer. Amy told my mother that she hated the name Diddy because the other children used to tease her, saying: "Well? Did he?"

67. Oregon Death Index 1903-1998: Jay B Ripley died 25 May 1915 in Grant County. Notes from conversations with my Granny regarding his death say, "Bit by a spotted tick".

68. "The Diddy Family of Flintlock Inn," p. 46.

69. 1920 U.S. Federal Census (Sacramento Assembly District 14, Sacramento County, California).

70. Eleanor E. Manning, The Edgar Hardy Maylone Story, Chapter IV, George Washington Maylone II, page 2. A photocopy section of this manuscript was kindly given to me by my cousin, the late Mildred Hizer Cuellar.

Notes to Part Three:

1. 1920 U.S. Federal Census (Cosumnes, El Dorado County, California).

2. 1920 U.S. Federal Census (Cosumnes, El Dorado County, California).

3. George Lloyd, "Daisy Miller: Former school teacher recalls life in South County," *El Dorado County Mountain Democrat,* Nov. 19, 1998, p. A-14. (Available on Ancestry.com)

4. Ida May Calkins appears in the 1900 U.S. Federal Census for Buckeye, Shasta County, California. She is listed as having been born in Iowa in May 1870, and as having been married to Wm A. Calkins for 12 years. One online genealogical source, the Fister-Riley-Baker Timeline, states: "1887: Ida May Brown married William Albert Calkins on May 22, 1887. Calkins died on January 20, 1934, at the age of 70, leaving behind his widow named Ida. He had farmed in the Bella Vista area and had owned a store in the mining town of Ingot." (http://www.farwestern.com/learnmore.pdf [4 Feb. 2010]) Amy, in her

recollections of childhood in Ingot, names Ida Calkins as one of their "closest neighbors". Elouise Shuffleton, "The Diddy Family of Flintlock Inn ... As Recalled by [Amy] Emma Diddy Papineau" in *The Covered Wagon* (Redding, Calif.: Shasta Historical Society, 1984), p. 45.

5. World War I Draft Registration Cards, 1917-1918.

6. 1920 and 1930 U.S. Federal Census (Placerville, El Dorado County, California).

7. Eleanor E. Manning, The Edgar Hardy Maylone Story, Chapter IV, George Washington Maylone II, page 2.

8. World War I Draft Registration Cards, 1917-1918.

9. 1920 U.S. Federal Census (Portland, Multnomah County, Oregon).

10. 1920 and 1930 U.S. Federal Census (Portland, Multnomah County, Oregon).

11. 1910 U.S. Federal Census (Bear Valley, Grant County, Oregon); 1920 and 1930 U.S. Federal Census (John Day, Grant County, Oregon).

12. 1920 U.S. Federal Census (Precinct 3, Lane County, Oregon).

13. Eleanor E. Manning, The Edgar Hardy Maylone Story, Chapter IV, George Washington Maylone II, page 2.

14. George Lloyd, "Daisy Miller: Former school teacher recalls life in South County," *El Dorado County Mountain Democrat,* Nov. 19, 1998, p. A-14 (Available on Ancestry.com).

15. Eleanor E. Manning, The Edgar Hardy Maylone Story, Chapter IV, George Washington Maylone II, page 2.

16. 1930 U.S. Federal Census (Cosumnes, El Dorado County, California).

17. 1920 U.S. Federal Census (Plymouth, Amador County, California).

18. Ontario French Catholic Church Records (Drouin Collection) 1747-1967.

19. "Sudden Death of Mrs. Papineau," [Placerville] *Mountain Democrat,* June 26, 1897. (Available on Ancestry.com)

20. Elouise Shuffleton, "The Diddy Family of Flintlock Inn ... As Recalled by [Amy] Emma Diddy Papineau" in *The Covered Wagon* (Redding, Calif.: Shasta Historical Society) 1984, p.42.

21. Eleanor E. Manning, The Edgar Hardy Maylone Story, Chapter IV, George Washington Maylone II, page 2.

22. 1930 U.S. Federal Census (Sacramento, Sacramento County, California).

23. http://www.thepeoplehistory.com/30s-homes.html (29 Oct. 2009)

24. For those who are interested in the history of the Sacramento River, the California State Map of 1893 on Ancestry.com might be of some help (Historic Land Ownership & Reference Atlases, 1507-2000).

25. http://www.stocktonet.com/stockton.html (31 Oct. 2009)

26. 1930 U.S. Federal Census (Stockton, San Joaquin County, California)

27. I have deduced this from the 1930 U.S. Census (Portland, Multnomah County, Oregon) where Dorothy F. Ripley, a widow, is living with her son Terrence Frank Bennett, and her mother, Margaret Guernsey. Leo sadly died in 1929 (Oregon Death Index, 1903-98).

28. 1930 U.S. Federal Census (Burns, Harney County, Oregon)

29. Yolo County Genealogy: Yolo County Place Names of Past and Present, www.pa-roots.com/#yolo/maps/locations4.html (4 May 2009).

30. www.pa-roots.com/#yolo/maps/locations4.html

31. 1920 U.S. Federal Census (Grafton, Yolo County, California) and 1930 U.S. Federal Census (Grafton, Yolo County, California)

32. "The Diddy Family of Flintlock Inn ... As Recalled by [Amy] Emma Diddy Papineau" in *The Covered Wagon* (Redding, Calif.: Shasta Historical Society) 1984, p.42.

33. 1930 U.S. Federal Census (Tracy, San Joaquin County, California).

34. Eric W. Ritter, "The Historic Archaeology of A Chinese Mining Venture Near Igo In Northern California," Bureau of Land Management, 1986, p. 7-8. (www.blm.gov/heritage/adventures/research/StatePages/CA_pubs.html, [2 Nov. 2009])

35. 1930 U.S. Federal Census (Township 1, Shasta County, California)

36. 1870 U.S. Federal Census (Township 1, Shasta County, California)

37. 1930 U.S. Federal Census (Township 1, Shasta County, California)

38. 1930 U.S. Federal Census (Township 1, Shasta County, California)

39. 1930 U.S. Federal Census (Redding, Shasta County, California)

40. 1930 U.S. Federal Census (Township 2, Shasta County, California)

41. Elouise Shuffleton, "The Diddy Family of Flintlock Inn ... As Recalled by [Amy] Emma Diddy Papineau" in *The Covered Wagon* (Redding, Calif.: Shasta Historical Society) 1984, p. 42.

42. Ruth Dozier O'Donnell, "The House on the Hill" in *The Covered Wagon* (Redding, Calif.: Shasta Historical Society, 1984), pgs. 20 and 21.

43. Eleanor E. Manning, The Edgar Hardy Maylone Story, Chapter IV, George Washington Maylone II, page 2.

44. 1900, 1910 and 1920 U.S. Federal Censuses (Round Mountain, Shasta County, California)

45. California Death Index, 1940-1997.

46. 1920 U.S. Federal Census (Igo, Shasta County, California).

47. Ruth Dozier O'Donnell, "The House on the Hill," *The Covered Wagon* (Redding, Calif.: Shasta Historical Society, 1984), p. 23.

48. 1900 U.S. Federal Census (Marysville, Grant County, Oregon) and 1911 Census of Canada (Yale and Cariboo, British Columbia). I have constructed this branch of the family tree with help from letters written by Inez Pearl Ripley Smith (John Henry and Ann's daughter) to my grandmother, in which Pearl lists all her siblings.

49. Family trees on Ancestry.com list Julia and her husband as both born in Cass County, Missouri. Marshall Webster Adkins' death date: Oregon Death Index, 1903-1998. Julia living with Ray and Maude Ripley: 1930 U.S. Federal Census (Portland, Multnomah County, Oregon).

50. 1930 U.S. Federal Census (Township 1, Shasta County, California).

51. Eric W. Ritter, "The Historic Archaeology of A Chinese Mining Venture Near Igo In Northern California," Bureau of Land Management, 1986, p. 7-8. (www.blm.gov/heritage/adventures/research/StatePages/CA_pubs.html [2 Nov. 2009])

52. Despite his stomach problems, Alexander Francis Johnston (b. 1885) lived until 1971. (Johnston Family Tree, Ancestry.com)

Notes to Postscript:

1. 1930 U.S. Federal Census (Redding, Shasta County, California).

2. 1930 U.S. Federal Census (Portland, Multnomah County, Oregon).

3. "Mother of Mrs Ed Hall Died Here Last Saturday" – newspaper obituary from John Day, Oregon, June 1932. In my possession.

4. Dorothy F. Ripley, Terence F. Bennett and Margaret A. Guernsey, 1930 U.S. Federal Census (Portland, Multnomah County, Oregon).

5. Great Register Index, Trinity County California, General Election November 8, 1932. Available on Ancestry.com: (California Voter Registrations 1900-1968, Trinity County 1900-1944, image no. 572.) Oddly, May does not appear on this register.

6. Eleanor E. Manning, The Edgar Hardy Maylone Story, Chapter IV, George Washington Maylone II, page 2 – 3.

7. As above, page 3.

8. State of California Department of Public Health, Standard Certificate of Death for Mrs. May Maylone, Rural Route #1, Redding, Calif. Signed by Mrs. Amy Papineau and filed Sep 9, 1933. In my possession.

9. There is some confusion about May's actual final resting place, as her death certificate states that she was buried in Redding, and my mother seems to remember seeing her grave there. I haven't been able to visit the Redding cemetery; perhaps there is a marker stone there. Doreen Rothlisberger and Millie Hizer Cuellar took me to see her grave in the Fairplay Cemetery.

10. Eleanor E. Manning, The Edgar Hardy Maylone Story, Chapter IV, George Washington Maylone II, page 3.

11. "The Columbia Broadcasting System inadvertently launched [Parran's 1932] campaign after radio executives censored the phrase "syphilis control" from a talk, leading Parran to cancel his appearance. Newspapers across the Nation reprinted the censored speech." From U.S. Dept. of Health & Human Services, Office of the Surgeon

General, biography of Thomas Parran, Jr. (http://www.surgeongeneral
.gov/about/previous/bioparran.htm). [23 Nov. 2009]

Lightning Source UK Ltd.
Milton Keynes UK
10 August 2010

158177UK00001B/406/P